Frolic, Fervour and Fornication

and Fornication

an alternative history of Suffolk

Woolpit Horse Fair
E.R. Smythe

Pip Wright

Other books by Pip Wright

Exploring East Anglia by Bus Pass
Exploring Suffolk by Bus Pass
The Watery Places of Suffolk
News from Essex
Daniel Malden
Lydia
Death Recorded
I Read it in the Local Rag (pub. by Poppyland Publishing)
Thomas Slappe's Booke of Physicke
Lucky is the name
A Picture History of Margaret Catchpole
The Chantry, Sproughton (for 'Sue Ryder Care')

Books by Pip & Joy Wright

The Amazing Story of John Heigham Steggall,
'The Suffolk Gipsy'
Newspapers in Suffolk (6 vols)
Grave Reports
Witches in and around Suffolk
Bygone Cotton

See all these at
www.pipwright.com

& The Diary of a Poor Suffolk Woodman
(with Léonie Robinson, pub. by Poppyland Publishing)
See **www.poppyland.co.uk**

Contents

A Village in the Woodlands (believed to have been Onehouse)

No gilded roofs here strain the gazer's eye,
No goblets flow with noxious luxury;
Sleep, balmy sleep here rests his downy wings,
Nor waits the purple pomp of gorgeous coverings:
No gems here dazzle the offended sight,
No trilling airs inspire unchaste delight.
No servile bands with crouching necks appear,
Not flattering's self can find admission here,
But lofty groves of beauteous forms are seen:
The builder oak, the fir forever green,
The towering ash whose clustering tops receive
The rising sun and deck the ruddy eve;
The alder brown that loves the wat'ry vales,
The asp' light quivering to the summer gales,
The willow pendant o'er the mazy stream,
The poplar huge, the elm's extended beam:
Their different colours here display and vie
In all the tints of varied harmony...
Earth spreads her charms, with flowers the meads are crowned,
And smiling Ceres pours her gifts around.
How sweetly does the love-lorn nightingale
Tonight's dun shades repeat her mournful tale,
And when the ruddy morn appears in view,
The painted tribes their cheerful notes renew.
From every copse they fly, on every spray
Swell their gay throats and hail the rising day...
Far from the madding people's furious strife,
Far from the anxious cares of busy life,
Beneath this straw-thatch'd roof, this humble cell,
Calm, peace and friendship pure, delight to dwell,
And when retir'd to rest, soft dreams employ
the slumb'ring thoughts and tune the soul to joy,
Which wrapt in bliss through airy regions flies,
Quits the dull earth and claims her native skies.

Benjamin Batt c1800

The preface, introduction, first bit,
(call it what you will) - the part of a book that most people skip and don't bother to read...

...which would be a pity because a great deal of care and thought has gone into it.

I started to collect the material for this book at least ten years ago; and still the book remains unfinished. Of course it does. There is almost no end to what I might have included within its pages. There is a gigantic wealth of history out there. Collecting it is the easy bit. What is infinitely more difficult is filling in the missing details. All too often only a part of the story survives and it's left to us to interpret what has come down through the centuries and attempt to plug the gaps as honestly as possible. Sometimes that means listening to tales that have found their way into the collective memory of the county, and seeing how they might fit with what can be shown to be true. In other words, just because there is no written proof that an event or even that a certain person existed doesn't mean they never did. Whilst being utterly sceptical, you still need a healthy respect for a story that has survived when so many did not.

So you'll find here a cornucopia of Suffolk tales and characters, most of whose existence can be verified by contemporary accounts; but occasionally they appear alongside more hazy stories where the truth is much harder to determine. I've tried to make it clear which are which.

Finding out about history is all about knowing where to look. The sources employed in this book have been many and varied, and to a large extent define, chapter by chapter, the layout of the book. The very oldest of these sources are the most difficult. They are often harder to access, tucked away in libraries and collections such as the British Library or the University of Chicago. They may be written in an unfamiliar hand in Latin, Norman-French, Middle-English or a combination of all three. Sometimes they were written by a scribe whose own command of these languages may not have been that good. In such cases, I have put my faith in transcribers and historians far more eminent than myself. But even then, we are at the very beginning of an understanding of these ancient documents.

It is only as we climb a little closer to the present day that we have the advantage of being able to examine first-hand evidence; the words of the people themselves, or at least their representatives. Still however, we may be reading the past through eyes of the present.

In 1412 in Acton near Sudbury, Dame Alice de Bryene, widow of Sir Robert de Bryene, had her Steward keep accounts of the guests fed at her table, the food and drink served to them and purchases made.[1] Doubtless, household books like this were kept as a matter of course on most estates, this being a rare survival. Attempts have been made to flesh out the matter-of-fact material contained in the household book; to draw conclusions as to how these people lived, their state of health, the relation between landowner and those beneath her, and to draw even more day-to-day conclusions. But it is all supposition.

Monks and priests regularly ate at her table. Feast days and fast-days were properly observed. Dame Alice gave freely to religious causes as well as to the poor on her doorstep. On her death, she left in place a 'chantry,' whereby money would be provided to pay, after her death, for a Mass to be sung for her soul every day for evermore. (This turned out to be a little more than a hundred years as such 'superstitious practices' became outlawed following the dissolution of the monasteries)

Did all this mean she was particularly pious or just following the normal practices of her day? And here is another thing. Almost certainly, she sat down at table with people of all ranks and classes, from knights of the realm to itinerant workers who had come to mend the roof. Did this make her a bit of a socialist, or merely demonstrate how different life was, even for the wealthy, when their living space was just one large open-plan room?

Her brass in Acton Church is 4 foot 9 inches tall. She looks gentle and kindly. The dog at her feet (not easily spotted here) symbolises fidelity, so maybe she was a person you could trust. But she was 75 when she died, so she

probably looked nothing like this. Maybe she or her heirs popped along to the nearest memorial brass shop (Brasses R us?) and chose one they liked the look of, regardless of whether it matched its recipient in any way.

The trouble is, it is so hard not to fill in the missing details with familiar twenty-first century values and ideas. It would be lovely to know more than we really do about our predecessors, but we can't dig them up and ask them, so we just have to make the most of what they have left behind. Then we should temper everything we think we know with a huge measure of scepticism.

We often have counter claims to the same story. When Anne Boleyn was executed in 1536, we are told her head and body were interred in the chapel of St. Peter at the Tower of London. However, there have been countless fairly plausible tales of parts of her, especially her heart being spirited away and buried at Salle in Norfolk, Horndon-on-the-hill in Essex and at Erwarton in Suffolk. Accounts dating from soon after her death lend support to

Legend has it that Henry VIII visited Anne Boleyn when she was staying here in an earlier house with her uncle, Sir Philip Parker. The Hall we see today dates from 1575.

any or all of them. But she only had one heart, so they can't all be right, even if heart-shaped caskets have been found at these places and re-interred at certain times. There may even be other parishes dotted around the country with claims to parts of her anatomy. And we'll all continue to be none the wiser.

An intriguing ghost story surrounds Boulge Hall near Woodbridge. Known primarily as the home of the eccentric poet and translator of Omar Khayam, Edward FitzGerald, (Old Fitz) the house was reputed to be haunted by its previous owners, Colonel Henry Short and his wife

Eleanor. FitzGerald, who grew up in the house during the mid-nineteenth century, remembered it as 'a house of banging doors.' According to the writer Peter de Polnay who lived there just after World War II, rather than the spirit of 'Old Fitz' inhabiting Boulge Hall, something altogether more malevolent stalked the place.

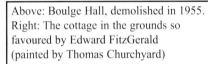

Above: Boulge Hall, demolished in 1955.
Right: The cottage in the grounds so favoured by Edward FitzGerald
(painted by Thomas Churchyard)

Henry Short had married Eleanor Whitby (previously Eleanor Plummer) before moving from Edlington in Lincolnshire to Suffolk, where she had already inherited Boulge Hall. This was not a marriage made in heaven. As a result, Eleanor had a thatched lodge constructed in the grounds, to ensure she didn't have to meet her husband too often. It would be this very lodge that would later appeal to Edward FitzGerald as a young man, living something of a hermit's life despite having inherited great wealth. Though he married in middle age, the union would be short-lived. He was not a ladies' man after all. A lot has been written about FitzGerald and his somewhat alternative life-style, but it is the previous owners of Boulge Hall that I find much more interesting.

Eleanor Short would outlive her husband Henry by another twenty-four years. As this was the third husband she had buried before his expected span, there were doubtless those who felt she might have had a hand in hastening his demise. However, by the time of his death, he had moved well away from this virago of a woman, and his most fervent last request was that he should **not** under any circumstances be buried at Boulge.

Eleanor Short was, by all accounts, a difficult lady. There had been legendary accounts in the village about her temper and the violence of her actions. On one occasion in January 1800, four servants (Wm. Walker, Richard Jackson, Wm. Southgate & Sam Baldry) were tried but acquitted at the Ipswich Quarter Sessions for the assault and confinement of Mrs. Short. They had tried to disarm her as she threw things through windows and brandished a knife. Other details are more hazy, but even murder has been attributed to Eleanor Short. Suffolk historian, Vincent Redstone was not usually drawn to flights of fancy, but sixty years after her death, he described her as the 'Queen of Hell' and related sightings of her carriage being pulled by headless horses. Servants at the house during the late nineteenth century spoke of their reluctance to work there, as spirits pervaded the place.

The FitzGeralds, knowing by the 1820s that Mrs. Short was not long for this world, had moved into lodgings nearby in anticipation of being able to buy the property: but the awkward old lady, it is said, refused to die, and hung on out of spite, until she was in her eighty-fifth year.

Somehow you just can't ignore the importance of superstition in Suffolk history. Which is why I have given over a short chapter to a collection of items on that subject that will show how closely linked our past is to the beliefs of the people who inhabited it.

Even sensible, rational, educated people have reported remarkable things. According to Rev. F.B. Zincke of Wherstead,[2] a farmer and churchwarden he had known described entering the house of a wizard by the name of Winter at Aldeburgh and seeing half a dozen imps, as black as your hat, resembling something between rats and bats and communicating with their master through twittering. The Rev. Hollingsworth of Stowmarket also wrote of *'Old Winter of Ipswich.'*[3]

In his collection of Suffolk illustrations at Ipswich Record Office, Willam Stevenson Fitch[4] includes this water-colour of the old manor house below the church at Shotley.

150 years ago, Fitch tells us, it was *'going fast to decay.'* It was moated and *'believed to be haunted by spirits.'* Fitch himself is far too interesting a character to leave there. He will appear again on page 222.

Quite bizarre too are a few stories that feature in the appendix to Rev. A.G.H. Hollingsworth's *'History of Stowmarket,'* regarding the observance of witches and fairies. It is surprising, in a way, to think that an educated man was prepared to include such stories in this volume. Presumably he was suitably convinced by the words of those he quotes here.

Fairies frequented several houses in Tavern Street about 80 to 100 years since. They never appeared as long as any one was about. People used to lie hid to see them, and some have seen them. Once in particular by a wood-stack up near the brick-yard there was a large company of them dancing, singing, and playing music together. They were very small people, quite little creatures, and very merry. But as soon as they saw any body they all vanished away. In the houses after they had fled, on going upstairs sparks of fire as bright as stars used to appear under the feet of the persons who disturbed them.

An old woman named Wix was reputed a witch. She was drowned at night in crossing the river near the mill, and when found her body was swimming on the top of the water, which was thought a good confirmation of the suspicious.

On old woman used to frequent Stow and she was a witch. If as she was walking any person went after her and drove a nail into the print-mark which her foot left in the dust, she then could not move a step further until it was extracted. The same effects followed from driving a knife well into the ground through the foot print.

Stowmarket

Above all, this is a book about Suffolk's past and its people. Yes, especially the rather more eccentric ones. But also it is about events and the places where they once happened. This book has had a number of titles since its inception. Several now appear as chapter headings. But also, it is about the sources you can use to dig into the past and where you might find them. This is reflected in the layout of the book and the importance given to first-hand accounts of the world of our ancestors.

Suffolk Towns and villages, parishes and manors: and those who lived there

As most of us know, when Duke William arrived from Normandy in 1066, after dealing with King Harold, he set out to establish precisely what he had taken on. So, a survey, often referred to as the Domesday was carried out. In Suffolk, we are quite lucky, because ours is rather more detailed than much of the rest of the country. This may reflect the high value placed on the land in this area, or maybe the team who came to our part of the world were a bit better motivated.

When you look at an amazing document like the Domesday Book, it seems astonishingly organised, as if the county had just been waiting for a man like King William to drag it out of the Dark Ages. In actual fact, much of the administrative organisation was already in place, which is why it was possible for the Domesday survey to compare England before and after the Norman invasion. Viking England was already arranged in Manors, grouped together into Hundreds, which in turn were arranged in Counties, not very different from those we know today (Though I doubt if even the Vikings had dreamed up Cleveland and the County of Avon).

Our familiar towns and villages sometimes consisted of a single Manor. Stowmarket was one such town. Yet Stowupland, just up the hill, would be divided into three. Cavendish, by the end of the fifteenth century would number as many as ten. This had nothing to do with the acreage. Cavendish is smaller than Wickhambrook with its three manors, in spite of the fact that Wickhambrook had a more than a handful of hamlets and greens attached. Several of the giant Breckland parishes have the fewest manors.

Villages as we have come to know them have generally been defined as parishes formed around a parish church. Yet a few of our villages have two churches and are really two parishes (for example, Icklingham All Saints and St. James), though one may have fallen into disrepair as at Stanton, where All Saints survives; St. John's is derelict. Some parishes, and their churches have disappeared completely: they have become almost forgotten as they have been absorbed into a larger nearby parish - Fordley has become part of Middleton. The monastic villages of Creeting All Saints and Creeting St. Ovary have been absorbed into Creeting St. Mary. Capel St. Andrew is now a hamlet attached to Butley. Buxlow has long since become a corner of Knodishall. And there are many others like them.

We are now used to one parson serving a number of parishes. But as some villages shrank in the early decades of the twentieth century, this was already happening then. Linstead Parva, Linstead Magna and Chediston combined. Bucklesham, Foxhall and Brightwell became a united benefice.

Linstead Magna Church just before 1924 when it was finally demolished.

Many of our towns, being larger, can be expected to have more than one parish, though towns like Woodbridge Southwold and Lowestoft found one parish church sufficient for many hundreds of years. Even Bury only boasted two until 1841. Ipswich alone in the county of Suffolk could lay claim to a dozen or so medieval churches and their attendant parishes.

Some Suffolk parishes are tiny. Wordwell had just 44 inhabitants in 1881, Gipping had 54; Easton Bavents, already fast disappearing into the sea, had only 13 (In 1600, Easton was referred to as the most easterly parish of England). Mind you, people did live in some odd places. In 1881, six people were living on Havergate Island.[5]

Boundaries did not always separate places tidily. Historically, parts of Thetford lay in Suffolk, and one Newmarket parish, along with its racecourse were in Cambridgeshire. More neatly separated by the River Stour, Bures St. Mary is in Suffolk, whilst Bures Hamlet is on the Essex side of the divide. Some of our expanding towns have now absorbed what were once quite separate villages: for example, Kirkley is now part of Lowestoft, parts of Combs and Stowupland are now in Stowmarket, and Whitton has been gobbled up by Ipswich. Boundary changes have even deprived Suffolk of a parish or two. Fritton and the town of Gorleston are now in Norfolk, having once been part of Suffolk.

It is to the many Suffolk places we can turn to tell our story. White's directory for 1885 speaks of the county being composed of some 500 parishes. There are stories in this book from about two thirds of them; further evidence that the book is incomplete. And the longer time goes on and the more we consign to 'history' the more incomplete it will become. Sorry about that!

Pip Wright

Ipswich was once famous
for its corner-posts.
These were two of them.[1]

Chapter 1
Mostly about Ipswich

A book by G. R. Clarke, published in 1830 contains an intriguing story. In the seventeenth century in Ipswich lived a very odd family. They all experienced problems on odd days and all had Christian names with odd numbers of letters. The husband was Peter, his wife Rabah. Their seven children were named Solomon, Roger, James, Matthew, Jonas, David and Ezekiel. According to this account, the husband had one leg, his wife one arm. Solomon was born blind in one eye; Roger lost his sight in an accident; James had his ear bitten off in a quarrel. Matthew was born with only three fingers on his right hand, Jonas had a stump foot and David was a hunchback.

All were remarkably short with the exception of Ezekiel who was 6ft 1 in. The husband had black hair, his wife, white, but all the children were red-headed. The father died in 1701 after falling into a deep pit. His wife refused to eat or drink and died five days later. Ezekiel enlisted as a grenadier and was wounded in 23 places, but survived. Roger, James, Matthew, Jonas and David all died on the same day in 1713, but in different places. Solomon and Ezekiel drowned crossing the Thames in 1723. Clarke's book goes on to comment, *'Never was such a collection of mishaps experienced by one family.'*

Unfortunately, Mr. Clarke fails to tell us the name of the family (unless it was 'Odd') and it is all too vague to be able to trace whether it has any truth in it whatsoever.

An equally bizarre story is easier to trace. The same book by G. R. Clarke tells of an eccentric character by the name of Thomas Colson who met his end in 1811. The Suffolk Chronicle for October 12th that year includes this story...

Thursday sen'night, Thomas Colson, (more generally known by the appellation of Robinson Crusoe) a disordered man who was originally a woolcomber, for many years had followed the occupation of a fisherman on the River Orwell, was lost near Levington Creek; his little shattered bark having got upon a mud bank, was afterwards sunk by the ebbing of the tide. Having been attacked by a nervous fever about 18 years ago, his mind has been in a state of derangement ever since, nor could he be persuaded but that he laboured under the power of witchcraft; and to guard against its effects, he constantly wore the bones of animals and old iron sewn up and bound round him, which made his appearance very romantic.

Notwithstanding his mind was evidently disordered, he yet retained a strong mechanical genius: he was the builder of his own craft: had also learned to weave; nay his ingenuity even extended to the construction of musical instruments, having made many violins for sale: an organ which he had brought to tolerable perfection was his last attempt in that line. Poor Robinson's boat has been raised, but his body has hitherto eluded the most vigilant search: it is supposed he was washed off the deck. This eccentric character was in his 57th year, perfectly inoffensive, and free from that sin of blasphemy to which seafaring men are too often addicted.

According to the New Suffolk Garland,[3] Colson was tall and thin with piercing eyes. His whole body, it was said, was encircled with charms, bones, stones with holes in them and spells and verses to protect him from his tormentors.

The story continued to intrigue people. An article published in the Stowmarket Recorder as late as 1936, includes the old charm reputed to have ensnared Thomas Colson, which required the enchanter to...

'take new wax and the pouder of a dead man, make an image with the face downward, and in the likeness of the person you wish to have; make it in the ours of mars and in the new of the mone, under the left arm poke a swalers hart and a liver under the rite; you must then have a new needal and a new thread; the Spirit name must be menchened, his Sine and his Character.'

Following Colson's disappearance in 1811, Mrs. J. Cobbold of Holy Wells, Ipswich wrote this poem...

I may not sleep - with hellish pow'r
The wizard works in secret bow'r
I saw the wretch a mass prepare
Of melted wax and dead men's dust;
From mould'ring skulls he scraped the hair.
And worms from eyeless sockets thrust;
Then shap'd - distinct and true;
I saw my very image rise;
My swelling brow, my sunken eyes,
Too soon to dreadful likeness grew;
And as the plastic form he prest,
Some magic word he mutter'd o'er;
Then from a living swallows breast
The reeking heart and liver tore:
The bleeding spoil on either side
Beneath the moulded arms he tied,
And from a cobweb curtain'd nook,
Some half burnt bones the wizard took,

I shudder'd for I knew them well,
The bones of her who on the heath
In flames resigned her wicked breath.

The power of such a spell was said to have caused him great torment and he is reputed as saying, *'It is hard to kick against the pricks.'*

The suggestion is that the *'pouder'* described in the spell would be ground from an executed felon. The article names Elizabeth Wilkinson who, with her husband, hanged on Rushmere Heath for the murder of her daughter in 1785. As the poem suggests a burning, it may refer to Margery Bedingfield who was burned alive on the heath in 1763 for Petty Treason (the murder of her husband).

What we can say from all this is that Thomas Colson was very much a real person, written about in his own lifetime and afterwards. He plays a fairly major role in the *'History of Margaret Catchpole'* by Reverend Richard Cobbold, who probably remembered him from his childhood growing up beside the River Orwell in the first decade of the nineteenth century.

The Orwell foreshore around 1830

Ipswich has been a significant port for centuries and during that time, Ipswich has produced its share of boatbuilders. According to Robert Reyce, in his Breviary of Suffolk: in 1359, Ipswich furnished King Edward III's fleet with no less than 12 ships. A further six came from Dunwich and three from Orford. The Spanish Armada in 1588 were repelled by a fleet including that included two ships well victualled, armed and manned at the expense of the town of Ipswich. Yet by the time Daniel Defoe came to the town in 1724, he saw an industry in decline. On a positive note, he said he saw no reason why the building of large warships should not be possible again.

Perhaps his words were taken to heart as in August 1817, the Suffolk Chronicle reported the launching of *The Orwell*, a great East Indiaman of 1335 tons with a keel 153 feet in length. It had taken just 15 months to build and used 2000 loads of oak, 100 tons of wrought iron and 30 tons of copper. It had been built at Mr. Bayley's Nova Scotia yard (below) on the banks of the Orwell.

This seemed to herald a new dawn for ship-building at Ipswich, but only ten years later, Mr. Bayley was offering his Halifax yard for sale or rent.

Other Suffolk ports built an assortment of vessels. Aldeburgh supplied three ships of over 180 tons for Sir Francis Drake's voyage to Portugal in 1589. Woodbridge too was renowned for its boatbuilding as this item from a 1764 Ipswich Journal shows:

On Wednesday, a ship of 240 tons burthen, designed for the Jamaican trade, and built by Mr. Turner of this town was launched; being the largest that has been built here these 60 years.

* * * * *

One of the great chroniclers of Suffolk in times past was John Glyde, an Ipswich librarian and publisher. He wrote a number of books and articles for newspapers under the pseudonym 'Silverpen.' In his 'New Suffolk Garland'[3] he tells of an unsuccessful auctioneer who became something of a laughing stock in the early years of the nineteenth century. Someone keen to make merry at this poor man's expense circulated a hand-bill to the businessmen of Ipswich. This is a copy of that notice.

TO BE SOLD AT AUCTION,

BY PRIVATE CONTRACT,

AT A REPOSITORY NEAR THE POST OFFICE,

IPSWICH,

BY SIMON NEVERSELL

ON SATURDAY, THE THIRTY-SECOND INSTANT.

*The sale to begin precisely at five minutes past Ten o'clock in the Afternoon

———————

LOT.

1. A Copper Cart Saddle, a Leather Hand-saw, two Woolen Frying-pans, and a Glass Wheelbarrow.

2. Three pairs of Pease Straw Breeches, a China Quarter Cart, and two Glass Bedsteads with Copper Hangings.

3. Two Marble Bonnets, a Feather Cap, an Iron Gown, two Straw petticoats, and three Glass Shoes.

4. Deal Coal Grate, with Paper Smoke Jack, a Mahogany Poker, China Tongs, Cotton Shovel, and a pair of Gauze Bellows.

5. Two Second-hand Coffins with Glass Nails, three Glass Coach-wheels with Cambric Tire, two Persian Saddles, and a Wooden Bridle.

6. A Leather Tea-kettle, an Iron Feather-bed, six pairs of Brass Boots, and a Steel Night-cap.

SUNDRIES.

Pewter Waistcoat and three Flint Wigs. A Bell-metal Caff-sieve, and Calimanco Hog-trough. A Buck's-skin Warming-pan, and a Pewter Looking-glass. A Japan Cleaving-beetle, and a leather Mattock. Three Silk Hog-yokes, and a Pinchbeck Swill-tub. Four Sheep's-skin Milk Pails, and a Wheat-straw Trammel. A Lamb's-skin Grindstone, and a Horse-leather Hatchet. A pair of Pewter Pudding-bags and a Canvas Gridiron. A Dimity Coal-scuttle, a Wooden Timber Chain, and a Brass Cart Rope.

*A FEW more articles, too NUMEROUS to mention.

John Glyde's notebooks and collections of historical trivia are well worth trawling through. You will find a number of items in Ipswich Record office[4] including a file he kept for each of the main Suffolk towns. In the file marked Stowmarket is a newspaper cutting relating to a scandal that never quite broke, but happened nevertheless...

In 1861, the Daily News reported that a small market town in Suffolk was about to face a problem. Following the death of one of its leading inhabitants, a shortfall of sixty thousand pounds had been detected in the accounts of the bank he had managed for a number of years. No mention was made of which town was

Stowmarket

referred to, but John Glyde clearly knew, as he filed this cutting in his Stowmarket collection.

After that, it was easy for me to discover that this coincided with the death of John George Hart, the manager of Oakes & Bevan's Bank in the town.

Hart had been post-master in the town before he had managed the bank. He was widely respected and had been a key figure in bringing the railway to Stowmarket. His obituary in the Suffolk Chronicle stressed his good works and his discharging of his responsibilities.

Three thousand came to pay their respects, including all the local dignitaries. However, it seems to have been true that sixty thousand pounds, an enormous sum, was unaccounted for, and apparently lost in a series of bad investments involving the bank's money. Today, it would have been a national scandal, but it appears to have been hushed up. Hart's employers and friends could see no advantage in blackening his name at the expense of public confidence. Cautious newspaper accounts, which promised further details to follow, were soon forgotten and no further revelations were published. The Oakes family took personal charge of the bank from then on. Stowmarket vestry records[5] show that some consternation was caused on the discovery that £111 was missing from Hart's vestry accounts. This money too was replaced by his friends and nothing more was said.

That was the way you did things then. In a similar case, Henry Cronin Pratt, manager of Pratt's Bank in Sudbury absconded in 1893 with about £17,000 of his customers' money. He had been altering pass-books and helping himself to small amounts for years. He was highly respected and, until his disappearance, nobody suspected a thing. Again, it should have been a great scandal, but Pratt was a Freemason and, within a short space of time, the money was put back by his friends in the Lodge and the whole affair buried with a minimum of fuss. There were reports from time to time suggesting he had drowned himself by jumping off a cross-channel ferry and other such explanations for his complete disappearance, but to this day it remains a mystery what actually happened to Henry Pratt after 1893. Peter Thorogood, author of a book on the story, *'The Earl, the Rector and the rogue,'* believes Pratt died penniless in New York about thirty years later.

Reading John Glyde's handwritten notes from over a century ago gives you a marvellous insight on life as he knew it. In what are filed at Ipswich Record Office as 'Miscellaneous notes'[6] are buried tales of Ipswich residents from the early nineteenth century. Describing his schooling in the 1820s in a premises in St. Helen's Street (Head-teacher Mr. Long), Glyde tells of a peculiar punishment known as 'The Cage.' It was a great wicker basket suspended from the roof by rope and pulley where boys were punished by being drawn up and left there throughout dinner time.

One Dr. Stebbing (pictured below), who lived in a house 'in front of the Catholic Church', was a crack-shot and greatly looked forward to the start of the shooting season on September 1st, to such an extent he was reluctant to treat patients that day.

Any who did seek his attention, would get short and summary treatment. He was a man accustomed to rising early and believed others should do the same. As a result he refused to pay any tradesman who appeared with a bill after eight in the morning, saying they were lazy and needed to get up earlier if they expected to be paid by him.

(This is the same George Stebbing who appears in Rev. Richard Cobbold's *'History of Margaret Catchpole.'*)

John Glyde's notes describe the town watchmen, who, for pitiful wages patrolled the streets of Ipswich by night, calling the hours and state of the weather. They were meant to deter criminals, but most were elderly and received regular abuse and ridicule from those to be found wandering the town late at night.

John Soar, one of the Ipswich Town watchmen during the mid-19th century

There is a delightful tale of one Samuel Tydeman who was brought before the magistrates for an assault on a watchman. The sentence came in the form of a fine which, as he couldn't pay, meant an alternative sentence of 7 days in the Bridewell (prison). The parish constable sent to take him to the Bridewell knew he had a job on his hands. Tydeman was a big and a violent man. So, the Constable told Tydeman he would pay him two pence to deliver a letter to the governor of the gaol and wait for a reply. The governor duly received the letter and sat Tydeman in a cell whilst he wrote the reply. After some time, Tydeman asked how long he would have to wait.

"Seven days," was the answer.

Of all the many items I've seen relating to Ipswich's very own Cardinal Wolsey, this has to be the best. It is a newspaper article from the Ipswich Journal of November 10th 1900...

Some enterprising individual has been digging up a skull of the late lamented Cardinal Wolsey, and it was on sale in a window in that salubrious thoroughfare known as Rosemary Lane the other day. But the price was far too high. It is not as if Cardinal Wolsey's skulls were at all scarce. I have several myself. In fact I can supply them in a very good state of repair from ninepence a-piece. Superior ones with his autograph on, at eighteen pence, their genuineness guaranteed.

On January 29th 1846, a stag hunt, which began at Kesgrave continued through and around the town of Ipswich to the amazement of all who saw it. There were reports in the newspapers of the time, but the best account has to be one written by Mrs. Hanbury,[7] told as if she were that stag. Two of these illustrations are by Edward Robert Smyth and are reproduced here from copies held by the Cobbold Family History Trust...

Having slowly finished my repast at Witnesham, I stretched my limbs upon the earth that I might ruminate at leisure... I was awakened by the well-known signal of the huntsman's horn, and I started up to escape my pursuers. From Kesgrave first I bent my rapid course, and through the prickly furze and over verdant turf with eager haste I made my sudden flight. Behind me soon the many-coloured pack were scattered on the heath around; and soon I heard the full-mouthed dogs approaching in my rear. I tried in vain to fly from their pursuit; for leaping over bush and briar, they still hung on my track. I heard the hunters' cheering shouts; and as their noble coursers swept along, how fleetly did I hasten from their shining hoofs across to Foxhall Hall. Through Rushmere next, I left the pack behind; but still the noise of trampling hoofs rung in my ears; and urged by that dread sound to quicken still my pace, I hurried past Hill House until St. Clement's hamlet met my view. To Ipswich driven down, I marvel I had the strength to flee through the intricate mazes of this chartered town; for I had heard of Corporation Feasts, and knew that Venison was true Aldermanly fare, I boldly too resisted the Police, and I fear I might have injured even the Mayor; but children only hindered my impetuous flight. How much I yearned to join the happy deer which grazed in Christ Church Park, but frightened at the busy haunts of men, I gazed with wildness as I dashed along the crowded pathway to the Common Quay. I passed the newly-built Custom House and could not speculate upon the corn-law bill, nor judge how good it was for trade, that those tall ships within the dock had wafted to our shores the distant produce of most foreign climes; enough for me that verdant pasture clothes our native plains.

But Wolsey's Gate appeared in sight, and visions of an age gone by with vivid colours to my mind were brought... much bewildered by the crowded streets and by the huntsman's clanging whip, I rushed with hasty steps along the streets to gain some more open space, and soon the River Orwell met my anxious gaze, I sank into its cooling waves and swam quite proudly till I reached a friendly shore... I bounded on again passing behind the Griffin

Inn; I had too often shed my horns to venture near the railroad shaft, which crowns the hills of Stoke, so bursting through the crying pack and being closely pressed around by daring horsemen, I approached the strand, where some small bathing houses rear their humble heads, and once more sought refuge in the Orwell's tide. The crowding pack now reached the margin of the shore, then dashed into the flood, three hounds alone pursued me through the liquid waves, and a small boat impelled by sailors eager to obtain me for their prize, followed me swiftly. I could hear the sound of horses floundering in the mud...

The tide had turned from the Orwell's banks and helped to favour my advance towards Hog Island, where I swam ashore. Here some ragged urchins tried to compel me to pass Greenwich Farm, but turning from their shouts, I jumped a chain which moors a crazy vessel to the beach and fled toward the Cliff. Here my career was stopped by the rude onset of two savage dogs; and bursting from their hold I sprang with quickened pace towards the Fountain Cottage. Passing a low-roofed lodge, I crossed the grounds near Holywells. There swam a pond, seeking for refuge in a grove of alders, where a narrow stream bursts from a craggy bed. I found that I had distanced my pursuers, and for a while I panted on the brow of a steep bank, then spying a small cottage, I stealthily approached and bent my head into a pail beside the open door.

A group of happy children dwelt therein... they saw me glancing timidly around, and uttering sounds expressive of alarm, they startled me from my too brief repose and hastily I leapt the gate which leads to Bishop's Hill. The dogs behind me now were joined by all the pack. I then perceived a motley company had joined the chase; and calling up my courage quite afresh, I fled across the fields with breathless speed, pressed by the new relay until I dashed past Cauld Hall Farm.

But soon I heard the coursers in swift pursuit, and the dogs madly pursuing their wild career. After I had rushed over it, the Woodbridge Road looked gay with prancing steeds and well-trained hounds, and still the varied group kept on their rapid course. The Round Wood passed, the huntsmen still untired had me full in view. The huntsman too with his unerring hounds followed my tread; but I was faint and flagging in my pace; and as I crossed near Westerfield, I made one desperate effort to escape my foes. But my strength failed me, and when I came to Witnesham my weary limbs could hardly bear me on.

I would proceed, but sobs quite choke my voice, and large round burning tears roll down my burning cheeks........

The banks of the River Orwell, just downstream from Ipswich in 1840

To end the chapter in a more cheerful mood, I turn to just about the only twentieth century story in this book. The autocar was a pretty recent invention in 1903, so any local paper was keen to write about such things. Botwood & Egertons in Ipswich were agents for the Primus, and to put it through its paces, Mr. Reginald Egerton decided to drive from John-o'-Groats to Lands End. For some inexplicable reason, he and Warren his 'mechanician', chose to have the car delivered to John-o'-Groats in mid-January to begin their journey. In spite of the predictable difficulties (predictable to anyone but Mr. Egerton), they were well prepared. Petrol stations hadn't been invented, so taking a full tank and another 30 gallons in cans, Mr. Egerton also arranged for fuel to be delivered to significant points along the route. The East Anglian Daily Times was to be informed daily by telegraphed messages sent from Post Offices along the way.

The problems they encountered included punctures (*'driving over some newly-laid granites'*), a badly cracked radiator (no anti-freeze), a leaking fuel pipe (*'patched up with rubber-tape and solution'*) and of course, any amount of snow.

Also, in the dark, they ran into an unlit railway crossing gate (Egerton rather objected to it being unlit). Nearly the last straw was when the car caught fire but this was fortunately dealt with by *'two men with buckets of water'*. It **was** fortunate, as the Primus was still carrying umpteen cans of petrol. The paint and upholstery were scorched and the belt burnt away, but with true British grit they fashioned another from some belting they were carrying and continued. However, these and other problems caused them to revise their plans and to make for home instead of Cornwall.

The 870 miles they covered took them 6½ days (*'in all weathers'*), but the trip was regarded as a tremendous success. As Mr. Egerton commented, they had only got through one accumulator, though they had of course carried spare ones in case of emergency. Looking at their press photograph,[8] you wonder quite where they put all the stuff they claimed to have carried.

The yard of
the Neptune Inn,
Ipswich c1840

34

Chapter 2
Frolic, fervour & fornication

This chapter is about all the things you would never expect to find in Suffolk parish registers... but are there nevertheless.

In 1538, it became necessary for every parson, for the first time, to keep a record of all baptisms, marriages and burials in his parish. The law was not very specific as to how this was to be recorded and a variety of papers, parchments, rolls or books were used. Not every parish did as instructed. There were several attempts during the sixteenth century to standardise the way in such records were kept, but it wasn't until 1598 that everyone was brought into line.

The 1598 legislation made it clear that each parish would have a book in which these records would be written, and as a check, copies would be sent quarterly to the bishop. Also, parishes were instructed to enter any past records into this book, at least those from the reign of Queen Elizabeth I [God bless 'er!].

Norton Baptisms 1788, but including an unexpected item - details of a fire that devastated the village

So, some Suffolk records date from 1538, some from 1558: others are less complete. This page from the register for Little Livermere[1] is largely in Latin, but roughly imparts the information in the previous paragraph. It is beautifully written, almost certainly by a professional scrivener, as many parish priests did not want the bother of entering up all the past records themselves. It is noticeable that many entries from before 1598 are skillfully presented, but it is downhill all the way after that, as with many parsons, their handwriting left a lot to be desired.

Though hundreds of years had passed without written acknowledgement of those who had lived and died in a parish, it assumed a new importance with the introduction of the Poor Law of 1601. Desperately trying to come to terms with beggars wandering the roads and byways of Britain, the answer the country's lawmakers came up with was simple. **'The parish will look after its own.'** Therefore you needed to know who your own were - who was born there, who was married there and who wasn't there any more because you'd put them into a hole in the ground. It was almost as if the lawmakers of 1538 had anticipated the need for such bureaucracy.

But give an educated man a blank page and command him to write and you will almost inevitably find he will write things well beyond what is strictly necessary. Also, you give that man a remarkable amount of power - the power to write almost anything about anybody, and the guarantee that it will survive through centuries. The rector of Badwell Ash clearly demonstrates his disapproval following the baptism of Mary Thrower's daughter Sarah in 1825, as under father's profession, he writes[2]...

'A married woman parted from her husband & living in open & avowed adultery with a man of the name of Bullard.'
One entry from the Lavenham registers reads simply, *'11 Jan 1739 - buried John Clark, an old miser.'*

When Dan Wall, rector of Hintlesham filled up a register and was required to start a new one in 1795, he celebrated by writing a poem on the first page.[3]

Time registers thy Times in number Three,
Thy Birth, Life, Death are for Eternity.
Be borne, beare, & be borne againe and know
The world's as perfect, when thou'st not as now,
Live like a dying man, O Lord Love Death
Into thy hand conveigh my dying Breath.

It sounds a little morbid, but it was the style of the day; and he didn't have to do it. He just thought it would be nice if he did; and he'd probably be tickled pink to have known we would be reading it more than two centuries later.

Baptisms & Marriages

William Son of Thomas & Anne Bradford
Jan.ry ye 31st aged 3 years & an half
Susanna Daughter of Roger & Susanna Reason
March ye 23d. aged 3 months
A Bad Practice prevails in this Parish
that People after they have obtain'd
private Baptism for their Children.
are very negligent in bringing them
to Church, in order to be receiv'd into
the Congregation. Onings. 2.

Sometimes parsons wrote in registers to get things off their chest. This piece is buried in the baptisms for Little Thurlow near Haverhill[4] and was written in the year 1771.

Private baptisms were conducted in the home and were often performed by the local midwife rather than a parish priest. There is evidence at Hadleigh of a system whereby certain midwives were licensed to baptise. If a child was born alive but feeble, rather than let the infant die unbaptised, it was important to see this was done. The midwife, who may also have been the local herbalist, layer-out of the dead and many other things besides, would carry holy-water blessed by the parson especially for such occasions. According to Rev. G.H. Butler, writing about the parish church of Gazeley,[5] *'if a midwife baptizes an infant, the*

water and the vessel used are to be burned or brought to church.'
I'm not sure quite how you are meant to burn water, but certainly
she would inform the parish priest that she had christened a child
and he would enter it into the register as a private baptism. What
was expected after that was if the child survived, the mother
should bring the child to church to be formally 'received into the
congregation.' Unfortunately, for a short period at the end of the
18th century, a tax was levied on marriage (6d), burial (4d) and,
following a birth, churching (6d.) All too often the poor were
reluctant or unable to comply. The rector of Little Thurlow was
annoyed by the number that were only too happy to avail
themselves of the first part of the ceremony, but forgetful of the
second part.

The tax proved a good money-spinner for a while and was
even increased in 1783, as J. Smythe, curate of Cockfield, informs
us in an entry in his register. Special dispensation was made for
paupers and those on parish relief. Often, names in parish records
are accompanied by the word 'pauper.' The tax seems to have
been repealed in 1794.

Items relating to the parish of Freckenham[6] give details of
charges made in the 1670s for churchings, marriages and burials,
the most expensive of which was 10s paid by John Durrant for a
marriage under special licence. I hope she was worth it!

Some parishes seem to have specialised in private
baptisms. At North Cove near Beccles in the 1760s a long string
of private baptisms is indicated by children recorded as *'received
into ye congregation'* often many months after their births.
Perhaps their parents needed to save up first. At Fritton (now in
Norfolk), between 1800 and 1812, only three out of 85 baptisms
were conducted publicly. Now just what was going on there?

Baptisms, for the most part carry little information other
than the names and dates required by law. Occasionally, the
mother's maiden name, father's trade or precise place of birth are
recorded. It is rare to find as much detail as appears in the Thorpe
Morieux register for 1591.

One Marie Stamforde servant to John Hasell of this parish was brought in bedd of a bastard sonne on Thursday at night being the 18 of March, the same bastard was begotten as she laide by one John White singleman, sonne to William White of this parish, which John White did dwell as servant in Mr. Hasell's house at the tyme that the foresaide Marie dwelt there. The young bastard being very weake, and like to dye, was baptised at home privately in John Hasell's house upon Ffriday the 19 day of March and the name of it is George, which name was given hym by George Chamberlain who was his godfather Anno 1591.

Then the rector finishes with a flourish... *'this was a fruiteful yeare for bastards in this little towen.'* [7]

Baptism records yield all kinds of stories. I have used them myself to help recount the lives of people long gone. Some tales are sad, others merely intriguing.

There is an entry in the Hawstead register that reads...[8]

The following memorandum I made from the account of the clerk when I was a lodger at Hawstead Place, and had but a distant prospect of becoming Rector of the Parish.

On Tuesday 26 July 1759 was born in the Parish of Hawstead a child, or rather two children joined together with two Heads, four Arms, four Legs. The two Faces, which were quite distinct and beautiful, were opposite each other: the bodies were united from a little below the necks to somewhat lower than the Navels. Both the Children of which this monster was formed were males. It is doubtful whether it was born alive, however the mother was certain that it was alive the Day before its Birth.

Siamese twins are rare, but feature on a few occasions in Suffolk registers. As in the entry for Kelsale in 1545, (*a two-headed baby monster*)[9] the word 'monster' appears in all cases. Among the births noted at Woodbridge in 1661, we read of *'Burrows - a monstrous child having foure armes, foure shoulders, four thighs and four feet.'* In 1736 Dr. Studd of Saxmundham advertised in the Norwich Mercury that he had in his possession *'one of the greatest Curiosities in Nature, being a Double Foetus of a BOY and a GIRL, joined together.'* He had delivered them three months earlier and preserved them, so that *'Gentlemen and Ladies that are curious'* might, for a small fee, view them.

Baptisms weren't always simple. At Playford in1785... *'The frost was so intense that the basin of water on the font was frozen over during the morning service.'*[10]

And how about this for the start of a novel...[11]
Stanton All Saints: 29th March 1624: *'Baptised Mary daughter of John and Margaret Gould, Irishman, who then remained prisoner to the Turkes and Margaret Gould his wife who travelling in these parts by passport was delivered of her childe in the churchyarde of All Saints the 23rd March 1623/4.'*

The parson could, of course, choose to make his opinions only too clear. Bramford: 3rd February 1681: *'Ralph and Isaac Hood two base children of the common whore Sarah Avis baptized.'*[12]

41

On occasions, the information supplied can be quite remarkable...

Worlingworth

February 9th 1693: Baptized Elizabeth the bastard daughter of Sarah Downing by Robert Rous, the reputed father.
April 6th 1694: Baptized Margaret the bastard daughter of Margaret Baker by the aforesaid Robert Rous, the reputed father.
January 20th 1697: Baptized Mary the base child of Susan Briggs by Robert Rous the reputed father.
...then, as if that was not enough...
February 10th 1695: Baptized Drusille daughter of Robert Rous and wife. [Long-suffering wife!]
And just to show that sinners often outlive the righteous...
May 31st 1762: Buried Robert Rous.[13]

The 'powers that be' may have frowned upon those who wrote more than they felt was strictly necessary. Later registers were no longer filled with blank pages, but pages of forms offering little opportunity for additional information. That did not inhibit the officiating minister at St. James in Bury St. Edmunds in 1832 when presented with a situation that was truly amazing.

It was a marriage between Christopher Newsom and Charity Murrell. As can be seen from this register entry, Charity Murrell signed her own name whilst her husband could only sign his name with a cross. This is all the more remarkable in the light of what the minister wrote in the margin of the register...

Charity Murrell being entirely without arms the ring was placed upon the fourth toe of the left foot - & she wrote her name in this register with her right foot.[14]

Marriage usually requires the publication of Banns, which survive for a large number of Suffolk parishes. These are more familiarly read out on three occasions in church, but could be made all the more public, as is evident from Woodbridge registers...

1654: John Benns of Wickham [Market] *and Elizabeth Bobet of Dalinghoe, both single, were asked the 10th, 17th, 24th dayes of January in the open market at Woodbridge.*
1655: Henry Stebbing, of Woodbridge, and Elenor Sparham of Dunstall in open market three several market days.

In Aldeburgh in 1655, *John White of Knodishall, widdower and Anne Reynolds of this parish was published... but they relinquished each other and were never married. The purpose of marriage between Henry Downeing of Subborne, singleman... and Anne Fayrehead alsoe singlewoman was published on the 8th, 15th and 22nd days of March in the open market place at Aldeburgh 1655. And the said Henry and Anne were marryed.*

Reading of banns was the opportunity for listeners to raise objections to a marriage. However, if you moved far enough away from your first marriage, you might expect to get away with a second...

The first Woodbridge Register includes the marriage of Roger Leftchilde to Mary Sewell in October 1617. A note in the margin informs us his first wife, Margaret *'from Peterburrow'* turned up two years later (along with child), prompting the parson to comment in the register, *'Leftchild by name, Leftchild by nature.'*

Burials

Burial registers are often little more than lists of names and dates. For the most part cause of death is not mentioned, unless, of course, it is particularly noteworthy.

The following entries are all from St. Michael's, Beccles registers...

January 10th 1593: John sonne of John GILBARD and Elizabeth which was drowned in the river betwene Beckles and Oulton mouth out of a keel his father being with him at the same time in it about the 15 day of November.

April 27th 1595: A stranger which it is sayd came from Cambridge whose name we knowe not.

St. Michael's, Beccles

April 10th 1596: William WRIGHTE who was slayne as he diged sand the clyfe fallyng on him.

May 17th 1611: Thomas BILTON barber stirying abroad but a little more than one hower before he died

July 16th 1611: Margret wife of [space] *CODMAN (who dyed in childbirth but in common suspycyon the child was not hir husbands).*

1690: Will Wadkins came to an untimely end being killed by a gun

[An entry after October 1727] *Buried in the month of October were registered 53 persons. In the same month were carryed out of town 3 persons to be buryed in other places and one more child died in the town therefore not registered. The whole number amounting to 57 persons which great mortality might be imputed to a very uncommon and odd feaver.*
[Usually only about 7 or 8 were buried each month. This disease was clearly not one of the more commonly recognised killers and may well have been malaria. This was, after all, amid the marsh-lands of East Anglia.]

Louise Dahl in her book about Burgh Castle (pub. 1913) puts the high number of burials in 1657 down to a malaria epidemic, though she doesn't make clear where her evidence comes from. Burgh Castle, of course, has quite recently suffered the ignomony of being relegated to Norfolk.

I hope the following is a mistake on the part of the person entering names in the Somerleyton parish register...
May 29th 1612   Helen Dearinge a widow buried the 19 of May who dyed the 28 day of the same month.

Most burials in parish registers give no cause of death. Just occasionally are we treated to extra detail. St Nicholas's in Ipswich recorded in detail which burials in 1665-6 were from the plague and which were not.[15] The Wetheringsett register for 1863 records the deaths over one winter of over twenty children from scarlatina.[16] The minister for Monks Eleigh for a number of years in the nineteenth century gives causes of death for most burials, showing how many died (over a third) from consumption. Yet when 324 people died in the year 1570 in Aldeburgh (only 40 the

year before), we are left to guess what terrible epidemic must have struck the town. The Somerleyton register tells us that George and Mary Rivettt were buried together on the same day in June 1714, but gives no further explanation as to how this came about.
Some more unusual causes of death that are mentioned are these...

Bramford

Old Mother Abillone was killed, haveing by accident set her house on fire She was slaine by it, yet she was not burned to ashes, though all her household stuffe even the brasse and pewter were consummed, yet the greatest part of her bodie remained, a sadd spectacle to behold. This was a sunday about tenn or eleventh of the clock, morning, being the 21st of November 1675.
[This description appears among a host of smallpox victims][17]

Bramford c1835
painted by J. Thomas

Walton (near Felixstowe) *July 9th 1792: Buried: Man washed up on beach tied up in two sacks.*[18] [Seaside parish registers tend to contain any number of unnamed drownings. This one was clearly no accident.]

Bildeston
January 23rd 1731: Buried, John Broom, apprentice to John Webb, blacksmith, was shot dead upon a spot in shop of said John Webb, 21st 1731/2, by John Webb, son of said John Webb, who is a boy between 8 & 9 years of age. (Coroner's Inquest brought in verdict: Accidental death)[19]

Cretingham
Buried: May 20th 1836: Lucy Burrows, infant: (The first body buried in a New Poor Law coffin, a most disreputable specimen of modern liberalism).
Buried: September 29th 1835: Ann Nunn (Dropped down dead whilst dancing at the Bell).[20]

Thurston
November 22nd 1863: Buried, Jesse Shepherd aged 43 Killed instantaneously by falling over the bannister at the north side of the Railway Station whilst attempting, it is supposed, to slide down.[21]

Layham
Will Clover killed by the mill as it was grinding on a Sunday.[22]
Stratford St. Mary
July 26th 1621: Buried Peter Clarke, wente to steall cherries upon the saboth daye fill downe & maymd him selfe and died within three dayes after.[23] [a real pair of cautionary tales!]

Worlingworth
March 15th 1762: Lydia daughter of James Gosling and Mary his wife was buried - who dropt down dead in the churchyard as she was low'ring her mother to ye grave.[24]

Somerleyton

Feb 8th 1761: James Mickleborough aged 21, a servant of Mr. Bowgen, died 48 hours after both his legs were shattered by a loaded wagon.

Stoke by Nayland

Dec. 2nd 1603 Thomas Poulterer, servant to the Right Honble. Lord Windsor who by chance fell into the towne well and was so slain.

Burgh Castle

1905 George Charles Nelson buried, kicked by horse alarmed by motor car.

Creeting St. Mary

Feb. 20 1801 Elizabeth Wood of Creeting St Olaves [a parish that has now disappeared] *age 83 length of her coffin 3ft 4ins., width 1 ft. 1 ins., its depth 1 ft. 9 ins. This singular character lived some years in ye chimney of her home on Creeting Hills. This dwarf known as Sally Woods lived in the lane on Creeting Hills still known as Sally Woods Lane. When her cottage fell, she lived in the chimney.*

Sally Woods Lane, Creeting St. Mary

An early 19th century watercolour entitled 'Anne Woods of Coddenham,' almost certainly the person referred to here.

Pettistree

March 24th 1744 William Jaye was buried (being the last of his name in the parish and an end of a very worthless, malicious, ill natured family, having for ages being remarkable for oppressing, and as much as in them lay, for defrauding the ministers of this parish of their just dues, which character this person kept up to the last day of his life).[25] [The man with the pen was definitely in a position of power. He could write whatever he liked and it would probably survive through centuries.]

The deaths of accident-prone people of St. Margaret's, Lowestoft feature prominently in the burial registers. In the sixteenth century, at least three perished in wells. Others died in sand, water and lime pits. Other details include job and character descriptions. Here we read of *a chimne sweper, flaggraver, pilate of a shipp, marchant, proctor, surgen, knacker, haireweaver, tinker* and *fidler* as well as *a good virtuus and charitable woman, an honest and prudent man* and *John Wells, a miserable miser.* Somerleyton register records the burial of Richard Gillins in 1763. Though no cause of death is given, the parson sees fit to record that he was *a labourer and a young man, honest and industrious.* It is probably no surprise to discover that in the Napoleonic wartime period of 1805-10, at least a dozen unnamed sailors were washed ashore at Lowestoft and buried there.

The 1628-1785 burials for Preston St. Mary are unusually detailed regarding causes of death. In most parishes however, merely names and dates and little more appear. Sometimes, a hint of a sadder story may be entered up, such as at Tannington in 1589 where *William Strange, a poore child was slayne with a tree,*[26] and at Thorington in 1591, where *one Derrowe a lad of 8 yeares who as he saide came from Bunggay... died at our bricke Kell* [kiln]. In Rushbrooke's register[27] we read of Thomas Jermyn, killed by the fall of a mast which seamen were raising on a stormy day in 1692. Sadly, he wasn't even meant to be on that ship at the time.

Bramfield Church c1840

Probably the most remarkable remembrance of a life lost is to be found on a stone in the chancel floor of Bramfield church (pictured opposite).

Between the Remains of her Brother Edward,
And of her husband Arthur,
Here lies the Body of Bridgett Applewhaite,
Once Bridgett Nelson.
After the Fatigues of a Married Life,
Borne by her with Incredible Patience
For Four Years and three Quarters, bating three weeks,
And after the Enjoiment of the Glorious Freedom
Of an easy and Unblemisht Widowhood,
For four years and upwards,
She Resolved to run the Risk of a second Marriage Bed,
But Death forbad the Banns:
And having with an Apoplectick Dart,
(The same Instrument with which he had Formerly
Dispatch't her Mother,)
Touch't the most vital part of her Brain,
She must have fallen Directly to the Ground,
(As one Thunder-strook)
If she had not been catch't and Supported by her Intended Husband.
Of which Invisible Bruise,
After a struggle for above sixty Hours
With that grand Enemy to Life,
(But the certain and Mercifull Friend to Helpless Old Age,)
In Terrible Convulsions, Plaintive Groans, or Stupefying Sleep,
Without Recovery of her Speech or Senses,
She died on the 12th day of Sepr in ye year of our Lord 1737,
Of her own age 44.

At Stoke Ash, in October 1722, the relatives of Mrs Bridgett Smyth were unsure which of her two former husbands she should be buried with, so placed her body between the two of them. Thomas Howard, the fourth Duke of Norfolk outlived his three wives. The first two were buried in the same tomb in Framlingham church, a somewhat unusual economy.

Once you were buried, there was no guarantee that you would remain there. If they were short of space, you might only

get 50 years in the ground before you were dug up to make room for someone else. The medieval Charnel House at Bury St. Edmunds, shown here, would be the very last resting place of countless sets of bones disinterred over the centuries.

At St. Peter's Cretingham, the rector's displeasure at such a practice is made abundantly clear...

Burial: 6th September 1603: Margaret Cornewalleis. Many remains of the ancient and honourable members of this family were indecently and impiously exhumed to make a spacious vault for the vulgar family of Chenery of Eye, and among the relics, the skull of this lady, buried 223 years, having hair entire, of great length and nicely braided in the crown, was taken up, and the hair divided among numerous bystanders. A portion of it given to me Sept 28, 1834, is in my possession. N.B. The transaction took place before my Incumbency. R.B. Exton

The Rumburgh register recounts the finding of a stone coffin in 1895 during renovations to the church. It was almost certainly of monastic origin, as the church was formerly part of a priory. It was reinterred.

Other odd items

 Some entries appear in registers that clearly have no place there. The unhappy parson at Coney Weston in 1764, uses the pages of his parish register to feel sorry for himself...[28]
[The last line is from Psalm 120 v.5]

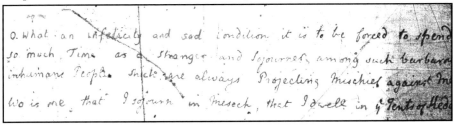

 Who is this man? Most likely, he is Sam Jonston whose name appears briefly between two more permanent rectors, Robert Sugden who died in 1662 and Rev. Gul. Cobbold who took up residence in the parish in 1665. I guess Rev. Jonston decided it was all too much of *'an infelicity and sad condition.'*

On a more agricultural note, the Finningham register recounts... *In the year 1799 Mr. Hunt of Gislingham cut & carried a field of barley on the 19th of November being as soon as the wetness of the season & the late ripening of the corn would permit.*[29] [Which may have delayed the payment of tithes.]

 The Beccles register offers cures for the bite of a mad dog. This is one of them...[30]

Take six ounces of Rue clean'd, pick'd and bruis'd, four ounces of Garlick peel'd and bruis'd, four ounces of Venice Treacle, four ounces of filed pewter or scraped tin. Boil these in two quarts of the best ale in a pan cover'd close over a gentle fire for the space of one hour, then strain the ingredients from the liquor. Give eight or nine spoonfuls of it warm to a man or woman three mornings fasting and cold to any beast fasting, eight or nine spoonfuls is sufficient for the strongest, a less quantity to those younger or of a weaker constitution as you judge their strength, ten or twelve spoonfuls for a horse or bullock; three, four or five for a sheep, hog or dog. This must be given within nine days after the bite and it never fails either on man or beast. If you can, conveniently, bind some of the ingredients on the wound.

In the Benacre register, you can find another such cure, along with a cure for stones.[31]

Letheringham Mill

And how about this grisly tale from the Letheringham registers...

John Bullard and son were tenants of Letheringham Mill. They were murdered in the night of 7th February 1698/9 by Jonas Snell, their journeyman, who was hanged for the crime at Wickham Market, Friday 14th April, 1699. His remains still swung from the gibbet at Poachards Green 50 years later.

It is easy to assume that people living in isolated villages over two hundred years ago were out of touch with what was going on elsewhere - even in their own county. Think again!

The rector of Stuston, near Diss, James Pawsey writes...[32]

Upon the 31st of October 1762 a Brief was read in this Church for building Colleges at Philadelphia and New York in America and upon ye 3rd of November a Collection was made from house to house, and seven shillings and one penny was collected.

Which proves that even small out-of-the-way villages had a knowlege of a wider world. This becomes even more clear when you examine three pages from the Belstead register of the 1660s detailing weekly collections being made for the relief of disasters in a wide range of places around the kingdom from Southampton to Lancaster, [the Great Fire of] London to Grimsby.[33] Cratfield records of the early 17th century include a payment of 2s 6d *towards repairing of a church in a feren shere* [foreign shore or shire?]. In April 1695, when the town of Warwick was almost destroyed by fire, Stoke by Nayland raised £1-1s-2d in a parish collection.

Briefs, as used above, were Sovereigns' Letters Patent, stamped with the Privy Seal, authorising charitable collections through parish churches. References to these survive in a number of parishes, notably Pettaugh and Barham.

The 1665 *'Booke of Towne Accounts for Denston'* lists collections for disasters in places as far apart as Shaldon in Devon, Morpeth in Northumberland, Thirsk in Yorkshire and Brecon in Wales, as well as for French and Irish protestants. There are also payments made *'for a fire near yᵉ sawmill yard in Lambeth'* and *'towards the reliefe of those that were sick of the plague in London.'*

It is not uncommon to find collections made for the redemption of captives taken hostage around the world. Rushbrooke[34] and Darsham[35] collected money to release *Christian captives taken by Turkish pyrates* in 1671 and *English captives in Algiers* in 1680. A Falkenham register[36] contains a memorandum relating to four shillings collected towards the repairing of St. Paul's Cathedral in 1633. A number of briefs are listed in the same register whereby collections were made for individuals around the country. Unfortunately, the reason for their suffering is not mentioned, nor is the means by which this knowledge was obtained, but here are a few examples...

May 17 1663: one published for John Ellis of Milton in the county of Cambridge collected 5d.

Aug 23 1663: one pub. for William Smyth & others of ye towne of Hexam in ye county of northumberland. collected 7d
Sept 18 1663: one published for Ed^w Chisham of Grantham in the county of Lincolne. collected 1d.
[Clearly Edward Chisham wasn't worthy of as much sympathy as the others]

In 1670, the people of Stratford St. Mary made contributions for the *'redemption of Turkish captives.'* [37] And at the end of the oldest Rushbrooke register[38] can be found subscription lists from the seventeenth century showing again an awareness of disasters as far away as Grimsby, Shropshire, Dorset & Scarborough.

People could be stunningly generous. In 1637, the people of East Bergholt collected over twenty pounds to help relieve the poor of Hadleigh as they suffered from the plague. In 1659 Wherstead collected five pounds, one shilling and threepence halfpenny towards *the releefe of the distressed people... of Southwold.* This is one of a large number of such collections made around that time, though far smaller sums were usually involved.

Gt. Whelnetham church

All manner of unexpected things appear in Suffolk's parish registers. The parson of Gt. Whelnetham, being unable to get to his church one Sunday, wrote...

Jan 2nd 1767: It began to snow very much this day. The wind blowing strong and heaping up the snow, continued at times snowing every day and on Friday the 9th it snowed all day, the wind blowing strong which gathered up the snow so much as to make the hollow roads level, all carriages laid by, the stage could get only from Bury to Bradfield Manger, forced to turn back again to Bury. In the Rectory garden at Great Whelnetham Jan 10th 1767 the snow before the parlour front measured 3 ft. 3 ins. deep... Jan 11th Sunday at 2 of the clock afternoon I attempted on horseback to get to church, could not ride as far as the Hall gate, with difficulty got back, the road being wholly covered and smooth, in places 4 ft. deep.[39]

An entry in the margin of one of the Burgh (near Woodbridge) registers recounts how the Rev. A. Maude, rector of that parish from 1876 until 1914 used to enjoy cycling. Unfortunately, whilst travelling at some speed, he had a serious accident with a horse and cart, which rendered him unconscious for six weeks. He was not expected to recover but, miraculously, he did. So, he dedicated a window in  Burgh Church to his fortuitous escape. As this picture shows, from that time on, he wore a station-master's hat to protect the wound.

The second of Bramford's registers[40] has a memorandum on the fly-leaf recounting the great storm of 1661. The fourth Bures register, at the back, tells of a great flood...

'that carried away ye chief of ye bridge, went into ye church and damaged ye floor, came into ye vacarage yards and barn but it did not, praised be God, come into ye house.'

The first register for Brandeston[41] contains an account of the Rector, John Lowes' execution for witchcraft in 1645. More detail of this can be found in my book, *'Witches in and around Suffolk.'*

Some years after the repeal of the Witchcraft Act, there is an entry in the Monks Eleigh register that reads...

Dec. the 19th 1748. Alice the wife of Thos. Green, labourer, was swam, malicious & wicked people having raised an ill report of her, for being a witch.

Probably the earliest mention of witchcraft in Suffolk I have been able to find appears in Ipswich Petty Plea Rolls from the reign of Edward 1, whereby Joan Haltebe obtained damages from John Gyn: master of La Garklande, John Sailyeur: baker of Oreford and others for calling her *'sorcerer and pympledhore.'*

And then there are the items with which someone seems to have been a little cautious about sullying the pages of the registers. What may have been too unpalatable for the register itself has been written on loose sheets and tacked to the inside cover of the book.

There is a long account attached to the inside of the Little Livermere register, detailing one of its most notorious ex-parishioners.[42] There seems to have been concern that Arundel Coke's name did not feature in the parish registers although he was known to have been born and probably buried there. Suggestions had been made that pages had been removed to eradicate his name. This was not so. Born just after the Civil War, his baptism, like others at that time, had been missed out. As a hanged man, he was

The ruins of Lt. Livermere church today

not supposed to have been buried in consecrated ground. Almost certainly he **was** buried there, but no record could appear in the burial register.

Arundel Coke, alias Cooke of the borough of Bury St Edmunds Esq. barrister at law. Not named in this register, from the year of our Lord 1641 to 1682, no baptisms are entered as the page is not filled on the left hand & no entry made in the year 1642 and as the opposite page is evidently blotted by the same ink with which the Baptism of Elizabeth Sucklinge 1639 was entered (see the day of the month) altho' that page be not of the same colour and dimensions there is no cause to suppose a page was taken out of the register to destroy any record of this unfortunate criminal's birth &c.

On Tuesday the 13th of March 1721. John Woodburne, late of the borough of St. Ed. Bury & Arundel Coke Esq. were indicted under the Coventry Act passed in 1670 for assaulting Edward Crispe Gent. of the borough of St. Ed. Bury, lying in wait, unlawfully and feloniously did slit the nose of the said Ed. Crispe with an intent in so doing to maim and disfigure. Coke, the brother in law of Crispe married to Crispe's sister bribed

Woodburne to murder his relative and invited Crispe, his wife and other friends to sup with him at his house, the corner of the Sparrow Hawk St. placing Woodburne in readiness in the porch of Mr. Morrice's house. In the course of the evening Coke went out and encouraged his accomplice, telling him Crispe was very jolly. Between nine and ten o'clock Coke lured Crispe into the church-yard, it being dark, to walk before Mrs. Monk [?]. He then whistled, the sign for Woodburne to execute his purpose. Mr. Crispe upon this signal and hearing footsteps was alarmed and hastened towards the wall. Woodburne came up to Mr Coke at the instant who bade him take cause not to hit him instead of Crispe, it being very dark. Coke took him by his sleeve and led him to Crispe saying, "brother stand still." Woodburne then struck Crispe two strokes with his hook - "though I never heard him swear." (Woodburne declared at his trial) He now swore, "God d**** him!" on which Coke said, "what doth he swear? Secure him, down with him." "He stood by as I gave him several blows and then he went away telling me to take away his watch - as to his money he don't carry above half a crown or three shillings in his pocket, and when I go to London I will sell the watch for you."

Leaving his brother-in-law for dead, Arundel Coke returned home after an absence of about ten minutes (as disclosed by Mr. Bemmer [?] who married Coke's sister and with his wife and daughters had supped with Coke and Crispe being nearly night) and seemed out of breath as if he had walked faster than usual. Then Coke drank a glass of wine and when asked what was become of Crispe answered, "I believe he is gone home in the dark" - in two or three minutes after that Crispe returned much wounded and bloody and that it was about half an hour between the time of Mr Crispe going out and returning again. Coke seemed in great consternation upon seeing Crispe come back to his house. Previous to the L. C. Justice summing up the evidence, Coke stated that he was much ashamed and very unable to defend himself. "I am," he continued, "ashamed to think I should be concerned in so heinous a crime against Mr Crispe's life. I am confounded at it. It is indeed a very great crime and I know not what to say for myself. As for Woodburne he hath asserted of me many things that are false."

L.C.J.:[Judge]   *I have told the jury what he hath said is no evidence against you.*

Coke: *When I first spoke of this matter to Woodburne he said he should value it no more than the cutting off the head of a dog. Indeed I did go out with Mr. Crispe that night but I was not near him when Woodburne struck him. I retreated to my own house in a moment. My Lord I am sensible that a point of law may arise on the statute whereon I am indicted.*

L.C.J.:   *Whereon?*

Coke: *With respect to my intention.*

At this point, Coke interrupted to make the most remarkable claim...

Coke: *My intention was to kill Mr Crispe and not to maim or disfigure him.*

Maiming and disfiguring had been a high profile crime of the time leading to 'The Coventry Act' that made it punishable by death. Coke still thought he might avoid a hanging. But...

...The Jury retired for half an hour, then gave their verdict, Guilty.

On 31st March 1721 they would both be hanged, and then their bodies handed over to local doctors to 'anatomise,'(see overleaf) before their 'bits' were handed over to their relatives for burial.

...Mr. A Coke was buried the same day in the church (east end of Church) of Livermere Parva.

Sexual Shennanigans

As with this previous case, the register of Gt. Whelnetham contains loose sheets appended. One reads...[43]

In the year 1701, six persons did their penance in the space of 8 days. They were these...
William Boldero & Elizabeth his wife
Ffrancis Ottewell & Rose his wife
These fore antinuptua fornication on Sunday April 13th
[presumably Latin for wife-swapping]
Robert Bray on Good Friday April 18
Elizabeth Harold on Sunday April 20 being Easter Sunday
These for fornication with each other [but on different days!!!]
Never was the like (I suppose) before in ye Town ffrom ffornication and all other deadly sin. Libera nos Domine
Two of these seemed very penitent especially the widow Harold But Boldero and Ottewell the two men appeared with an impudent whores fforehead [?]
Sunday Jan 31 1702   George Cason did his penance for committing ffornication with Mary Johnson but shewed no sign of penitence, rather to the contrary.

This intriguing item leaves you with the desire to know two things -

1. What kind of penance were they expected undertake? and 2. Why was it such a big deal?

You see, this was not merely a ticking-off from the vicar, but supported by the full weight of the Archdeaconry Court, which carried the power to excommunicate those who were not prepared to go along with the judgement and to do their penance (without giggling).

Fortunately, a second sheet is tacked inside the Gt. Whelnetham register. It is not from there or even from that part of Suffolk. It gives details of a penance performed at Ubbeston near Halesworth at around the same time. Possibly two parsons swapped ideas. By the way, this extract is also to be found in the Ubbeston Register.[44]

12 Sept. 1707   The form of penance to be performed by Sarah Edwards for committing the crime of Adultery as followeth. Imprimis [firstly] - *The said Sarah Edwards shall upon a Sunday after the second Peale of Morning Prayers come out into the Church Porch of Ubbestone and there shall stand until the second lesson be ended arrayed all the while in a white sheet down to the feet with a white wand in her hand and a paper pinned upon her breast expressing her offence and shall ask forgiveness of those that come to the church.*

Item - the second lesson being ended the Minister shall receive her into the Congregation and being placed before the Minister's desk with her face to the Congregation and standing upon a pesse [believed to mean a hassock] *shall make penitently the confession following saying after y[e] Minister in an audible voice.*

I Sarah Edwards do acknowledge and confess that I have most grievously offended Almighty God and provoked his just wrath and indignation against me by committing the sin of fornication - I am heartily sorry for this my great sin and offence and I do most sincerely beg of God Almighty pardon and forgiveness thereof and to grant his grace of true repentance and

perseverance therein and that I may never commit the like sin anymore but lead an honest and sober life for the time to come and that I desire this congregation to join with me in prayer to Almighty God saying...
Our Father, which art in Heaven &c

Willm. Edgar   Reg^r Dep.

The performance hereof to be certified
Under the Minister and Churchwardens
At Yoxford October 3 1707

Whilst this creates a great picture of the event, it doesn't fully explain my second question. Fortunately we have another such detail - this time from Lowestoft. Between 1751 and 1755, ten parishioners of Lowestoft were summoned to the Court of the Archdeaconry of Suffolk to answer charges of adultery and fornication (from Lowestoft Parish Registers Vol. 1, transcribed by Frederick A. Crisp). Lowestoft believed it had a problem, and indeed it did, as three of the accused women were widows who had between them seventeen illegitimate children as well as those born during their marriages - yes, I'd say they certainly had a bit of a problem!

In October 1753, Randal West confessed that he had committed the crime of fornication with Mary Cobb and was given a schedule of penance.
In December 1755, Mary Balls, Judith Brame, John King & Nathaniel Newon did not attend the court and were excommunicated. Margaret Newton did attend to do penance. She was required to repeat after the minister this statement...

I... do here in the presence of Almighty God and this congregation here present humbly confess and acknowledge that I have most grievously offended his divine Majesty in defiling my body by the heinous Sin of Fornication for which my said foul offence I am hearytily sorry and do sincerely repent thereof and beg of God mercy and forgiveness for the same; desiring all you here present to take warning at this my punishment, for the avoiding any the *like wickedness and pray to God for me that his wrath and plagues threatened against Whoremongers, Adulterers, fornicators and all such Unclean Persons may be turned away from me **and this town where I live.***

The way I see it, the important words for those officiating are the last six. They believed that if they tolerated what they saw as sin, they would all suffer God's wrath. Less than a century before, the great plague had been accepted by many as punishment sent by God for just this kind of transgression. They were no longer prepared to turn a blind eye - you did your penance or you were excommunicated; simple as that.

As has been shown, Archdeaconry courts had a great deal of power. Fines or penances could be demanded and in extreme cases, excommunication, which could make it hard for those so punished to find employment. Most commonly, they dealt with non-attendance at church, improper behaviour in church and non-payment of dues. But immorality too was high on the agenda. Hadleigh, Moulton and Monks Eleigh, by virtue of their monastic attachment to Canterbury, continued even after the dissolution of the monasteries to belong to a separate Deanery (Bocking). Their court records survive and make interesting reading.

Between 1637 and 1641, sixteen Hadleigh cases of adultery and fornication came before this court. John Porter and wife appeared to answer questions as to why their child was born just fourteen days after their wedding (the answer to which must have been pretty obvious). John Mickfield was cited for publishing banns of his marriage whilst *'living suspiciously'* with the woman and subsequently *'hath put her away.'* More unusual was the acknowledgement of lesbian activity, but in 1640, Philippa Long, widow was charged with *'incontinency with Margaret Fuller.'*

Other misdemeanours include John Merril's *'coming late to church and behaving irreverently when he is there.'* Also the unfortunate Anne Glasse was caught a bit short during a long sermon, *'having beastly made water in the church at service time.'*

Sometimes, it was not only the parishioners who came under scrutiny. An ancient document of 1333, describes how the Priory of St. Peter in Ipswich was visited by order of William, Bishop of Norwich to investigate a number of troubling accusations...

'Henry of Kerseye, prior, denies having relations with Margery Starlynge, Joan Wypelwasshere, Mary Shirneve, and purges himself of the charge... He admits he has rendered no account of the revenues for 6 years past; that with brother Thomas of Verdone, cellarer, he has taken away a lamp from the church... that he unduly favours William of Derby, porter, who lives with Agnes, daughter of John of Hadeleye. Robert of Thorndone, sub-prior admits that he has differences with the prior; that he has beaten brother John of Rungetone and also Robert of Kenbrokes in St. Peter's church. He denies having relations with [blank], wife of Geoffrey Bulloke of Ipswich.... Brother John of Brysete denies that he has conspired with the sub-prior and four others against the prior and Thomas Verdon, cellarer.; or that he was discovered by William Spyrone of Ipswich with Mabna [?] daughter of Thomas Maijors and Patience Andrews when he was chamberlain and guardian of St. Clements church, or that he has had relations with Joan of Cloptone. He admits relations with Agnes, daughter of John Blunt and [?].

As a result of all this, a series of demotions, penances and more rigorous punishments followed.

Missing history

A good proportion of our parish registers survive, which means we have a fair chance of finding Suffolk baptisms, marriages and burials when we go searching for them. The Parish chest seems to have been a safe haven for our documents prior to the Record Offices taking charge of them. Of course, there are reasons why some records don't survive. Hundon Parish Church suffered a terrible fire in 1914. The register page pictured is one of the good ones.[45] Much was destroyed.

I have an advertisement from a 1777 news-paper offering a 25 guinea reward for the return of register pages stolen from Wroxham in Norfolk. Vermin, floods; all manner of disasters could befall our parish records. But often gaps in our knowledge today are down to simple human error.

An entry in the Stuston register for 1756 reads...[46]

From this Time [1753] to 1756 the Rev^d Mr Oldfield enter'd nothing in this Register as it appeared to J. Pawsey who succeeded him in this Rectory.

As if to make his point, J. Pawsey writes everything down from tiles falling off the church roof to listing candidates for confirmation, something rarely included (though Pakenham's second register names those taken to be confirmed at 'Tosticke' [Tostock] in 1636). One West Stow parson refers in his register to how badly it has been kept for the years 1675 - 1724. As if to verify this, only seven entries cover those 50 years.

Being able to confirm that you had been baptized was important. Confirmation, marriage and burial were only available to those who had been christened into the church of England. In 1761, a correction appears in the Reydon register admitting that William and Brame Bradwell had been omitted from the record *'either by the mistake or the forgetfulness of the officiating minister.'* A similar mistake is owned up to regarding the daughters of William and Alice Hazell. As these was only shortly after their baptisms were supposed to have happened, it is not clear whether the man writing this is that same forgetful parson.

The records for Bacton in the 1780s seem incomplete and so they are. Filed amongst documents that once dwelt in the parish chest are what the Ipswich Record Office describes as *'assorted pieces of paper.'*[47] These include a wonderful example of the 'piece of paper from the parson's pocket'. Bacton Parish Chest has three locks requiring three keys to open it. These were traditionally divided between the rector and his two church-wardens. This meant they all had to be in the church at the same time, having remembered their keys in order to open the box. It is well documented that in such cases, parsons tended to write details intended for the parish registers on pieces of paper, pending transferring the information onto the appropropriate pages. In this case a number of names and dates never made their way into the register of baptisms, marriages and burials, especially for the years 1786 and 1787. Perhaps the parson forgot, or couldn't be bothered, or thought just slipping the paper into the book would suffice. Fortunately in this case, that separate sheet of paper has survived over two centuries. But if the maid had washed his trousers without looking in the pockets, those names would have been lost forever. Think how often that must have happened.

Most of the parishioners of Suffolk parishes were to all intents and purposes illiterate throughout earlier centuries. Until schools became more plentiful in the nineteenth century, most couldn't even write their own name. So they were reliant on others to interpret what they (with a broad Suffolk accent) called themselves. Hence, spellings of names vary immensely. When researching a family called Allington, I found the name variously spelt Allerton, Ollerton, Alderton, Alderson, Ollerson etc. Rolfe was also Ralph, Raffe, Relf and so on. Some names, once common in our registers, have almost disappeared since families settled on a more acceptable form. There used to be a lot of Pricks about. Now, mysteriously, they nearly all seem to be Prykes. Hardly surprising really!

During the Civil War years, many of our parish registers were hidden away and there may be a gap of ten years or so. William Dowsing, responsible for the puritanisation of our churches was a Suffolk man, and statues, stained glass, wall-paintings etc. were removed from most of our churches. In many parishes, items still viewed as valuable were spirited away just in case. At Euston, near Thetford, the registers[48] were 'lost' for over nine years and there are no entries for that time. It was only at the restoration of the monarchy such books were mysteriously 'found' again. To celebrate, someone in 1657 (possibly the parson) has written this magnificent poem.

When Traytors domineere in Saints disguise
And Hell-gott Presbytereans made their prize
Of Charles the first then Church & State were torne
And in black stormes of warre lay both forlorne
Then Loyal Priests in their just rights were crost
And then this booke nine years & more was lost

If thou art greived cause here thou hast noe place
And caust not find thy yeare & daye of Grace
To King and Keyser render still whats due
And curse that Hell-gott Presbyterian Crue

Not all missing registers survived that confused period of our history. All Felsham registers before that time, for example, were lost and never re-emerged. What is clear is the value so many parishes put on their history, seeking to protect it at any cost.

A final thought for this chapter is a warning that what may appear to be an original inscription in a parish register may not be all it claims to be. Above the burials for the parish of Stowmarket in the year 1665 are the words... *'the year of the Great Plague... the tradition is it did not reach Stow¹ but it was at Needham... The people of Stow carried provisions half way to Needham for the people there who had the plague.'* [49]

The hand in which this is written seems strangely out of place beside the 17th century script of the rest of the page.

Stowmarket rectory 1840

Almost certainly, it is the work of Rev. A.G.H. Hollingsworth, historian, writer and rector of the town in the 1840s, and it is a reminder that not every old piece of writing is necessarily quite as old as it may appear at first glance.

Chapter 3
The Parish Notices[1]

Civil unrest and other unpleasantness

The parish chest was, for centuries, the repository for all manner of paperwork - parchments and scrolls, booklets and letters... for example, this one from 1626 which, until modern times, resided in the Earl Stonham parish chest.[2]

At first glance it appears difficult to decipher, but look at the second line and the words *'require you to appointe one able man to watch the beacon for one weeke'* emerge. Why, fifteen years or so before the English Civil War, were the constables being instructed to protect the beacon from being lit? Was Earl Stonham such a hot-bed of dissent that it was seen as the possible focus of a new peasants' revolt?

The likelihood is that this letter was just one of a host distributed around the county. Anyone who has recently cleared out their kitchen-drawer knows the amount of stuff they have that they end up throwing away - that is just how it must have been with our parish-chests. As they became full and unmanageable, unnecessary clutter was disposed of, taking with it any amount of valuable historical documents. I cannot be sure this is the only surviving letter of its kind, but it is the only one I've seen - a rare survivor from what was originally widespread. And it tells us something we would not have known otherwise - they were beginning to feel troubled all that time before Oliver Cromwell justified their fears. Remember - this page comes courtesy of the good people of Earl Stonham who kept this letter for four hundred years. It's a message to all of us - never throw anything away without giving it a great deal of thought!

Far more predictable is an order contained in the Mickfield papers, dated 1642 instructing the constables to '*prepare for riot and disturbance.* '[3] The Civil War was beginning.
Long Melford has an earlier warrant simply instructing constables '*...to be ready.*' It is dated 1601. This was following the intro-duction of what would later become known as the 'Old Poor Law.'

So what else survives from the parish-chests of Suffolk? What else tells us first-hand about life here centuries ago? The things that most appeal to me are those that are the most basic and parochial; those that, bearing in mind parish-chests did get cleared out from time to time, are surprising survivors.

The 3 lock chest at St. Cross South Elmham

There is a warrant addressed to the Constables of Rattlesden dated 1713 instructing them to... *'bring before us... Justices of the Peace... Ann & Mary Pulford... they are always quarrelling & threatening to murder each other.'*[4]

A similar order relates to petty crime in Mendlesham in 1595 and instructs the constables... *'to put John Dam into the stocks from eight of the clock in the forenoone in the most open place in your market there to contynue soe untill two of the clock in the afternoon of the same day'*[5]

Back Street, Mendlesham
from an original pyrography
picture by Daniel Wright

Once, trial and punishment could be a very local business. Courts Leet handled lesser offences and made sure they were equipped to deal out the necessary retribution. Woodbridge Churchwarden's Acounts for 1596 include an entry *'to John Henlington for making a place upon the Pillarie for the witches to stand on.'* Geoffrey Pocklington's book, 'Chelsworth' describes a payment made to Jno. Rudland *'for building Stocks and a whipping post.'*

The Court Leet of Clare in the seventeenth century comprised of a panel of 18 'headboroughs' who ruled upon such matters as the height people might build their chimneys and how they might choose to dispose of unwanted offal.

Recalcitrant animals could be as much a cause for concern as troublesome humans. Mendlesham again[6] has an order to the pound-keeper to shoot *'a pony with a contagious disease.'* And much more recently, (1940s) the West Suffolk War Agricultural Committee sent a memorandum to Great Livermere[7] concerning a reduction in the number of rooks.

Even more basic and parochial is a cluster of letters from Pakenham[8] in 1832. These relate to a number of poor families forced to share one stinking privy, a cause of some concern. Unable to write their own complaining letters, the same hand penned the words of five householders. They each signed with a cross.

I, Mary Sheckle declare that I cannot bear to have my door open in hot weather for Mr. Kemp stirs the Privy up in hot weather and putrifies us... In Frosty weather he stirs it up very often and then it is worse than in hot weather.

I, Susan Stannard say there are disagreeable smells again & again... there are about 45 persons who use this privy.

I, Maria Sexton must say that the smell is a deal worse in summer than it is now. I hope it will be better now that it is covered with faggots [some hope!] *...there are 5 different privies but they all drain into one place.*

I, Susan Stannard say that the smell is disagreeable in summertime... we are obliged to live in such places because there are no others to get.

I, Jane Burroughs declare that my Husband is in summer time forced to get up from his dinner on account of the smell. I think just the same as he does very uncomfortable as I am there longer than my husband.

The remarkable thing to me is that these have survived the parish-chest clear-outs.

Charity Schools

A somewhat less remarkable survivor is a book from Earl Stonham[9] relating to the management of a charity school set up in the old Guild Hall near the church to educate eight boys from the parish at any one time. It is the panache with which these accounts are recorded that impresses me. Candler Bird, the treasurer responsible for this page, gives us everything we need to know - the names of those educated, how the money for their schooling was received and how it was spent - and all recorded with such flair and delight. Boys (and it **was** only boys) usually stayed for 2-3 years around the age of 8 or 9.

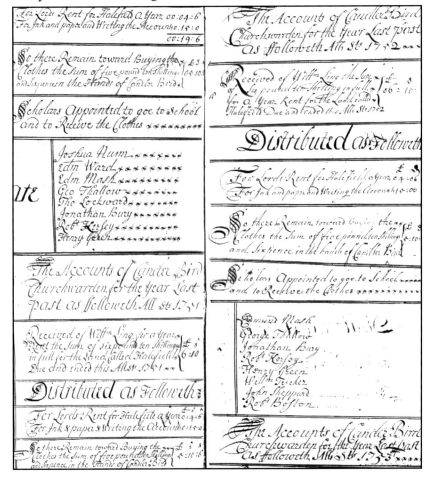

Other charity schools are recorded in different ways. Holton St. Mary near Hadleigh had a school in the eighteenth century where the master was to be paid £7 a year to teach 18 poor children. However, if he could *'procure a school mistress'* to join him, his salary would rise to £9. Also, he would have a house and the opportunity to hire *'Town Ground'* for £18 a year.

Holton Charity School in the early nineteenth century.

Boys were to learn to read, write and *'cast accompts.'* Girls, instead of accounts were to learn to knit and sew. Added to this there was a fair bit of Catechism to be administered, and correction of *'those in the beginnings of vice, such as lying, swearing, stealing, particularly stealing wood, prophaning the Lord's Day and disobedience to parents.* Part of the master's job was to check up on how often children attended the parish church. At the end of their schooling, children were to receive a Bible into which they were to sign the following note...

'I promise with the consent of my parents if ever I shall please God to make me worth £50, to give £10 for ye use & improvements to the Charity School in Holton where I received my education and

this Bible, for which I bless God and thank my benefactors stead-fastly purposing by ye assistance of God's grace to be charitable in proportion to my abilities.'

Education was patchy and schooling 'a bit of a post-code lottery', to use a modern phrase. A letter at West Suffolk Record Office dated 1819 describes a Dame School at Flempton and Hengrave, *'that has on average about 12 scholars.'* [10] A number of parishes including Rougham, Bradfield St. George, Rede, Brockley and Thurston benefited from the Thomas Sparke charity that set up a school in 1721 to educate poor boys of those parishes. In Mendlesham, a building and lands left by one Peter Duck were to provide housing for, and a school to educate, 'the village paupers.' Redgrave and Botesdale were to benefit from the illustrious Sir Nicholas Bacon having once lived there; setting up a Grammar School that catered for fee-payers, boarders as well as six free places. This had begun as early as 1561 in the former chantry building pictured below.

A small table is included in 'The History of a Parish' by G.H. Butler (1910) and looks at how marriage registers were signed across two decades, a century apart. In 1799 - 1808, in Barrow, Gazeley, Kentford and Moulton over 50% of those signing, merely 'left their mark.' By 1899 - 1908, only about 4% appear to have been unable to write their name. We are unsure, of course, whether all of those in the past were quite that illiterate. It is possible, especially in an estate village, they were made to feel that to write your name when you were of labouring stock was 'getting above yourself.' Signing with a cross was what people like that were expected to do.

The Militia

Sometimes stories emerge from parish papers. Or at least, parts of stories. Take this sad tale from the papers of Groton in Suffolk.[11]

Saml Clark (Married a woman from Boxford, by the name of Mattock) & serving as substitute in the Militia left his wife in the Parish of Groton, from whence she duly Rec^d the legal allowance for herself & children which has been refunded from the Parish of Bursham [Garboldisham has been crossed out] *Until the man enlisted into some Regiment & went in the expedition against Holland & which place he was kill'd*

where do this man's wife & family belong, is much the Desire of our Parishioners to know - now the woman will not own anything about it any more than he was an apprentice to some man as shoemaker at garboldisham who she says, was a Certificate man of that Place & if so...

Here the letter ends. You can sense the parish's confusion. The date is probably about 1805 and under the old poor-law the parish was supposed to look after its own. The trouble is with something like four parishes to choose from, nobody wanted to take responsibility for another poor family with no breadwinner.

The Militia was a kind of Home-Guard and all parishes were required according to size to supply one or more Militia-men each year. The family support on offer was poor and it was not a

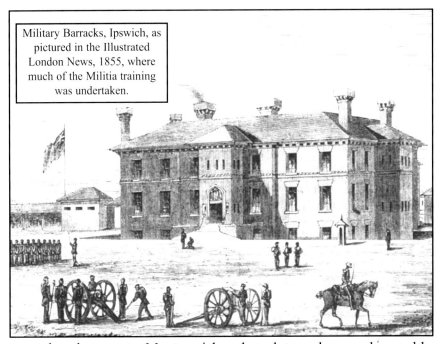

Military Barracks, Ipswich, as pictured in the Illustrated London News, 1855, where much of the Militia training was undertaken.

popular placement. Most parishes drew lots and men who could afford it paid a substitute to take their place if their name was drawn. Samuel Clark, like many, was then recruited into a regular army regiment whence he died fighting abroad. Lt. Glemham papers[12] refer to the need to seek a substitute for the militia, and Haughley[13] have muster papers for the militia dated 1803 (Napoleonic War time). Badwell Ash[14] has lists of militia payments and relief of wives dated 1795. Great Glemham had to look some way afield to find their substitute. For at least four years, (1795 - 99) they were re-imbersing Bildeston for paying the wife and child of Philip Hammond, as he served in the Militia, representing their parish.[15]

Mellis records state... *On April 1th 1643, Edward Gibes of Thrandeston was slayne at a muster, being shot through the bowells, and another of Wortham was shot in the thighe and three others were shot through theyre clothes.* It wasn't the enemy you needed to fear. You were more likely to be killed by your own side if you joined the Militia.

Gleaning

Poverty gave rise to any amount of paperwork as the needy were always in need of support. It seems to have been assumed from Biblical times that one perk available to the poor was gleaning rights; gathering what was left after the harvest was completed. What was not widely understood was that this was not enshrined in law and was at the discretion of individual parishes and their farmers. For example, a Brundish document of 1820 describes the rules by which the practice was governed there[16] (following the recommendations of a meeting of Grand Juries at Bury)...

'That the Church Bell shall be Toll^d every morning during Harvest at eight o'clock as a notice to begin gleaning & at seven in the evening as a notice to leave off gleaning... That entering or quitting the fields otherwise than by the gateways is strictly forbidden... That no young woman or Lads above the age of fourteen who are capable of service or are out of employment by any misconduct will be allowed to glean.'

At the very end of this book, in the Suffolk Anthology, appears a short poem entitled, *'Gleaning time'* that gives a fuller and more vivid picture of the way this was practised.

However, it didn't always work like that. A document dated 1788 from Groton[17] begins...

'Whereas the Poor of Groton and the Neighbourhood thereof have for some years past unlawfully and without any ancient customary Right what is not only made a practice of Gleaning Barley and other soft corn without the leave of the Owner, but have in a most insolent daring and riotous manner assembled taken and carried away large quantities of corn in open defiance of the owner... [Following a recent court case] *the learned Judge confirmed... There was no positive Law on usage upon which a right to Glean could be ascertained - the Soil and the Culture belonged to the Farmer and he had an exclusive claim to all the Fruits of his Own Soil... The permission of the Poor to Glean was merely an Act of humanity on the part of the Farmer but could not be claimed as a Right.'*

Gleaning from the fields was not the way they did things along the coast. As well as the occasional wreck, there was a constant procession of collier ships passing places like Pakefield and Kirkley. If the sea was rough, lumps of coal would be washed ashore and provide useful fuel for families that would go 'a-poltering', as it was called locally.[18]

Emigration abroad and strikes at home

Dealing with the poor in your parish could be an expensive business, even after the establishment of workhouses serving Unions of Parishes. Covehithe followed the lead of a number of parishes by raising a loan to send two of their most poverty-stricken families far enough away to cause them no more concern. In 1836, James & Mary Aldred and their seven children; Samuel & Mary Harbour and their six children were encouraged to emigrate to Canada. The Allendale would convey them from Lowestoft to Montreal.[19]

There are plenty of other cases in Suffolk of parishes sending their poor to Australia, South Africa, Canada etc. The Wetheringsett archives include a letter and circular from the Colonial Emigration Agency (dated 1836) offering *'gratuitously, every possible assistance'* should the parish wish to encourage people emigrating to the United States or any of the colonies.[20]

This was not a cheap option as the formerly mentioned circular from the Blything Union to Covehithe Overseers shows. Though the Union was to bear the cost of passage to Montreal, the parish was required to ensure all emigrees had food for the voyage - each adult minimum provision to be composed of 70 lb. of bread, biscuit, oatmeal or flour, and 7lb of potatoes for each lb of bread. Also, appropriate clothing was expected and enough money to enable them to get to the interior of the country.

Thorndon papers from 1836 include references to charges on the rates for £600 + interest to be repaid in five years towards *'the expenses of emigration of several persons from the parish.'*[21] Campsea Ashe was borrowing money around the same time and for the same purpose.[22] Drinkstone records include a subscription list *'to clothe John Broom, a pauper... for a voyage on the sea.'*[23] George Fisher of Sotherton was sent at the parish's expense to Van Diemen's Land in 1836. A paper survives in the Bacton archives suggesting four adults and eight children were sailing aboard the Brunswick to New York in 1830 and listing the food they were to take with them.[24] The excellent little book 'Stradbroke Notes', produced by the local history group and published by S.A. Bryant, has a chapter by Gwenllian Jones full of detail about the 200 or so parishioners encouraged to find a new life abroad.

One of the best accounts regarding emigration appears in Rev. Zincke's History of Wherstead. In May 1832, Samuel Rich, his wife and four children were enabled by the parish to depart for Quebec. Though their passage costs were under £20, the total cost involved was nearly £50. Amongst the essentials allowed for their trip were tobacco, rum for the voyage, tools and tin-ware.

At least their £50 paid for a whole family. When William Cable was enabled to leave Theberton at Michaelmas 1835, his bill alone would amount to £29-13-2.   In 1836, nearly a tenth of the small village of Horham left England for a new life in Canada. The parish would be paying for years!

Emigration got an additional boost from time to time. In 1874, the relatively young agricultural union, under their leader Joseph Arch, decided to flex their muscles and take on the farmers over pay and working conditions. Around Newmarket, Bury and Woodbridge, labourers threatened to strike. The farmers then responded by locking out union members. As one farmer stated,

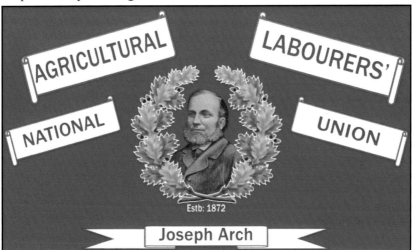

Locked out workers near Bury St. Edmunds as shown in 'The Graphic' 9th May 1874

"I shall let my horses stand idle in the stable and allow my land to run to grass before I will submit to be dictated to by an irresponsible body." This wasn't just a case of bosses versus workers: it was often Anglicans versus Methodists, and the dispute became both bitter and widespread.

It wasn't easy for either side as this illustration from 'The Graphic' entitled *The farmer his own labourer* suggests.

The Dalham school log book refers to this, as 'four big boys', having been locked out of their place of employment decided to return to school. Some villages, Dalham included, recognised the need to improve the education of those employed, and ran evening classes for labourers who wanted to improve their lot. They were taught arithmetic, reading, essay-writing, physiology, science, hygiene and book-keeping.

After twenty weeks of the lock-out, the members of the Amalgamated Labour League (A.L.L.) were allowed back on terms no better than before. In fact, this would be the beginning of a real slump in farm prices, and wages would fall. William Banks, the General Secretary of the Suffolk A.L.L. posted front page adverts in local papers claiming a great victory, but he was also admitting that the best way workers could improve their situation was to emigrate to 'The Dominion', which for many at that time meant Canada or Australia. Thousands took up the offer.

Poverty and the poor of the parish

As was shown earlier, parishes would take a harsh view regarding other parish's paupers. From 1697, the poor needed an official 'settlement order' to move into another parish, however temporary their stay might be. Removal orders were drawn up on a regular basis, and people returned to where they belonged, if necessarily, forcibly. Matching orders would be sent to the receiving parishes. Mendlesham includes amongst its orders, the removal of Susan, wife of John Smith from Clacton in Essex following his arrest and transportation in 1833 for burglary.[25] Mary Race and her infant child of Felsham were removed from nearby Bradfield St. George in 1805, as husband Ezekiel was serving time in Bury gaol.

My own book, Lydia, describes the removal of the family of Robert Saunders' family from Debenham to Cotton in 1810. St. Margaret's parish in Ipswich[26] demonstrates this admirably, with over seven hundred assorted settlement and removal orders. Wetheringsett has over 150 surviving documents.

And give some thought for poor Martha Wells, removed from Pakenham in 1733 because her husband had run away on the day of their marriage.[27] As Haughley was his last known domicile, they were sending her there.

Sometimes a sweetener was necessary - especially if you wanted to get rid of someone quickly...

The Woodbridge Churchwarden's Accounts include a payment of five shillings to '*Grosse woman that came to depart the town.*'

Woodbridge

The Guild of the Holy Ghost: Beccles accounts for 1637 include the following item... *given to John Brvmwell & his wyfe wch came from Hadley in the time of sickness* [it was a plague year] *to ridd them out of towne, 1s 0d.*

Beccles clearly did not need other parishes' problems. They had enough of their own. Just down the road at Bungay, a century later, they had other ways of dealing with such problems. The Quarter Sessions Records for 1760 describe the trial of Mary Grimes, who was convicted of wandering and begging in Bungay with a counterfeit pass. Her sentence was to be '*publickly whipped next market day until bloody.*'

In the reign of James II, Hessett's accounts refer to *John Hales and Margaret his wife both sturdy vagrant beggars... aged about 35 years were... openly whipped at Hessett* [and sent back to Cambridge where they belonged].

A parish could be put to some expense removing a pauper, especially if the two parishes were far apart. Francis Lewis of Brandeston was brought from Rochford in Essex in 1718 by John Beard, overseer and churchwarden at Rochford. In a letter where he described[28] *'the worst journey of my life,'* he attempted to lay a significant claim on Brandeston parish for *'legitimate expenses.'* Not surprisingly, they disagreed and offered the not insubstantial sum of seven guineas.

Settlement papers for the town of Brandon include what amount to potted life-stories. In each case there would have been an examination of those to be moved on and their tales read like the plots for historical novels. One has to have a certain sympathy for Lucy Carpenter, singlewoman aged 18. To achieve a settlement in a place other than your place of birth, you might marry or find a position of work lasting a significant time. The length of time necessary to give you a right of settlement in a place grew as time went on and came to be accepted as a year and a day. Employers were often discouraged from employing people for longer than a year as they might ultimately cost the parish money...

She let herself as a servant to Mrs. King of Brandon, four days after Michaelmas 1798, as a result of a conversation with her a few days earlier. Her mother made an agreement with Mrs. King that Lucy should be paid 2 guineas for her service to Michaelmas 1799. The day before this Michaelmas evening, her mistress had a disagreement with her, and in the evening paid her 2 guineas and discharged her. The J.P.s decided that she had not gained a settlement in Brandon but belonged to Santon Downham, the place of her father's settlement.[29]

Henry Crissell, formerly of Stoke by Nayland posed a problem for the overseers in 1808 when he claimed that his continued employment as husbandman for James Goad gave him the right of settlement in his new parish. Unfortunately, his employer's house in which he resided was built across the boundary dividing Bures St. Mary and Wissington. The decision reached was that as he slept each night in Wissington, that should now be his place of settlement.[30]

It could be a thin line that might be drawn between a travelling musician, an itinerant pedlar and a beggar.

Great Glemham papers include an unusual one, a 'vagrants pass'[31] awarded in June 1809 to Eleanor Herron and her two children. This family came, we are told, from Tenterden in Kent and were not to be instantly moved on. The clue is in the name.

Herron, a variant of Hearn is a gipsy name. The Herrons may, like other travellers, have been regular visitors at that time of year, working on haymaking and harvest. More curious is the vagrant's pass awarded in Burgate just before Christmas 1781 to Robert Sheenman of Petersfield in Hampshire. Was he a peddlar, or perhaps an entertainer? ... Another tale where only part of the story survives.

In Nigel MacCulloch's book, *'Haughley, Past & Present,'* you have the opportunity to see the expense one pauper's sickness and death could land on a parish (over £8). And even after the death of Francis Mudd in 1772, further payments were made to his widow and family. At Bungay in the winter of 1743-1744, we can read from the Overseers' accounts of a payment for the removal of Goody Watt's bed to the workhouse. She must have died shortly after, as there are further payments for Goody Wyatt's coffin, her winding sheet and even beer for the bearers at her funeral.

Apprentices, Bastards and 'Houses of Industry'

One way of dealing with the children of paupers was to apprentice them to a trade, in the hope of raising them out of povery. But just in case, many were apprenticed at a distance so the parish could regard them as somebody else's problem should things not work out.

Orphans Jane and Susan Grisson of Bradfield St. George were apprenticed in 1698 at an early age, this being convenient to the parish who did not have to pay further for their keep and lodging. Aged about 10, Jane was bound to Thomas Avis, who was to instruct her in the ways of good husbandry, for which he was to be paid £9. Her sister Susan was less fortunate, in 1703 successfully freeing herself from the abusive Thomas Clarke, finally enabling her to move on to another apprenticeship.

Hacheston papers include an indenture for 1820 apprenticing a boy in the parish to a chimney-sweep.[32] Stowmarket apprenticeship indentures boast a wonderful assortment of trades - housewifery, husbandry, worstead weaving, say & bay weaving, chairmaking, tobacco pipe-making; as well as youngsters sent as far away as London to become blacksmiths, fishmongers, glovers, gardeners and even watermen on the Thames. Polstead apprentice indentures[33] include placements in Mellis, Manningtree, Norwich, Colchester and Bury.

The churchwarden's accounts for Wenhaston describe the expense to which the parish might be required to accept to send an apprentice away properly kitted-out. In 1602, there are fifteen separate entries relating to the *'apparelling of Katherine Eves'*, totalling over one pound. Bradfield St. George accounts show that even though Edward Hayward, cordwainer of Tostock was prepared to take on 11 year-old Thomas Coker without any charge, it still cost the parish £1 - 7 - 8d to supply the boy with clothes to send with him.

An apprenticeship indenture or a service contract was a legally enforceable document and contained a certain protection for both parties. An indistict warrant survives from 1814 to apprehend

Thomas Ashfield of Hopton, cordwainer, for not instructing his apprentice, Robert Fill the younger. A paper from Wetheringsett dated 1790 describes the reason for the discharge from service of Elizabeth Bambridge[34] being... [she] *had been guilty of divers misdemeanours paricularly that she hath been very negligent in milking his Cows, whereby he has suffered great damage.* One of several discharge documents for Burgate[35] describes how in 1726 William Hayward was able to dispense with the services of Sarah Alston as she was *'sickly and unfit to perform her work as a dairy maid.'*

One simple way of helping the young unemployed of the parish was for everyone who could afford it, to employ them as servants. Marlesford has 26 hiring papers[36] from the years 1804-1824. It seems, a number of better-off parishioners were prepared to do their bit for the parish.

Children born out of wedlock were a major concern as they could be a drain on parish funds for up to sixteen years. It was important to identify the 'reputed' father and force him to reimburse the parish. Bastardy orders are amongst the commonest surviving parish documents. Some parishes have large numbers of these, especially from the early nineteenth century when the level of bastardy reached epidemic proportions and was one of the major reasons for the drafting of a new poor-law in 1834. Elizabeth Saunders/Alexander of Mendlesham had at least five illegitimate children by at least three different men, yet never married. [Read more of her in *'Lydia'* by Pip Wright] Hannah Humphreys of Polstead[37] managed to be the subject of four bastardy orders in eight years, naming Thomas Bedford and Henry Martin as fathers (twice each). Elizabeth Downing of Shotley baptised six illegitimate children in ten years (1787 - 1796), three of them called Mark. The Assington papers include orders to the constables to arrest the fathers of bastards in the parish.[38] And Hepworth[39] has surviving accounts of expenses attending to the births of bastard children dated 1825-1834.

Parishes like Mendlesham and Cotton, where over a third of the children were being born to unmarried parents, could no longer cope with 'looking after their own.' From that point on, there was a more punitive approach to poverty and, with all unions of parishes having access to a Work-house, the complaints of rate-payers that they were being forced to pay to keep the idle and irresponsible were being addressed. Parishes did their best, of course, to persuade fathers to face up to their responsibilities and there is plenty of evidence of *'knobstick weddings'*, so called from the churchwarden's staff of office. These were the Suffolk equivalent of American 'shotgun weddings.' When Mary Allington of Gedding became pregnant in 1831, pressure was applied to encourage her to marry the father of her child, Charles Debenham. When he wouldn't have her, she married **his father** instead. Around the 1820s, it is remarkable how many births are recorded to parents married for less than six months.

The New Poor-Law of 1834 might be described as *'nobody gets anything for nothing.'* Also it meant that parishes were grouped together in *'unions'*, each parish contributing to a shared Union Work-house. Some Unions had already been going for a long time. The Bosmere & Claydon Union House at Barham had opened in 1776. Stow House of Industry at Onehouse opened in 1781. They were never meant to be comfortable places. There are plenty of records of people breaking windows in the workhouse in order to be sent to gaol, where the food was better. There was resentment over workhouse creation from the outset. Mobs attempted to disrupt the building of Nacton and Tattingstone work-houses and even tried to pull down what had been started before soldiers from Ipswich were dispatched to disperse them. Disturbances at Union Workhouses were not uncommon. The mob was more successful at Bulcamp workhouse where, accord-ing to the London Magazine of August 1765, a thousand men caused damage amounting to over £500.

I P S W I C H, *August* 16.

Yesterday Daniel Manning, and Benjamin Preston, of Theberton, Labourers, and James Strowger, of Wenhaston, Carter, were brought to our Goal by a small Party of Light-Horse, being charged with having been feloniously concerned in pulling down a Building at Bulchamp, called a House for the Poor, within the Hundred of Blything, in this County.

On Wednesday four Companies of the 43d Regiment of Foot came hither, and this Day one Company and a Detachment of Grenadiers marched for Bungay, Beccles, and Lowestoft.———The Remainder of the Foot will march To-morrow for Saxmundham, Halesworth, and Southwould.

We do not hear that any Disturbances have been made by the Rioters in this County, since those mentioned in our last Week's Paper.

Ipswich Journal August 17th 1765

Those sent to the work-house could expect only the most basic of provisions. Burgate records include the diet expected to be received in the Hartismere workhouse,[40] where inmates could be required to carry out work of the most unpleasant kind. Mind-numbingly repetitive and boring tasks were order of the day, though as time went on, some of these were removed as a result of lobbying by social reformers of the day.

Picking oakum

Picking oakum was the picking of tar from tarred ships' ropes in order to recycle them. Other hated jobs were roadbuilding and the grinding of bones for manure. A document from Mendlesham dated 1845 specifically forbids anyone demanding that paupers carry out bone-grinding.[41]

Really caring for the needy

We often assume these were less-caring times, but parishes often took their responsibilities seriously. Weybread records include a letter from Leiston,[42] identifying their responsibility for *'the child of Margaret Chisnall'*. Their payment of one shilling a week was less than the mother thought she should receive, and clearly threats had been made by her to abandon the child. Leiston made it clear they would not see the child suffer...

'You say she threaten to leave the child with you... Let her do it (if she be so much of a brute). If you send it to us by some safe hand we will receive it and take care of it till our House is fill'd up.'

In a case that sounds not dissimilar, a fragile document survives from Bacton[43], describing the finding of *'a strange child in the church porch'* in October 1632. The whole tale is unclear, but a further detail describes the arrival of one Rose Blackcroft from Needham in Norfolk to claim the child, being his god-mother. Another such foundling, left beneath the overseer's window, was baptised at Capel St. Mary in November 1731 and given the name *'Mary Capel.'*

In his nineteenth century book on the history of Wherstead,[44] Rev. F .B. Zincke recounts a dispute between Sir Robert Harland (pictured below) and one of his labourers, Jerry Double. When they were both quite young men, Sir Robert had insisted his men carry on with the harvest work even on Sunday whilst the weather held good. Of all his men, only Jerry Double refused, and for that he was discharged.

We don't know how hard he found it to get another job, though he did have the advantage of being the only labourer, in what was an estate-village, to own his own house. The heart-warming part of this story is that Sir Robert thought long and hard about that decision and in the end, not only reversed it, but paid Jerry Double a pension of ten shillings a week for the rest of his extremely long life.

Churchwardens' vestry accounts show that they too were often not immune to a hard-luck story. Bungay, in 1703, gave a shilling to *'a poore woman which lost all she had by fire and her husband was burnt and left her five children.'*

Bungay 1818
painted by
Lady Palgrave

In the Woodbridge Churchwarden's Accounts, there is an entry for 1651 that reads... *'Paid two men watching Widow Curly when she was distracted 1s 0d.'* I take this to mean they were on suicide watch. And Cotton mention in the overseers disbursements the payment in 1806 of a shilling *'to a traveller in distress.'*

There were ways of helping the poor to help themselves - John Rampling of Gedding in 1780 was forced to give an undertaking that he would maintain his family if the parish lent him a bed.[45] Bedding belonging to the parish is the subject of a list in the Barnardiston archive.[46] The Overseers Account Book for

Great Glemham[47] includes inventories of goods and chattels belonging to the parish for the use of the poor in the seventeenth century. Items include beds and other furniture, cooking pots, bedding, a spinning wheel, looking-glass and candlesticks.

Long before the Union work-houses, most parishes had 'Town Houses' for the poor and elderly. These had to be furnished. Great Glemham's accounts for 1750 include the following entries...[48]

To a bed for the town house	*1 1*	*0*
A journey to buy it	*1*	*0*
For fetching it home	*1*	*3*
Setting it up and mending others	*1*	*6*

[By the sound of it, flat-pack furniture is nothing new]

As regards poor-relief records and Overseers' accounts, some of the most revealing are to be found at Ipswich Record Office regarding Sibton,[49] and Peasenhall.[50]

In a sixteenth century churchwarden's book for Wenhaston, we see how the parish paid to maintain its Town House. In 1594 the building was thatched for 20d; in 1595 the chimneys were swept for 2d and in 1596 the door was fixed for just 2d. The language used in these books can appear to us quite quaint. In 1701 in Sudbury, a vestry meeting agreed that...

Henry Pleasance shall well and workmanlike and with his best skill and art make and frame one substantial church clock with a pendulum to the same, as large and good, or rather better, for such uses as are generally made, and shall set up and fix the same.

It was also agreed that for winding and maintaining the clock he should be exempt from paying rates.

Other alterations to the church were often made at the parish expense. In 1589, Wenhaston had a new bell cast, costing in excess of £3. Other costs involved were...

For our charges at Sowtholde   4s 8d
For carying of the bell to Sowlde and home agayne   4d
For bere when the Bell was hanged   2d
For meate & dryncke ffor the Bellfownders
    when they ded hange the bell   2d
For making a newe bell rope   6d

Bell metal was expensive. There is reference to the casting of another bell, but to save money the parish purchased from someone in the parish a large cooking pot, to melt down in the course of manufacturing the new bell.

Recycling was certainly expected at Metfield. Nothing went to waste when clothing those unable to clothe themselves...
Richd Aldous to have Saml. Smiths Duffen Waistcoat
The shirt of the Late Saml Smiths for Jonathan Masterson
Yes, the poor wore dead men's (and women's) clothes.

William Bowers of Fornham St. Martin received relief payments in 1824 for injuries sustained from a fall from a windmill.[51]   Felsham records include bread charity tokens awarded as late as the twentieth century.[52]   On the other hand, John Hull of Hepworth in 1756 found himself in Bury Gaol and receiving a bill from the parish for the maintenance of his destitute children.[53]

There was less sympathy for those who would not (or could not?) work or live honestly. Quotes from the Overseers book for East Bergholt appear in Paterson's book, 'East Bergholt in Suffolk.'[54]   A ne'er-do-well called Tredget is the subject of a number of entries from 1748...

a cheen and Lock for Wm Tredget 2. 0
staples, bars, nails &c   3. 8
for lengthening the chene for Tredgett   10d
for two new locks for Tredget   3. 0

...instead, to help the more deserving... There is an entry for 1704 that reads... *'A pair of stilts* [crutches] *for Wid. Powle 6d'*

Health and other matters

There was an element of economic sense in keeping your poor as healthy as possible. Haverhill records have a list of *'persons innoculated at the expense of the parish.'*[55] Two superb documents from Lavenham dated 1635 list parishioners unable to support themselves because of an outbreak of smallpox. The names of all paying the poor-rate are there.[56]

Lavenham from an original pyrography picture by Daniel Wright

There is a note in the Newmarket St. Mary vestry minutes of 1777, authorising a surgeon to innoculate the poor at the parish expense.[57] Brandon vaccinated the entire parish in 1825. It certainly wasn't cheap! Richard Priest was paid over £16 to innoculate 155 Metfield inhabitants following an outbreak of smallpox in 1792. They had to nearly double the Poor-rate to pay for it. Hadleigh paid around £95 in 1778 to innoculate 700 patients, after which they were able to announce in the Ipswich Journal that the town was free of the disease. It was good for business!

Stowmarket suffered greatly from a smallpox epidemic in

1691-2 and according to accounts[58] received money from other parishes in the Hundred by way of relief. Smallpox was regarded by many as the plague of its day and people would go to a lot of trouble to avoid coming into contact with anyone who might be a carrier. If someone had already had the disease and survived, it could work to their advantage. This advert is typical of a number appearing in local papers in the 1700s...

Wanted, a housekeeper to a Gentleman's family.
She must be of the Church of England and have had the small-pox.
Apply to Mr. Alderman Oliver in Sudbury Suffolk.
Ipswich Journal: October 28th 1775

From time to time, the parish would be put to some expense regarding the health of one of their number. Doughty's Chronicles of Theberton quotes from parish accounts over the treatment of John Haggudday's leg...

Paid to Dr. Peak for cutting of the leg	*5 - 0 - 0*
to John Thorn for healing it	*5 - 5 - 0*
for bere for his doctor and the	
tounnesmen at 2 several times	*7 - 0*
For wooding legg for him	*5 - 6*

In 1753, James Goleby, the Theberton overseer was paid for *providing a place to dip Ann Clark in order to recover her of her lameness.* This is intriguing. Was this a sea-water cure or was it harking back to the healing powers of an ancient holy well? And I'd love to know what Bradfield St. George got for their 6d in 1798 when they paid a doctor for *'attenuating powders.'*

In the churchwarden's accounts for Orford, a surgeon by the name of Edward Riches seems to have agreed a kind of double-or-quits, no-win-no-fee arrangement, whereby in 1697, if he managed to make a cure of Margaret Hudson's leg, he would be paid the enormous sum of 50s., but should he fail, he would be paid nothing.

There were times when a parish could end up paying for things that were out of their control. In 1553, Mary Tudor, soon to become Queen, made her base at Framlingham Castle.

Framlingham Castle c1820

But she brought with her a bit of a rag-tag army that wasn't too popular around about. The Worlingworth churchwarden's accounts for that time include money *layd out for butter, cheese and ayle* supplied to *ye soldyars whylst ye Quene remayned at Framygam Castle*, as well as 1s 2d for *a shovel lost at Framygam* and 6d for *mendyng of a mattock*.

As can be seen, a lot of parish administration fell on the shoulders of the churchwardens and the overseers through the centuries. The wheels of administration need oiling (well!) so it comes as no surprise to read that at Theberton in 1827, they ran up a bill for drinks at the Lion totalling 8s 3d. I'll bet that was a meeting and a half!

So much of this book is about the poor of this county that you might forget there were those whose demonstrations of wealth could be positively obscene. Sir William Rowley of Tendring

Hall, Stoke by Nayland had this fine building (pictured above) erected on his estate around 1795 to house his dogs in rather grander style than most of his workers.

Still this material is just scratching the surface of the wonderful array of achives that have passed down through the years in Suffolk. And there is so much more. Bildeston had troubled times with its clergy. Henry King of Bildeston Lodge, lay-reader of that parish, was excommunicated from this office in March 1885, so wrote a letter to inform the churchwardens that... *'the sitting hitherto occupied by myself and family in the parish church will no longer be required by us.'*

Unable to get on with his organist, the Bildeston vicar, G. Clenaghan, in 1917 typed the following letter to his church-wardens.[59]

This is only about a quarter of it; the rest includes the line, *'when I came here, I was told Mr. Hurley was a man who would cringe before your face and then stab you in the back.'* In other words, he didn't like him very much.

```
                                        August,10th, 1917.

My Dear Churchwardens,
                    PRIVATE & CONFIDENTIAL.
I am more grieved than I can tell you to be obliged to call your
attention to the following matter. Last Sunday morning I went
behind the organ to give Mr Hurley instructions about the War
Anniversary Service. The moment I appeared he asked me in a most
excited and angry manner about the Psalms. I replied that I was
come to give him directions about the whole Service and we would
begin at the beginning. He would not listen to me and tried to insist on being
told at once about the Psalms. I was not inclined to be dictated
to like that and tried to tell him how the Service would begin.
He hardly listened to what I had to say about the National Anthem
and would hear no more,but raved on about the Psalms. I told him
at this point there would be no Psalms,but he would not hear. I
tried to reason with him and said it was too bad of him to treat
me in this way when I wanted to be calm before beginning the
Service. He would not listen,so in despair I had to leave him,
and the last thing he shouted after me as I went away was,"What
about the Psalms?"
```

There is an intriguing item of correspondence (1871) from Bedfield's records,[60] whereby the rector is being informed that a certain Mr. Smith should not be permitted to marry again as his wife and child were still alive and living in Syleham.

Education

Records from the early days of compulsory schooling make fascinating reading. A complete set of school log-books survives from Palgrave from 1863 until the present day, giving us a wonderful sense of what school-life was like through the years...

Mar. 9th 1863: Children dismissed at 1 o'clock. Puddings & tea given to inhabitants of parish on account of Prince of Wales wedding on 10th.

Apr. 17th 1863: Thin school on account of Diss Races
>   [This is a regular theme with thin schools reported
>   on account of sickness, snow, rain, heat, Diss Fair,
>   market-day, harvest or just because it was Friday]

Feb. 23rd 1864: Amelia Copping punished 2 handers for
>   *swearing.*

May 25th 1864 [following the death of the rector] *...poor children*
>   *unfit for work, crying bitterly for the loss of their reverend*
>   *and a very very dear friend.*

Crossing the
Waveney
at Palgrave

At least the inspection reports for that school seemed quite acceptable. There are school inspectors' reports dated 1877-92 from
Redlingfield[61] that under present circumstances would have seen
the school placed under special measures...

>   'Of Geography the children are still almost entirely
> ignorant and do not shew much general intelligence.'

'The present mistress only took charge a fortnight before the end of the school year... and cannot be considered in any way responsible for the miserable results.'

'If the school does not materially improve, it will soon be impossible to recognise it as any longer efficient.'

Damning reports over a period of time related to almost every subject from maths & English to needlework & singing.

The new head at Fornham St. Martin in 1882 reported[62] ...

the children appear very rude and unseemly in their behaviour. Their knowledge of tables is nil but their methods of copying and conniving are certainly amusingly ingenious."

The Head at Dalham wrote in the log book in May 1897...

This morning, on examining the children, I found Alfred & Frederick Kemp not clean - their necks especially being very dirty. They were sent home to be washed and returned again with clean necks and faces. Their mother sent an indignant note with them threatening to keep them at home if they were sent again.

A lot of the time, the children just weren't there. Mass absenteeism could be for a variety of reasons, including acorn picking. Bardwell seemed to expect absenteeism in September when gleaning was happening. The Dalham school log book explains the absence of large numbers of children away in the fields at various times of the year harvesting, turnip-singling, pulling 'carlic', shelling walnuts and 'brushing' (beating at autumn shoots). At Haverhill, an acceptable reason for the absence of over half the pupils was the Christmas Fatstock Sale held in the town.

It was no good. The law might say you had to send your children to school, but most village schools struggled to keep attendances up. At Dalham, even school manager Mr. Templeton was reluctant to send his sons when he needed them for on his farm for 'field-work.' Sometimes it even extended to the teaching staff. Bardwell had to admit defeat and close in February 1890 as the Master, Mistress and both assistants had been taken ill with *'la grippe'* [whatever that was].

At Westleton, a flag was finally hoisted in 1912, being the first time all the children in the school were present. The school had opened in 1863.

But the genuine reasons for absenteeism could be many. Dalham is a pretty village with a stream running through it. Flooding seems to have been a serious problem at least once a year according to the school's nineteenth century log books. Epidemics too brought about lengthy closures of Suffolk schools. Bardwell school was closed in November 1875 as most of the children were suffering from measles.

Scarlet fever at Dalham in October 1895 closed the school for over a month. It had to be disinfected before reopening. Then in 1897, a flu outbreak forced the school to close again. The following year, it was whooping cough. The worst time must have been June 1886 when diphtheria took the lives of five children in the village. The medical officer shut the school for 13 weeks.

Most nineteenth century school log-books show the emphasis that was put on examination standards and inspections. Descriptions of certain children's abilities were not exactly PC...

Haverhill 1886:[63] *Samuel Beavis (no capacity whatever) and James Henry Osborne (water on the brain) are quite as hopeless as they were last year and will require exceptional treatment. Admitted George Wm. Boreham aged 7½ who knows nothing whatever and will therefore most likely require the protection afforded by Article 109b.* (A kind of Statement of Educational Needs)

However, other problems loomed large. At Haverhill, overcrowding was the main problem in the girls' school, whereas the boys' school seems to have suffered from inadequate heating... *'There were 6 degrees of frost at 8 a.m. with all the fires going.'* There was a back-up, but that meant *'lighting the gas,'* a luxury to be avoided unless absolutely necessary. Local epidemics of scarlatina, measles, mumps, and *'low fever'* (whatever that was) get a number of mentions in the log book for Haverhill girls' school.[64] One more unusual entry informs us that a pupil, Harriet Barber had died from eating some poisonous fruit. Also, a couple of lines from 1878 say...

Many girls are absent owing to bad eyes... which is put down to... *cold easterly winds which have been felt very keenly of late.*

So, she goes on to say... *Gave the children half an hour's play on Thursday.* [Well, that ought to help!]

Highlights of village life sometimes crop up in school log-books. At Bardwell in September1887, we are told Mr. D.W. Taylor, owner of the local water-mill, was presented with a Royal Humane Society Testimonial for his bravery in saving one of the pupils, Edward Feakes (The Bury Free Press calls him *Edward Fakes*) from drowning whilst bathing in the mill pond earlier that Summer.

Punishment books were made a requirement around 1907. Fornham St Martin[65] includes the following entries...

Florence Emmerson (13) - a rap on the knuckles for 'prying'
Charles Emmerson (11) - two stripes for coming with dirty hands
Edward Pearce (5) - one stripe for being a very naughty boy
Bertram Plume (10) - Two strokes for running behind a motor
Charles Murrell (10) - 1 stroke for 'dirty trick
                              - spat in drinking mug'

Other common sins were *'misbehaviour,' 'inattention,' 'being persistently late,'* and the book also includes seven boys caned for stealing turnips.

Pakenham's book[66] begins in January 1908. Amongst the dastardly crimes contained within its pages are Sidney Twite (11) caned on both hands for smoking cigarettes in the dinner hour (and persuading Edward Marsh to do the same). Corporal punishment applied to hand, buttocks or shoulder could be for *'throwing boy's hat into urinal, stealing fruit from the school garden, chewing gum during lessons, snowballing in the street* and *making blots on another's book.*

The Head of Hawstead School brought out the cane for a range of sinful activities described by a single word - naughtiness, laziness, insolence, dishonour, disorder, meanness and, in the case of Danilla Gill, aged 7, irreverance (12 stripes). The book tells us that Harry Wright got his 10 stripes *'in the proper place'* (I don't think she meant the classroom). As for Elijah Bumpstead (aged 12) for his impudence, the Head records, *'2 boxes of ear, unlawful, admitted.'* Many of the Hawstead punishments were for the mistreatment of school property - *spilling ink; destroying india rubber, biting pencil end off.* But one of the most serious offenders appears to have been Ethel Mortlock (12) who was caned for *'writing love letters to a boy.'*

I don't know what Ethel wrote in her love letter, but they seem to have been a pretty unromantic lot at Hawstead. According to the log book of Dalham School[67], it was a tradition in the village to give a holiday on February 14th to allow the children to go *'Valentining.'* Even throughout the 1890s after the school no longer allowed time off for such frivolity, there are entries saying that most children were absent on Valentine's Day. Dalham, though not far from Newmarket gives the impression of having been a bit removed from the rest of the world even then. I like the way, the Head comments in 1876 that there appears to be some considerable difference between... *'school time and village time.'*

Many punishment books do not have a great number of entries and use of the cane may have been less common than is often supposed. There is an entry in the Haverhill Girls' School log book dated 1879 where the headmistress comments, *'Spoke to 2 of the teachers about striking the children.'*

Punishment Books do tend to highlight the same few names. In the Brandon High St. Infants School book[68], one Herbert Thompson has the first four entries, his favourite activity being *'throwing stones with malicious intent,'* (two strokes on the hand). Other dreadful crimes include other children throwing a boy's cap over the wall and stealing school crayons. I notice that one child in that infant school was 9 years of age. You couldn't progress unless you achieved the necessary standard.

The first page of the 'Little Learners Alphabet Book' from 1873.

109

In Ampton Endowed Church School's punishment register, several members of the Garnham family grace the pages.[69] Thomas Garnham was, at the age of 4, *'a very cruel child'* and was *'shaken and whipped'* for hitting other children with a stick. His sister, Ellen Garnham aged 6 *(of very dirty habits)* was guilty of *'filthy and indecent conduct'* and *'a dirty action in the W.C.'* Among a group of thirteen *'given strokes with a small stick'* for *'rebellion and defiance,'* one John Booty is marked as the ring-leader with asterisks round his name. He received 6 strokes.

The Rev. Hugh Pigot, rector of Hadleigh, wrote in 1857 of severe punishment carried out about fifty years earlier by the superintendant, Mr. Leatherdale...[70]

Mr. Leatherdale would seat himself in a chair, stretching his knees rather wide apart; the offending boy would then be forcibly seized by his assistants, and made to sit on the floor with his head on a level with Mr. Leatherdale's knees: Mr. Leatherdale would then place the backs of his open hands against the insides of his knees and then bring his hands and knees together, pressing hard upon the boy's ears. This would have been bad enough,; but this was not the worst; for while pressing hard inwardly with his knees, Mr. Leatherdale would rapidly move his hands horizontally backwards and forwards, rubbing the boy's ears, and causing the most intense pain by the rough friction. The howls of the boy who was being thus manipulated, are said to have been dreadful.

Looking a bit like cheeky children, brackets from the roof of the chancel of Hadleigh Church

There is a letter from the early 1900s about the ill-treatment of the schoolmistress at Braiseworth,[71] suggesting with some cause for concern that this might be used to force a closure of the school (It finally closed in 1919).

There is a terrific book relating to a parish survey of Hitcham[72] dated around 1861 (with later additions), whereby you can see listed the names of the people in the parish, stating which children attended school and levels of literacy. Other information deals with church attendance, health problems and who was the illegitimate child of whom. Once again, tucked amongst all this, we have half of a story. I'd love to know the rest...

Emma Jane Preece (wife of schoolmaster) late Syer. Her grandfather possessed 2 cottages which were taken possession of at her grandmother's death by Bond, grocer, Stowmarket who married 2 of her mother's sisters in succession. She thinks herself wronged and wants to see her grandmother's will. She keeps a small shop.

One last thought on education comes from T.F. Paterson's book, *'East Bergholt in Suffolk'*, where this old rhyme is quoted...

'Understand:
Larning is better
*   than House and land.*
When House and Land is
*   Gorn & Spent,*
Then Larning is
*   most Exelent'*

The tomb of Edward Lambe at East Bergholt, who also believed in learning; leaving a deed in 1594 for the education of boys in the parish.

Last requests and other oddities

One significant piece of our history is largely missing from this book. Last Wills and Testaments! Whole volumes have been written on wills, yet I have found little room for them here. For the most part they are serviceable and predictable. This doesn't make them boring or irrelevant, but they deserve more attention than I'm in a position to give. Yet there are aspects of wills through the centuries that fascinate me. Before Henry VIII's Reformation, we were all Catholics. After you died, it was believed your soul spent an undefined period of time during which your performance in life was weighed up by the celestial 'powers that be' to decide which way you went next. If you were bound for Heaven, but needed further purification before your soul could be deemed acceptable, you would spend a while in purgatory.

The time spent in purgatory was understood to be rather unpleasant - it was a kind of half-way house, a bit like being on remand before your trial, where you hoped someone might put in a good word for you and hasten the move on to higher things.

Now I guess bribery was frowned upon, but you could put in place measures that improved your chances of getting a favourable hearing, especially if you were rich. Therefore lots of medieval wills, as well as deciding who inherited the *messuages* and *pightles* people owned, left money in the form of rentable land to pay for smoothing their way to Heaven.

Thomas Herte of Wetheringsett died in 1487, leaving enough to pay a priest to say masses for himself and his family for two years. John Rolfe in 1792 died, requesting a candle be burnt *'afore the crucifix in Thorndon Church every Sunday and Holy Day in the year for seven years.'* Others left money for masses to be sung and prayers said for varying lengths of time. Sometimes a trental (30 masses) was paid for. John Crapenell of Winston asked in his will of 1472 for it to be arranged for two masses to be sung for him at Scala Celi in Rome. If you were really rich, the money you left covered *'all time until eternity'*, though Henry

VIII, Edward VI and their ministers made sure it would be a good bit shorter than that.

Another common request was to ask beneficiaries to go on pilgrimages for you. I hope the heirs to Christopher Benytt's fortune (1477) were well recompensed. He wanted them to make pilgrimages on his behalf to St. Mary's Walsingham, the Shrine of Thomas à Becket at Canterbury, Thorpe St. Peter, Norwich, the Holy Crucifix at Beccles, Blessed Mary at Aspal, St. Mary of Grace, Ipswich and the Maiden of Manston (whoever she was).

In the county archives may be found all manner of oddities, from a copy of the Act for the Suppression of Profane Swearing (Lt. Finborough 1729)[73] to a gospel pierced by a bullet from 1915 (Bardwell)[74]; from letters to the Forces Committee in 1945 giving thanks for gifts of cigarettes (Ipswich St.Helen's)[75] to a Nettlestead register note from 1941 relating to the church being closed due to damage caused by enemy action... to the downing of a German airship at Theberton and the subsequent graves.[76] There are streetsweepers' accounts (Ipswich St. Margarets)[77] and Constables' accounts (Mickfield)[78]; surveyors' accounts (Cockfield)[79] and the erection of the parish pump (Lt. Thurlow).[80]

There are licences granted in 1631 to permit certain people to eat flesh on fast days (Cowlinge).[81] And there is all the fun and celebration of a Royal Coronation (Queen Victoria) recorded in a special 1838 book by the parson at Stonham Aspal.[82] Pettistree demonstrate they too knew how to have fun,[83] detailing their Silver Jubilee celebrations in 1887. There are accounts of parish teas and fancy-dress winners at Bardwell[84] in 1910.

Festivities to commemorate an earlier Coronation appear in a Somerleyton register, celebrated on April 23rd 1661. Listed are all the ingredients that made for a fine party - *two barrels of beer, 9 duzzen of bread for the poor, tobacco, pipes, pruens, sugar and an hundred of faggot wood* (presumably for a good bonfire).

A good frolic was had by all! This watercolour is believed to represent celebrations in Christchurch Park, Ipswich for the Coronation of Queen Victoria.

A hand-written memorandum exists in the archives for Stansfield,[85] detailing *'A parson's difficulties in the eighteenth century.'* It deals with the valuation and handling of tithes, and even of parish boundaries. It was usual at Rogationtide for the beating of the bounds to take place, sometimes referred to as *'the perambulation of the parish.'* Tithes were due according to the acreage somone might hold in that parish. But farms were no respectors of parish boundaries and farmers could owe tithes in more than one place. Field margins and marker trees were subject to adjustment on occasions and in this document, the parson describes markers that have become *'bumped a bit.'* These could cause friction between the clergy of adjacent parishes.

Accounts of a variety of kinds were once housed in the parish chest. Where churchwarden's accounts survive, they can give us a marvellous insight into the workings of communities centuries ago. Dennington's accounts date back to the reign of Henry VIII and include references to the brewing of church ale, the appointment of a *'Lord of misrule'* and witchcraft in the parish. Just across the border in Norfolk, the Redenhall accounts include a note... *Ite*[m] *payd for the witchcrafte of the cort at* [Long] *Stratton.* (probably for the warrant to bring to trial someone from the parish). Though witchcraft wasn't strictly illegal until 1563, heresy was.

St. Mary's, Bungay

Entries in the Bungay St. Mary's accounts[86] include 4d paid in 1576 for a basket for carrying muck out of the church and 12d paid to someone for *'whipping Doggs out of the church.'* A further 4d was paid to *'pore women that layde forth of the bodyes of ye ij* [2] *men that were strycken deade within the steple of ye churche at ye great tempest that was ye iiij* [4] *of August in AD MCCCCC seventye & seven.* And in the margin are details that seem to tie up with one of the great Suffolk legends - Black Shuck. *'A great, terryble ferful tempest at the time of procession upon the*

Sundaye, such darknes, Rayne, hayle, Thunder & lightnyng as was never seen the lyke. Never to be forgotten,' Other reports speak of a fierce dog that appeared at the time of the storm and attacked worshippers first at Blythburgh, then six miles away at Bungay. A less violent entry in the same book speaks of one penny paid in 1544 to Raffe for... *'stppyng of hoolys alofft on ye steple where the caddows* [jackdaws] *come in.*

In Blythburgh Church

At Aldeburgh, as well as several entries relating to ridding the church of dogs... *with the whyppe* (1567), we read of Robert Fowler being paid in 1636 for *looking to the clock and for killing owles.* It seems unfortunate that almost any form of wildlife that was inedible was regarded as vermin. I have seen Elizabethan papers offering payments of 12d for every fox or badger killed, but also 1d for *'a polecatte a raven or a wyldecatte'*, 2d for the head of *'an otter, busard, schagge or cormorant'*, and 4d for an osprey. In 1663 churchwardens in Wetheringsett were buying nets to catch choughs [probably meaning jackdaws rather than choughs], crows and rooks that were invading the church. The sexton had a special payment for removing ivy from the church walls. Nature could be quite a threat.

Some of the earliest surviving papers relate to the parish of Cratfield with payments being made in the 1490s for a *Cherch ale mad*[e] *on Passion Sonday and Pentecost Sonday* and *a Welle rop*[e] *and an heke* [hook]. Entries before the Reformation of the Church include payments for items that would not have been required in the new Church of England...

a pelow of blew sylke
towells for the preste to wype on his hands at the lavatory
a pecke [basket] *for holy bread*
on[e] *holy water sto*[o]*p of Glas with a fotte*[foot] *of iren*
A payment of 12d was also made in 1557 (Mary I) to Gregory Rowsse for *makyng of a pulley for ye sacrament.*

Cratfield Church

117

Presumably payments that appear in Aldeburgh church acounts for *'pfume oyle'* and *'Franckensense'* in 1589 and 1625 were to ward off *'bad air'* in time of plague and other disease rather than a return to *'popery.'*

In 1538, at Cratfield we learn that 3s 8d was paid to Master Everard for a bow & arrows. This is one of a number of weapons references and is not as surprising as might appear. Churches often contained parish armouries. The one at Mendlesham survives to this day. During the time of the Civil War, parishes often hedged their bets and waited to decide which side to support. Cratfield chose in 1642 to make a payment towards arming the Parliament forces of Oliver Cromwell. Support for the monarchy appears in Woodbridge Manor Rolls which give 1660 as the twelfth year of the reign of Charles II. They chose to ignore the Cromwell years.

Again with Cratfield, as early as 1603, carpenters making church stalls were being supplied with tobacco as they constructed a sawing pit in the churchyard.

The Churchwarden's Accounts for Wenhaston go back to 1585, but a few pages have been torn out and should probably go back twenty years earlier. A number of entries emphasize the role played by the keepers of the purse-strings in the entertainment of the parish.

Wenhaston is famed for its painted 'Doom'. Whitewashed over centuries ago, it has now been restored and is one of the finest of its kind in the country.

118

Parties were organised called 'Ales'. In 1586, Goodwife Buke received 5s 4d for *'keeping two bride ales,'* which I take to be acting as hostess at two wedding celebrations. There is another entry for 1590 that just says *'16d for baytinge of the beare.'* The Boxford accounts seem to suggest it was part of a churchwarden's duties to arrange Ales. Churches had very little seating - only around the edge and the church and its churchyard (with few gravestones) until that point were the centre of parish social life.

Theatrical presentations were traditionally associated with the parish church. Aldeburgh's accounts include payments amounting to over two shillings in 1581 for the making of *'the devills Coate'*, almost certainly for a Mystery Play to be performed there. The Bailiff's books contain names of a number of groups of visiting players, along with payments to the town crier to bid people to come to performances. Unsurprisingly, there are no such entries for the more austere Cromwellian years between 1645 and 1657.

The sixteenth-century churchwardens' accounts for Boxford[87] includes both 'Ales' and Plays. These accounts are particularly interesting because they cover the parts of four reigns from the Tudor period, when huge religious changes were happening. Likewise, the records of the Churchwardens of Mildenhall[88] cover a similar period, and speak of sums of money raised at such Ales. Larger towns such as Bury, Ipswich and Bungay have evidence of plays, pageants and processions. But the times they were a-changing: by the the end of Elizabeth I's reign, the role of the church building had changed and was less of a social meeting point; more for religious ceremonies alone.

Many entries in our various parish account books refer to the expense of keeping medieval parish churches standing, making what were viewed as improvements or repairing what damage had been done by those who were less than appreciative of their history and their beauty. In an accusing tone, a group of entries from 1649 at Aldeburgh inform us that... *to paye for the windowes being broken when travelling people were in Towne called Egiptians* [gipsies] a sum of nearly two pounds was spent.

The vestry account book for Santon Downham[89] tells a good tale or two amongst the normal details of surplice washing and organ tuning. There is an account taken down from one James Lingwood, born 1840. He told of a man named Bowers who was taken against his will by the Press Gang and put before the examining board to see if he was fit for military service.
They tried to ascertain his age. After asking once or twice, and getting, *"What do you gentl'men say?"* by way of an answer, one of them tried shouting in his ear, *"How old are you my man?"* Answer: *"Thass fifteen miles to Brandon."*
They came to the conclusion he was quite unfit for active service and he returned to [Santon] *Downham where he appears to have recovered from his deafness.*

Throughout the centuries, there are references in our parish papers to public roles that don't exist any more. We no longer have parish constables or overseers of the poor. Beadles and ale-tasters (both mentioned in Stowmarket records) are a thing of the past. Some titles have vanished into antiquity - Hadleigh records include the *Alnager* - a kind of weights-and-measures man for locally-made cloth.

There are all kinds of writings buried in our parish records, and not all are to be treasured. The transcribed pages of a diary written by Miss H.B. Alderton[90] describing her last days at the rectory at Risby are of the most flowery kind. She was the daughter of the rector who had died in 1863. Two years later, on leaving Risby, she wrote...

Never more would the song of birds and the rising sun come streaming through that window to wake me. Never more would the sweet morning air play upon my brow... (It goes on like this for a number of pages)

Never more would we wander in the eventide with noiseless tread and admire the effect of the still foliage, so distant and yet so soft, like the exquisite mosaic, or rather, like the most delicate moss-agate, relieved against the clear sky... (Yes, dear, we get the idea!) *...Never more would father and mother dear come out of the garden door, cross the gravel... on to the high grass terrace raised by three deep steps, upon which were planted sweet-scented Shumacs, their lovely bloom glowing like a rosy sunset cloud...* (Please stop, I'm losing the will to live!)

Risby
Church

Rather more interesting is the article in the Lt. Bradley papers[91] that describes how the Rev. Francis Lyte wrote *'Abide With Me'* on leaving the deathbed of his friend William Augustus Le Hunte, formerly of that parish.

But, I think my favourite has to be an order in the papers for Clopton[92] requiring the return of lands designated for the poor, won on the toss of a coin in 1637. It appears that William Ellenger had come by the land known as Chaserods, following an evening's gambling. Though this had clearly been willed to the parish in 1489 by Margaret Gardiner and John Pelse, an unnamed gambler had seen fit to lose it in a wager. Subsequently, Ellenger had... *'taken a great part of the profittes of the said houses and grounds'* which had previously been used for the relief of the poor. The Clopton papers show that Ellenger failed to attend the hearing. However, some time later, Chaserods is recorded as being... *'in trust for use according to the wills of the donors.'* Like many stories from the past, it is incomplete, but there is enough to permit us a glimpse of the schemes our forebears got up to. Yes, all human life is there in our parish records!

Chapter 4
Directories

One of the most frequently referred-to books in my house must be White's Directory of Suffolk[1] for 1844. From at least as early as 1784, Suffolk towns appeared in trades directories, which listed businessmen and tradesmen. Some gave brief, not always glowing, desciptions of places listed. For example, The National Directory of 1794 described Ixworth as... *"a dirty, ill-built town with a mean market."*

Ixworth Mill

White's (1844) is different. The descriptions are altogether more whimsical, not necessarily to be relied upon, but fascinating nevertheless. I don't quite know how William White (who lived in Sheffield) gathered his information, but he must have relied upon the veracity of vicars, parish-clerks and others with whom he corresponded. As a result, tucked away amongst the accurate and believable are little snapshots of the bizarre, and myths paraded as fact. There is the tale of a swarm of bees, which apparently settled on the west wall of Redlingfield Church, having followed a corpse being brought for interment. Supposedly, in the seventeenth century, an ancient silver crown belonging to one of the kings of East Anglia was ploughed up at Mendlesham. Somewhat more doubtful is the reference to the wife of Henry Howard of Bacton, who died in 1739 (aged 95) who had given birth to a son at the age of 58.

Much of the 'history' White published is concise and entertaining; the problem comes in deciding which pieces are to be believed. Therefore, this chapter comes with a warning. Unlike most of the evidence I publish in this book, I can in no way vouch for many of the tales taken from White's Directory.

What White's does very well is to remind us of trades that flourished in days gone by - the lime-kilns and whiting manufactory at Claydon, the silk throwsting mill at Glemsford, the manufacture of drabbets and smock-frocks at Haverhill and the soap manufactory at Nayland. We are reminded of the many employed at Stanningfield and Clare in making *'Tuscan Straw Plat'* and how Brandon was once the centre of gun-flint manufacture, just as Sudbury was famous for its *'bunting for ships' flags.'*

Blacksmith shoeing a railway horse at Cotton

HISTORY, GAZETTEER, AND DIRECTORY, OF SUFFOLK, AND THE TOWNS NEAR ITS BORDERS; COMPRISING, UNDER A LUCID ARRANGEMENT OF SUBJECTS, A GENERAL SURVEY OF THE COUNTY, AND SEPARATE Histories, & Statistical & Topographical DESCRIPTIONS OF ALL THE HUNDREDS, LIBERTIES, UNIONS, Boroughs, Towns, Ports, PARISHES, TOWNSHIPS, VILLAGES, & HAMLETS; SHEWING THEIR EXTENT AND POPULATION; Their Agriculture, Manufactures, Fisheries, Markets, Fairs, Trade and Commerce; their Charities and Public Institutions; their Churches and Chapels; the Annual Value, and Patrons and Incumbents of the Benefices; the Lords of the Manors and Owners of the Soil and Tithes; the Civil and Ecclesiastical Jurisdictions; the Addresses of the Inhabitants; the Mediums of Public Conveyance, by Land and Water; the Seats of Nobility and Gentry; MAGISTRATES AND PUBLIC OFFICERS; And a Variety of other AGRICULTURAL, STATISTICAL, & BIOGRAPHICAL INFORMATION. In ONE VOLUME, with a MAP of the County. BY WILLIAM WHITE, AUTHOR OF SIMILAR WORKS FOR NORFOLK, LINCOLNSHIRE, YORKSHIRE, AND OTHER COUNTIES. PRINTED FOR THE AUTHOR, BY R. LEADER, INDEPENDENT OFFICE, SHEFFIELD; And Sold by W. WHITE, 200, Brook Hill, Sheffield; BY HIS AGENTS, AND THE BOOKSELLERS. Price to Subscribers, 13s. 6d. in Calf Binding, or 12s. in Boards. 1844.

Charities are given a good deal of space, and involve mainly money donated for housing, clothing, food and coals for the needy. In a number of cases, the day of distribution is given - significant days like Lady Day, Michaelmas, Plough Monday and Christmas Eve to name but a few. At Yaxley, a charity existed to pay the Constable's expenses and in Fornham All Saints, a charity was founded to pay for a sermon to be preached four times a year against popery. And just to show that such foundations are not all ancient, the archives for the village of Melton include a record that couldn't have appeared in White's - a charitable fund on John Thos. Roper's death[2] dated 1951.

Amongst the titbits of local trivia, a number of items relate to **extreme weather and other such disasters**. We can read of Bawdsey Church suffering from a terrible fire in 1841 when some boys climbed the tower to set some fireworks off and ended up destroying it. The great fire of Bury St. Edmunds in 1608 was hugely destructive, but the town was rebuilt, we are told, with wood supplied by King James I, *'who was a great benefactor to the town.'* A fire at Bures St. Mary's church in 1733, we are informed, was so

THE

Woefull and Lamentable

wast and spoile done by a suddaine Fire in S. Edmonds-bury in *Suffolke*, on Munday, the tenth of Aprill. 1 6 0 8.

LONDON

Printed for *Henrie Gosson*, and are to be solde in Paternoster rowe, at the *Signe of the Sunne*. 1 6 0 8.

fierce that it melted the six bells. In August 1843, Thetford experienced such a fierce hailstorm that one man in the town picked up 100 dead sparrows from his garden. A huge inundation of sand at Santon Downham in 1668 threatened to overwhelm the parish, burying houses and completely blocking all access to the largest farmhouse in the parish, belonging to a Mr. Wright.

Hadleigh suffered such a deluge of rain in 1843 that punts were seen rowing up the High Street.

Hadleigh High St.
in drier times in 1910

In the time of Queen Mary, Aldeburgh suffered a great famine. The starving people surviving by gathering the fruits of the sea-pea (*pisum marinum*) and living on them. The same story apppears in a far earlier document from the 17th century, now published as *'A Chorography of Suffolk'*[3] This earlier version of the tale suggests that in 1555, the life-preserving peas spilled out of a shipwreck and took root there...

'are we to consider the great goodnes of God who in that scarcitie in this mannour p'vided for the poore...'.
But as you can still find the

sea-pea growing in some profusion on the beach along Orford Ness and other Suffolk beaches, it seems more likely this wild pea was there all along.

A number of storms are mentioned, including one in 1577 that killed worshippers at Blythburgh and Bungay (St. Mary's) churches. The spires at Whepstead and Dalham were apparently blown down in a freak storm '*occasioned by Oliver Cromwell's death.*'

They liked their **archaeological finds** in Victorian times, so it comes as no surprise to discover that a number feature in this edition of White's. In 1828, we are informed, an arm-bone was washed up on Felixstowe beach with a gold bracelet still on it. The Lady Well at Woolpit was reputed to possess medicinal virtues for the cure of sore eyes. A battle was fought in 1173 at Fornham St. Genevieve on behalf of Henry II against the Earl of Leicester and '*many of the slain are buried in numerous barrows called Seven Hills, close by the Thetford Road.*' Labourers digging in a field near Eye in 1781 found '*a leaden box containing several hundred Roman coins and medals, well-executed and in high preservation.*' White's also reminds us of a tale of one of the lost treasures of Suffolk - '*One of the possessions of the monks of Eye was the site of the episcopal see at Dunwich till swallowed up by the ocean.*

 *They brought from that place St. Felix's book of the gospels and by which, under the name of the Red Book of Eye, the common people were accustomed to swear.*'

Greyfriars Friary, one of Dunwich's few surviving ancient monuments.

Possibly the most remarkable tale of this kind comes from the parish of Norton where, *'Henry VIII was induced by a credulous kind of avarice to dig for gold in this parish, but was disappointed in his search.'*

Suffolk legends are well covered in the 1844 edition of White's. The Hoxne claim to be the place of the martyrdom of St. Edmund is there, as is the curse put upon the bridge under which he is said to have hidden before his betrayal to the Danes. We are told that wedding parties on their way to the church would avoid using that bridge, whatever the inconvenience. Reputedly, the Saint's head was found by a dog, a scene shown by this stall end from Hadleigh Church.

In the entry for Orford is the commonly recounted tale... *'In the reign of King John, the fishermen took in their nets a sea-monster resembling a man an size and figure, with a long ragged beard and bald head, that ate fish and flesh and lay down on its couch at sunset and rose at sunrise.'* It remained but a short while before it escaped back into the sea.

There is the account of a medieval procedure by which barren women might become fertile, involving the leading of a white bull to the shrine of St. Edmund at Bury, involving ribbons and garlands and the procession of *'a numerous cavalcade.'*

One of my favourite tales involves Sir William Capel, native of Stoke by Nayland. He was a leading draper who rose to the position of Lord Mayor of London around the dawn of the sixteenth century and, to demonstrate his affection for the monarch Henry VII, dissolved a pearl worth hundreds of pounds in a glass of wine and drank it to the King's health. This is backed up by Charles Torlesse's book on the parish (1877) which says that Sir William also burned bonds relating to money the King had borrowed from him, so cancelling the debt.

At Hemingstone, the north side of the church had two porches, one now converted into a vestry (pictured below). By repute, the second, called Ralph's Hole was built by Ralph Cantrell who, being a Roman Catholic at a time when that was likely to see your property confiscated, used it to attend church (and not to attend, so to speak).

'At Lowestoft in 1664 dwelt Rose Cullender and Amy Duny, who were accused by a fanatical dissenter of witchcraft, as he imagined they had bewitched his two daughters.'

They were hanged at Bury, *'though their guilt probably consisted either in the deformity of their bodies or the weakness of*

Coming for the 'witches'

their understandings.' Yes I'm afraid lynch-mob law was something of a Suffolk speciality.

The stories that carry the most fascination are about the **people of Suffolk.** There is Thomas Cavendish, (then, of Trimley St. Martin) *'the second Englishman to circumnavigate the globe'* whom, at his own expense, fitted out three small vessels of 120, 60 & 40 tons manned by 123 men and boys *'for the purpose of annoying the Spaniards in their American posses-sions.'* Let's be clear about this, he was a pirate!

Less fortunate was Sir John Cavendish, in 1381, who had been dragged from Cavendish to Bury and *'his head struck off and set upon the pillory at the market cross.'* This was in response to the fact his son John, as esquire to Richard II had been responsible for the killing of the leaders of the Peasants' Revolt. Depending on which source you read, a Suffolk priest (or an Essex farmer) by the name of Jack Straw had led the East Anglian contingent to join with Wat Tyler's Kentish brigade, but it had all ended in bloodshed, with most of the blood shed being that of the peasants. Tyler and Straw were quickly identified as the leaders and executed. Others would be systematically rounded up. These included two men from Gazeley, Robert Tavell and William Cobbe. Tavell was found at Ramsey in Cambridgeshire and beheaded, but Cobbe seems to have been spared. This may have been because he was far from peasant stock. He was probably closely related to the Cobbes of Sandringham and this seems to have guaranteed his survival.

To return to Sir John Cavendish, his was not the only head to be exhibited in Bury at that time. Relations between town and monastery were often strained to say the least. Prior John de Cambridge, sensing trouble, set off from Bury Abbey along the road to Mildenhall, but was caught by the mob at Icklingham and beheaded. Reprisals this time were swift and bloody. Three peasants in Icklingham were randomly put to death. The spectre of a headless horseman has, from time to time been seen riding over the low meadows beside the River Lark. But whether the ghost is of the Prior or one of those who suffered on his behalf has never been determined.

Others getting a mention in White's directory include the Rev. Richard Lovekin, rector of Ufford, who lived to be 111. (nearly as old as John Gardiner Turner of Stoke by Nayland who, according to the parish register, died in May 1600, aged 116). He had been rector through the Civil War, *'when he was plundered of everything he possessed except one silver spoon, which he hid in his sleeve.'* Eccentric characters abound in these pages including Capel Lofft, barrister and writer of Troston, (pictured right) *'who is reputed to have inscribed every tree at Troston Hall to the names of classical celebrity'.*

The earliest account tells us the Raedwald, King of the East Angles, was reputed to have kept his court at Rendlesham where he received Christianity, *'but being afterwards seduced by his wife, he is said to have had in his church an altar for the religion of Christ and another little altar for the sacrifice of Devils.'*

Various distinguished persons are mentioned for a variety of reasons - Samuel Barnardiston of Kedington, who is supposed to have first coined the title, *'Roundhead'* for Cromwell's soldiers. The son of Francis Theobald Esq. of Barking was *'distinguished in his skill in oriental languages,'* and we are told that the Rev. John Boyse, born in Elmsett in 1560 was *'such a precocious talent'* that he could read the Hebrew Bible by the time he was five.

It is reported that upon an ancient monument in the chancel of Blythburgh church, *'two clumsy columns of brick'* had later been erected, *'giving rise to the comment that whoever resided in the tomb and whatever he might have been in his lifetime, he is a firm supporter of the church now.'*

We are reminded of less tolerant times... *'John Noyes, a shoemaker of Laxfield, after suffering imprisonment at Eye and Norwich for his adherence to the reformed religion, was brought back to his native place and burnt at the stake. Sept. 22nd 1557.*

NEAR THIS SPOT ON SEPTEMBER 22ND 1557

JOHN NOYES

SUFFERED MARTYRDOM AT THE STAKE.

AMONG HIS LAST WORDS WERE —

"FEAR NOT THEM THAT CAN KILL THE BODY, BUT FEAR HIM THAT CAN KILL BOTH BODY AND SOUL AND CAST THEM INTO EVERLASTING FIRE!"

BLESSED BE THE TIME THAT EVER I WAS BORN TO COME TO THIS!

"THEY SAY THEY CAN MAKE A GOD OF A PIECE OF BREAD — BELIEVE THEM NOT! GOOD PEOPLE BEAR WITNESS THAT I DO BELIEVE TO BE SAVED BY THE MERITS OF JESUS, AND NOT MINE OWN DEEDS"

THE RIGHTEOUS SHALL BE IN EVERLASTING REMEMBRANCE. PS. CXII. 6

...and clearly more tolerant ones - Etheldreda, born at Exning, daughter of Anna, Queen of the East Angles was canonized for a virgin by the Pope even though she had been married twice.

The story of John Noyes at Laxfield appears in number of places. The parish papers at Cratfield recount how all the fires in the village of Laxfield had been doused to make it difficult for the execution pyre to be lit, but one thin plume of smoke was spotted and the door of that house broken down to enable the executioners to find coals for their grisly business. As if being burnt alive wasn't bad enough, the Ipswich accounts for 1556 indicate that as well as wood being supplied for the *'exicusion'* of prisoners, green broom was also added to prevent the fire burning too quickly and to prolong the agony of those suffering such a punishment.

Noyes was just one of a number of Suffolk martyrs. The most famous, Dr. Rowland Taylor of Hadleigh is remembered by a memorial close to Aldham Common where he is said to have been burned (pictured below right) in a barrel of pitch [to hasten his death or to make it more intense?]. For many years, just a small uncut stone marked the place. The present memorial (below left) dates from 1818. Tradition has it that 'Bloody Mary' who

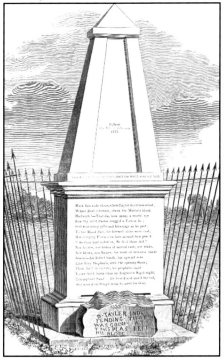

ordered these burnings was afterwards *'brought to bed of a viper,'* though this is probably just wishful thinking.

Back to White's directory, Captain G.W. Manby is listed as having a *'pleasant sporting cottage'* at Fritton. *'He was the ingenious and humane inventor of the apparatus for the preservation of lives from shipwreck.'*

We are also reminded of the other Gainsborough from Sudbury. The brother of the great painter was a dissenting minister at Henley on Thames but *'possessed as strong a genius for mechanics as his brother had for painting and one of his sun-dials of ingenious contrivance is now in the British Museum.'*

Finally, I have picked out items that relate to **Suffolk places.** All Saints church at Wickham Market was reputed to stand upon a hill and from its tower, fifty churches could be seen.

We are told of long-vanished castles - Offa, King of Mercia built a castle at Offton, *'after he had slain Ethelred, King of the East Angles, and seized his dominions.'* Lidgate Castle was plundered, even to its foundations *'for the reparation of the roads'*

Brent Eleigh had a parochial library furnished with books by Dr. Colman of Trinity College, Cambridge around 1700. Battisford once had a great wood that was cut down around 1545 by Sir Thomas Gresham, who was granted the manor after the dissolution of the monasteries. The wood was used in the building of the first Royal Exchange in London. Beyton church once had five bells, but four were sold in the late eighteenth century to pay for church repairs.

At Southwold, an area known as Fairy Hills is listed as the principal part of the east coast where swallows land on their arrival in England, and at which they take their departure.

A deep and ragged ravine in the cliff at Pakefield is known as Crazy Mary's Hole from its having been the favourite haunt of a deranged lovesick maid.

Low marshes, near the river at Syleham, were formerly so swampy that the *ignis fatui*, commonly called Syleham Lamps, were frequently seen and often led benighted travellers to their doom.

There are quaint tales of Suffolk villages and towns that must be included. At Haughley, at the time of Edward IV, William Baxteyn held lands by the service of finding a ladder for the Lord's gallows.

In 1832, Dunwich incurred a huge debt as result of a legal dispute with Southwold over a puncheon of Scotch Whisky which had been removed from Dunwich beach by the water-bailiff of Southwold. Though Dunwich won the jugement it cost them a thousand pounds in legal fees.

Middleton and the neighbouring hamlet of Fordley in 1620 had two churches sharing one churchyard. Complaint was made that if the services were not perfectly synchronised, the noise from the bells of one would disturb the congregation of the other. The answer the bishop came up with was that one minister should serve both, officiating in them alternately.

The advent of horseracing at Newmarket is put down to James I having been encouraged by the spirit and swiftness of Spanish horses which had been cast ashore in Scotland following the defeat of the Armada in 1588. Newmarket became a centre for racing as a result of his patronage.

And we are reminded of times past and places no longer as they were - The beautiful hanging gardens of Lowestoft, richly planted with trees and shrubs, interspersed with alcoves and summer-houses. There is also *'the uncouth figure of Hercules'* at Hawstead, which.. *'formerly discharged by the natural passage into a carved stone basin, a continual stream of water.'* It is suggested this had been a present from Elizabeth I following her visit in 1578 when Sir Robert Drury restored her silver-handled fan which she had dropped into the moat. However, in his earlier book on Hawstead, the Rev. John Cullum speculates that this might have been an attempt on the part of Robert Drury to prepare the place for a royal visit. Either way, he doesn't seem impressed...

ANCIENT · STATVE · AT · HAWSTED · PLACE · SVFFOLK
as it now remains A.D.1813 . Drawn to a Scale of 4 Inds to a foot .

"Modern Times would scarcely devise such a piece of sculpture as an amusing spectacle for a virgin princess."

Also there are the parishes that are no more, largely disappeared under the waves like Slaughden and Easton Bavents, or merely consolidated with other parishes - Dunningworth near Tunstall, Capel St. Andrew, now part of Butley, Little Oakley administered away into Eye. Others that once boasted churches and separate parishes include Haselwood (now part of Aldeburgh), Willingham (Beccles) Southelmham St. Nicholas (All Saints)

Little Horningsheath (Horringer) and the two lost parishes of Creeting (now St. Mary's).

Easton Bavents when it was still a separate parish

What William White did for Suffolk, he also did in the early edition of his directory for other counties. In his Norfolk directory of 1845, we hear of a servant girl who was boiled to death in Kings Lynn in 1531 for poisoning her mistress. We read of the eccentric Henry Lee Warner of Walsingham Abbey who would sleep all day and breakfast at midnight before working all night. Yarmouth, we are told, is a particularly healthy place to be *owing to the general salubrity of the air and wholesome exhalations, arising from the fish during the operation of curing...* [which are] *beneficial to the human constitution.*

Kelly's directories tended to stick to more verifiable data. However, the Kelly's directory for Suffolk of 1858 includes these titbits...

Elmsett - here is a dropping well which is said to possess medicinal properties.

Flixton - a charity was established here by Sir Robert Shafto Adair which stipulated that at his decease, £700 together with the amount in his charity bag should be invested and dispensed to the poor of three local charities. When he died £320 13s 7d was found in the bag and the total invested in New South Sea Annuities.

This would be hopefully a more financially secure investment than the one which had caused many speculators to be ruined in the South Sea Bubble of 1720.

An unusual entry relates to Shipmeadow, which instead of having a Lord of the Manor, had Mrs. A.M. Suckling as Lady of the Manor.

And of course, with the passage of time, names change. The public house close to Bourne Bridge in the parish of Wherstead is now known as the Oyster Reach. Yet throughout the nineteenth century, local directories referred to it as the Ostrich.

In this early nineteenth century watercolour, the pub by the Orwell is called 'The Ostrich'

Funnily enough, the present day owners seem to have it right. 'Ostrich' is a corruption of the earlier name 'Oyster Reach', a remembrance of a time when oysters could be gathered along the shores of the Orwell nearly all the way to Ipswich. As late as 1878, three mariners from Brightlingsea were found guilty at the Suffolk Easter Assize of stealing 16 oysters from the upper reaches of the Orwell and each sentenced to 2 months imprisonment.[4] Originally, oysters had been poor man's food. In the fifteenth century, they cost 2d a hundred, the same price as a couple of plaice.[5]

Bourne Bridge, Wherstead c1850

Though White, Kelly and others continued to produce county directories over a long period of time, later editions of this and other directories largely omit the more whimsical kind of material - more's the pity.

A pair of pictures of old Moulton (see story opposite).
Above: The village, painted by Hilkea Burgess in 1880.
Below: The 15th century packhorse bridge spanning the River Kennett.

Chapter 5
What the papers say

I have written a number of books full of amusing and entertaining stories from our old local newspapers. It would be a pity to publish a book like this without a chapter devoted to further discoveries gleaned from Suffolk's 'local rags.'

Many of these stories reflect the time in which they were written...

Under the headline 'AN UNFORTUNATE BEGINNING', the Newmarket Journal in January 1887 reported the story of *'a baker of Moulton named Hazard* [who] *attempted to deliver loaves with a pony and cart. but the usually gentle stream was much swollen from the melting snow and caught and carried downstream. With help, the pony and cart were saved.* [Which is more than can be said for the loaves, which were *'cast upon the waters'*].

At Ipswich Sessions a bill of indictment was found against the church wardens and overseer of St Mary at Stoke for conspiracy in sending an orphan pauper boy aged 8 years to a chimney-sweep and nightman in London after the magistrates had refused consent.

Bury Post: August 7th 1811

The Sunday train from Sudbury has been discontinued to the gratification of the inhabitants: it was opened for the accommodation of the graziers in sending cattle and sheep to the Monday market. Being so near St Peter's Church and at the time of starting during the afternoon service and the noise and bustle and cruelties exercised on the poor beasts in getting them into trucks, it was greatly annoying.

Bury Post: March 6th 1850

Last week a bear belonging to the Rev John Plamplin of Chadacre Hall, being at large in the yard, attacked a fine cow and mangled it so much that it died immediately.

Bury Post: April 26th 1820

There is Come to this Place and is now to be seen at the Griffin [Ipswich]

THE GREATEST CURIOSITY IN THE WORLD

The Miller that had his Arm and Shoulder Blade, with Muscles, Back and Breast, tore off by a Windmill at the Isle of Dogs; He walked afterwards about eighty Yards where he lay several Hours before his Wound was dress'd. He was brought to St. Thomas's Hospital the next Day where he was cured by Mr. Fern.

HE HAS HIS ARM AND SHOULDER BLADE WITH HIM,

where any Person may see him and receive further satisfaction. He has had the honour to be shown before most of the Royal Family and also the Royal Society, where it gave the greatest Satisfaction that could be express'd. N.B. - Upon giving notice he will wait upon any Gentleman or Lady at their own Houses or elsewhere.

Ipswich Journal: November 29th 1740

A young gentleman of Sudbury of considerable mechanical skill constructed a small steam engine and screw which he fitted up to a boat and thus formed a propeller on the river, finding velocipedes the rage, the thought struck him why not work one by steam, accordingly he attached a boiler and engine to a four wheeled velocipede by connecting the crank to the driving wheels The other day he started, seated on his steam carriage and to the great amazement of spectators proceeded down Melford road. He had however forgotten to fit a tap to turn the steam off, he was now at the mercy of the velocipede which had completely run away with him until it ran out of steam.

Bury Free Press: May 1st 1869

SUDBURY - RISKED HIS LIFE FOR A PENNY

A few days since, a party of lads were enjoying themselves on the meadows through which the Great Eastern Railway runs. It was suggested by one that he should lay himself on the railway for a train to pass over him for a penny. The feat was hailed with great enthusiasm by the others and it was arranged that the penny should be forthcoming. The lad who performed this silly act was called Heard. It is given as a fact that he did lay down in a 'gutter way' between the sleepers and that a train passed over him.

South West Suffolk Echo: August 31st 1891

A far less satisfactory ending happened to John Aldridge (aged 6), son of the goods porter at Eye railway station, who was

A magnificent early photograph of Eye railway station[1]

143

crushed to death by a train in September 1881. Safety issues were poorly attended to at that time. It seems that a number of children were regularly to be found in the station yard, riding on wagons being shunted. I'm sure it was common at that time for children to play in all kinds of dangerous places. This was just one of a number of similar cases. The jury at the child's inquest, warning of the danger of playing around shunted trucks said, *'the children had doubtless been admitted to Eye railway station by an oversight, or more correctly speaking, they had not been excluded with sufficient rigour.'*

Railways could be dangerous places, but for two station-masters, Gideon Hatchwell of Bury and James Cousens Wolton of Thurston, they found other forms of travel far more perilous. In October 1850 these two were riding on the roof of a carriage, sitting on a load of luggage, travelling between Elmswell and Thurston at about 14 miles per hour when they failed to take into account a low bridge.[2] They had already successfully ducked under three, but this was lower and both men were killed.

In the days before railway bridges, riding on top was a whole lot safer

The very earliest Suffolk papers published in the first quarter of the eighteenth century contain remarkably little local news, as they were largely collections of stories gleaned from

London papers the week before. However, the adverts are far more revealing.

Ipswich Journals of 1720 and 1721 describe *Ipswich Spaw Waters* - costing ½d for 3 flasks, *Samuel Cullum's gowns, cassocks etc.* & a runaway apprentice, William Cook (19) who had absconded from his master, Samuel Hardy (joiner). There is the opportunity *to view Mr. Moor's Astronomical Clock at the Great White Horse* (3d a look) and we hear of the execution of Christopher Welton *for robbing Mrs. Meagle at Rumburgh of £6*. Benjamin Barker of St. Mary Elms parish in Ipswich announced his wife Mary had eloped with another man and he was no longer prepared to be responsible for her debts.

As space alloted to local items grew, much local news was about crime. This was a subject that continually grabbed public attention. Crimes, arrests and trials soon filled the columns. Most of it was pretty trivial, but sentencing could be harsh.

At the Quarter sessions at Bury, William Ranson was found guilty of stealing 11 ducks the property of Ambrose Ruffel. He was ordered to be whipped in our market place this day until bloody. This sentence was carried out and he was discharged.

Bury Post: January 22nd 1784

At Bury Assizes - Isaac Skinner for stealing an elm plank and returning from transportation was capitally convicted
Peter Sparks was found guilty of sodomical practice to remain in Ipswich gaol for 12 months and to stand in the pillory twice at one hour a time.

Ipswich Journal: March 18th 1769

On Saturday last we hear that Peter Sparks stood in the pillory in pursuant to his sentence and suffered severe treatment by the populace. A soldier who was standing at a distance had the misfortune to lose an eye by a violent blow from a potato which he accidentally received. On Wednesday, Skinner was executed at Bury Gaol, he died very penitent at the gallows and exhorted

145

spectators to avoid bad company and Sabbath-breaking which he said was the cause of his untimely end.

Ipswich Journal:
April 15th 1769

A burglar sentenced by Mr. Justice Brett... to 7 years penal servitude offered to toss the bench whether it should be 14 years or nothing.

Suffolk Chronicle:
March 22nd 1873

Several gardens in this town [Bury] *have lately been robbed of early produce: perhaps the daring offenders are not acquainted with the punishment for the offence, this is no less than transportation for stealing one cabbage from a garden at night.*

Bury Post: July 9th 1788

Money Martin was charged with stealing a muck fork at Norwich Quarter Sessions. 14 years penal servitude.

Bury Post: January 10th 1855

Albert Sewell, 12, pleaded guilty to breaking into the dwelling house of Joseph Osborne of Thorpe Morieux and stealing there-from... half a suet pudding... for which he received two months hard labour.

Bury & Suffolk Standard: April 6th 1869

And punishment had to be administered, even in the most difficult of circumstances. At the Bury Quarter Sessions, in

February 1776, we are told by the Ipswich Journal that two thieves from Mildenhall and Newmarket, along with three from Lavenham Bridewell, convicted of cutting wood, were sentenced to be publickly whipped in Bury market square on Wednesday, being market-day...

Accordingly three of them were whipped, but as the fourth was going from the prison, the person who performed the office dropt down near our market cross and instantly expired; which caused a delay for some time before another could be procured to execute the punishment on the other two.

Some of the most surprising people made a habit of seeing themselves in the newspaper. The Suffolk Chronicle reported a case from the Ipswich Quarter Sessions in January 1873. It was a case that, in spite of its apparent triviality, lasted for six hours. Edgar Harvey was charged by the curate at Stonham Parva church, Rev. William Barlee of *'disturbing and disquieting the congregation assembled by singing aloud.'*

Stonham Parva -
the most idyllic of
country churchyards

In order to counter Harvey's lusty and tuneless singing, Rev. Barlee arranged for parts of the morning service, such as the *Magnificat*, to be spoken rather than sung, but Harvey had decided to sing anyway. The previous October, things had come to a head. Mr. Harvey's brief described Stonham as a place where his client's singing was infinitely more entertaining than sitting through a William Barlee sermon. On his being acquitted, the verdict was received with loud applause.

The following year...

The Rev. W. Barlee, curate in charge of Stonham Aspal, Suffolk was summoned before the Needham bench of Magistrates on Wednesday to show cause why he should not be bound over to keep the peace for six months. The complainant was a farm bailiff named Thomas Berry, who, it appeared, did not attend the defendant's church because he did not approve of the conduct of the latter. Defendant met the complainant last month, and, according to the evidence, became in a great rage with him, frothing at the mouth, and calling him a bad man and the father of liars, and saying he was going to hell, and that the door only need open to admit him. Mr. Barlee was bound over in the sum of fifty pounds and two sureties of twenty-five pound each, to be of good behaviour for three months... there appears to be considerable ill feeling against the defendant in the neighbourhood.

Lowestoft Weekly Journal: January 1874

This wasn't the end of Stonham's troubles. In September 1877, the Bury & Norwich Post reported that the Rector Rev. Richard Askew had been fined 40s at Needham Market Petty Sessions for being drunk and riotous. Apparently, *'some unpleasant feeling'* existed between the two clergymen and Askew had, while *'the worse for drink,'* called Rev. Barlee *'a _____ blackguard and a _____ Cambridge snob. &c. and tried to strike him, but was prevented by a policeman.'* The Rev. Askew would later be suspended from his parish for a year for a similar offence.

The full range of crime was there for all to read; and the consequences. When Freeman Howlett was convicted in 1793 for stealing a piece of wood, he was sentenced to be *'imprisoned for five minutes, then released.'* The purpose of this was to warn him that the next time he tried it, he would find himself on a boat to Australia. Amongst the cases that I found entertaining are these...

Last week a servant of William Corbould of Oakley near Ipswich was convicted of driving geese in the parish of Bramford upon the Lord's day and paid the penalty of 20s.

Ipswich Journal: July 7th 1764

Joseph Underwood a labourer of Cavendish was charged with wilful malicious damage in a disgusting way to a beer mug the property of John Martin Deeks, the landlord of the Bull Inn, Cavendish.

Bury Post: November 15th 1870

Two Cavendish Inns side by side. When this story was published, the Bull Hotel stood beside the White Horse.

Between 11 and 12 on Wednesday night, desperadoes numbering 7 or 8 entered the rookery at Shimplingthorne for the purpose of

149

stealing rooks, a man and a boy who were employed to watch the rooks were overpowered and obliged to retire: further assistance was obtained and Samuel Ruffell and his son received several blows. One of the ringleaders named Henry Steward of Lavenham was captured and another absconded.

Bury Post: May 10th 1837

On Friday evening disgraceful scenes took place at the Sudbury Union workhouse. On the morning of that day three men, Ralph Ardley, William Bryant and James Sargent who had been imprisoned for a like offence returned to the workhouse from Bury gaol and tore 300 feet of piping from the wall cutting off the gas, they were taken into custody and the Mayor committed them into custody at Bury gaol.

So long as Bury gaol complete with its treadle wheel is preferred to Sudbury Union these offences will be will be repeated.

Sudbury Post: November 24th 1847

[The food was better in gaol and good food was hard to come by...]

Mr Jarvis, a cowkeeper of Clare had noticed that his cow had 'fell off' recently very considerably in his supply of milk. He could not account for this, so one day he took a walk on the common and actually noticed a boy milking his precious liquid into his capacious mouth.

Bury Free Press: September 2nd 1871

But just to demonstrate this was not a totally uncaring society...

Alfred Baldry an 11 year old urchin whose father has been transported and his mother has almost forsaken him was charged with stealing a purse at Lavenham from Thomas Risby.

The lad confessed to stealing the purse which was hanging out of the prosecutor's pocket. The jury found him guilty and sentenced him to be whipped and discharged, they also gave directions that the poor little fellow who is without friends should be taken care of at the prison.

Sudbury Post: November 4th 1846

Love and marriage is another theme that filled the news-papers of the past, just as it does to this day.

Bacton: *On Monday a sprightly youth of 60 years with an old lady of under 20 summers went to Stowmarket and were made one. They returned to Bacton where the bride's father had prepared entertainment. In the course of the afternoon a slight affair brought out the gentleman's temper so much that he was quickly expelled from the house. His wife declared she would have no more do with him where a few hours before she promised to love and obey him. On Thursday she packed up and went to London to seek a situation: the husband is very desolate and very few pity him.*

Bury Free Press: June 10th 1871

On Saturday last a lad of about 18 years occupied as pot boy at the Angel Inn at Hadleigh, Suffolk, was married at Hadleigh church to a mere child in appearance. The parties regaled them-selves with gin before going to the church. When they returned, the bridegroom found he had lost his job, as his master did not want to employ a married man.

Bury Free Press: December 1st 1855

A disgraceful scene occurred at St Mary's church in Bury, a man named George Cooper presented himself at 8 a.m. for marriage in such a state of intoxication the Curate the Rev. Bearyman was unable to proceed with the service and deferred it until 10 am with the hope that the man might somewhat recover. At that hour the incumbent proceeded with difficulty throughout the service till he came to the words of the intended, (with this ring I thee wed). The man refused to proceed any further and left the church, free from the marriage knot which we trust will be a happy escape for the intended wife.

Bury Post: July 31st 1850

An over-indulgence in drink seems to have been a common feature in many of these stories...

151

Hartest: *There was a wedding of considerable amusement at Hartest on Tuesday last - the parties, James Garrad, aged over 60 years and Eliza Felton of about 40 years. The lady has been an inmate of the workhouse for the last 19 years and in the course of the winter Garrad through lack of employment took shelter under the same roof. He was smitten by the lady and made an offer of marriage which was accepted. The twain left the 'House' to be made one flesh, the Curate gave the funds for the banns to be published and the Rector consented to forego his fees. They were accompanied to church by friends; the gentleman who officiated in the parental capacity generally known as 'daddy', was adorned with sundry feathers after the fashion of a Red Indian or a New Zealand chief. When the party came out of church they went in different directions and retired to several houses but not long after the bridesmaid thought she ought to have 'stood a treat' and accordingly gave the bridegroom 3d with the requirement that he proceed to a public house and purchase one pint of beer to regale himself.*

He went, but while there, he was overcome by temptation to partake of refreshments with friends until he was overcome by drink. He essayed to go home with his beer but was found by the roadside in a state of intoxication. The bride's patience having been exhausted, went to search for her lord and reached the public house where she was also assailed by temptation and eventually rendered to the same condition. Such was the temptation of the first day of the foolish couple, thanks to the beer the drunken bridegroom escaped at least for one night without a certain lecture: the bride by her weakness sacrificed the right of reproof.

Bury Free Press: April 6th 1861

We never had prohibition in this country, but there were those who pressed for it. The nineteenth century Temperance Movement opened liquor-free pubs and held massive gatherings to encourage people to 'sign the pledge.' The Newmarket Journal in April 1887 covered a meeting of the local *Total Abstinence*

Society', where the speaker, Mr. Winston was reported as saying, *'The spirit is repugnant to the human blood, which endeavours to repel it.'* Appropriately, the prayers at the meeting were led by a **Mr. Pledger**.

Mind you, many local papers viewed the more enthusiastic abstainers with deep suspicion...

MILDENHALL - The Salvation Army - Two or three individuals belonging to this body have located themselves at the premises lately used as a Reading Room and Coffee House, where they occasionally hold meetings. [How dare they!]

Newmarket Journal: January 1887

"BRITISH WORKMAN" PUBLIC HOUSE.

*" A Public-house without the drink,
Where men can sit, talk, read and think,
Then safely home return."*

The success and blessing which has attended the establishment of " Public Houses without drink" in various Towns in England, and especially in Leeds, (where there are now 13 in successful operation), have induced some of the inhabitants of the Mayfair and Grosvenor Square District to endeavour to establish a similar place in this part of the Town where Working Men will be able to spend their leisure time in Reading and Conversation and Mutual Improvement.

It is intended that the house shall be open all day, in the same manner precisely as an ordinary Public-house, except that no Spirituous Liquors shall be sold there, but that Coffee, Tea, and other Provisions may be had, and that good cheap Dinners and Suppers shall also be provided for both Men and Women. Newspapers and Periodicals will be supplied, also Draughts, Chess and other Games.

This House would also meet the want, which is so much felt by many men, of some place where they can meet their friends; and where their Sick Clubs and Benefit Societies can meet for business apart from the temptations which await them at the Public House where they are expected to drink "for the good of the house."

It is desirable that the above should be the people's own, *not a* Charitable Institution. But a Capital is required for the commencement. It is therefore proposed to establish a Guarantee Fund for two years, to be managed by a Committee of Ladies and Gentlemen, including an Hon. Secretary and Treasurer.

These Houses have been established in other places at a very small expense, and have soon become self-supporting.

Combined with this Committee it is proposed to have a Managing Committee of Working Men, who should regulate all the affairs of the House. Their decisions to be confirmed by the Guarantee Committee in matters of outlay.

Under the Committee a man and his wife will be appointed to act as Salaried Managers.

The Managers will hand over to the Treasurer the Daily Takings for Entrance Money and Provisions supplied. They will have the charge of the House and be answerable for its cleanliness and good order.

Bye-Laws and other details with regard to Beer, Smoking, &c. will be decided by the Two Committees.

A Meeting of all Classes to consider the above scheme will shortly be held, of which due notice will be given. Meanwhile any person willing to Co-operate in this undertaking is requested to communicate with

CAPTAIN C. C. FITZROY,
28, Mount Street, **W.**

Mind you, the Sally Army could cut up a bit rough at times and there are quite a few newspaper references to altercations, punch-ups and riots involving General Booth's militia. Colchester and Sudbury saw violent street battles in 1883. Things had been a lot worse in other parts of the country, but their gatherings were viewed locally with suspicion. The Bury Post in 1887 described *the unmitigated nuisance of their marching bands and the accompanying noisy rabble attending their 'campaigns.'* In July

 1888, John Scotcher Jnr. of Bury would be charged with firing an air-rifle at the Band's drum, though insufficient evidence would see him walk free from the court. In September, an open-air street service would lead to two of the Army officers being fined for *unlawfully and wilfully obstructing the highway*. But, their recognition of the evils of drink proved to be an issue that many others would share with them.

Shimpling *When wine is in wit is out, this was instanced at a small wayside Inn not one mile from Shimpling when a sturdy young son of the soil, over ardent in his devotions to the god Bacchus, made a bargain he had wished to retract when awaking next morning.*

It was the painful recollections that the 'dear partner of life' by virtue of the last night's contract, was no longer his for he sold his wife for half a crown. The 'gude wife's' distress can be imagined when her would be 'Lord' arrived to claim his right with a heavy thump on the door, saying, 'I will have my bond like Shylock.'

Bury Free Press: March 10th 1866

I must have found at least a dozen **wife-selling stories** (What? No husband-selling tales?) in my researches. Here are a few of them...

Last week, a man and his wife falling into discourse with a grazier at Parham Fair, the husband offered his wife in exchange for an ox provided he would let him choose one out of his drove. The grazier accepted the proposal and the wife readily agreed. Accordingly they met the next day and she was delivered with a new halter round her neck and the husband received the bullock which he sold for 6 guineas. It is said the wife has since returned to her husband: they had been married about 10 years.

Ipswich Journal: Sept 29 1764

Not long since a man at Baylham in Suffolk having had a disagreement with his wife sold her to a farmer; the fee was 1s and he delivered her with a halter about her.

Ipswich Journal: June 21st 1783

Last week a disgraceful circumstance occurred at Sudbury when Henry Frost sold his wife (with the customary halter round her neck) to one Robert Whiting for 2s, but the bargain being offensive to a number of females present they would have given the new bridegroom a summary chastisement had he not taken refuge in a cottage nearby: but when they pursued him he was obliged to make his escape by jumping out of the chamber window.

Bury Post: May 16th 1821

Of course, relationships are rarely straightforward...

From St Edmunds in Suffolk we hear that an ancient gentlewoman of 72 years with an estate of £300 per annum had to defend herself from the extremity of the cold weather, in an honourable way: taken to bed a young fellow of 23 years.
Ipswich Journal: January 3rd 1741

On Wednesday at Ipswich, a young woman was to be married to a soldier: just as the service was about to begin the man changed his mind and walked away. The poor girl was so affected that she went home and hung herself, but being cut down before she was much hurt, and the man was prevailed upon to marry her
Ipswich Journal: August 10th 1771

William Day for throwing his wife into a well was ordered to prison and to keep the peace.
Ipswich Journal: July 27th 1782

The West Kent Militia, quartered at Bury, Sudbury and Melford, marched to Botesdale on their way to camp at Gorleston.

Gorleston

Their baggage waggon received an aquisition of several smart girls of this town of Bury and one servant maid much afraid of being distanced that she wanted the banns called which was not practicable; they appropriated her wages to purchase a special licence. The above are a regiment of fine men and it is thought they have left in the town many tokens of their gallant conduct which will be taken care of at parish expence.

Ipswich Journal: May 14th 1794

Not everyone was keen to join the militia, the 'home guard' of their day. But when jobs were scarce, at least the family was paid a subsistence allowance. Parishes were reluctant to be responsible for too many children, so men with more than one child were not usually accepted. In an Ipswich Journal story of 1794, we are told that a man from Horningsheath was asked how many children he had...

'One at home and two in the churchyard,' he said.
Assuming he meant that the latter two were dead and buried, he was appointed to the militia. Later the truth emerged. He had told the older two to go and play in the churchyard, so he could answer the question truthfully without putting himself at a disadvantage.

If a parish couldn't find a volunteer to represent them in the Militia, they had two choices - to ballot the available men or pay a substitute to serve on their behalf. It was not unknown for balloted men to fail to turn up. As a result, lists appeared in the papers naming and shaming those who had not joined the regiment on its being *'embodied for training.'* A typical list appeared in the Suffolk Chronicle in December 1831, naming and describing 69 such 'deserters', and offering twenty shillings reward to anyone prepared to apprehend and deliver any of them to the Commanding Officer.

Above all, it is the **strange and wonderful tales of Suffolk people and places** (and even their animals) that make the old papers such a darned good read...

Some days since a young farmer in the neighbourhood of Newmarket was ploughing near the road when he saw an oyster-man, he stopped him and pulled out his bread and cheese bought the barrel of oysters, paying him 3s 6d and sat down and ate the whole barrel of oysters and his bread and cheese and continued ploughing.   Bury Post: January 15th 1784

Ploughing by George Soper

A few days since, a blacksmith from Tuddenham drank some water from a well near his house when he occasioned sickness at his stomach for several days. In order to relieve he took some emetic tartar, and yesterday morning he voided a frog of more than an inch long which is alive, and he is quite recovered.
Bury Post: July 31st 1793

Glemsford. *The pleasure fair was held at Glemsford on mid-summer's day, there was an unusual amount of stalls with the green being completely full: the event passed over orderly which is an unusual thing to say about Glemsford.*
Suffolk & Essex Free Press: June 28th 1868

Whilst being a bit more complimentary about the entertainment on offer just up the road at Clare in 1844, the Suffolk Herald rather begrudged its workers having the money to attend at all...[3]

Clare Castle in 1800

CLARE.

The lovers of sights in this town had an opportunity on Friday evening of enjoying a treat, by witnessing the performances of Monsieur Ginnett's Equestrian troop in his Olympic circus, which arrived that morning, and was exhibited in the Castle Bailey. There were also gymnastic exercises, with other amusements. The feats of horsemanship were cleverly done, but could not be termed first rate. The Samson-like entertainments, however, of Signor Dipello, surnamed the "Iron Arm," were very extraordinary. He carried men with as much apparent ease as children carry dolls, and played with half-hundred weights with as little difficulty as cricketers use their balls. Amongst many other acts he rested on the ground with his hands and feet, his body forming an arch, and in that position supported *five men*, with the addition of four of the above-named weights; finishing his performances by placing his feet horizontally against the tent pillar, and then lifting and holding in the air a horse. The whole concern is respectably conducted, even the clowns are polished in their jests. One of them after having a pretended blow aimed at his face, sneezed, and exclaimed that he had taken a pinch of *rappee*. Exhibitions are frequently productive of singular phenomena in pecuniary affairs. In these (so-called) hard times, when there is a real scarcity of business and employment, and an *apparent* scarcity of money, almost every one complains of the difficulty of raising the means to pay rent, rates, tithes, taxes, and all other "just and lawful demands," and the collectors of these said dues are too often taught to feel the truth of these complaints in being directed to "call again to-morrow." But let some popular or fascinating place of amusement be opened, and distribute its handbills, or parade its music through the streets of the "dull town" or village, then, instantly, as if by magic, cares are banished, sorrows forgotten, purses opened, money found, and the inhabitants hasten in crowds to secure seats in the place of recreation. This is no picture, but a reality; for it is well known that in this town there is depression amongst all classes, yet on Friday evening nearly six hundred persons paid for admission to Ginnett's Olympic Circus. May we not ask then, *is* there a *real scarcity* of money?

The way I interpret it, those living in the metropolis of Bury looked upon places like Clare as the back of beyond. The same paper a few months earlier had reported...

Clare - The excessive dullness of this town was relieved last week by the arrival of 'Hunter's Museum' with the Panorama and Cosmorana. It rarely happens that so much amusement and instruction is contained in (comparatively speaking) so small a space and viewed at such a reasonable charge...[4]

159

Which is why they assumed that places like Glemsford and its inhabitants, written about so disparagingly on a previous page, were worthy targets of mirth, as the story here shows.[4]

In March 1843, local papers took great delight in reporting the conviction of an inept burglar named James Brown of nearby Hawkedon who had broken into a beer house in Glemsford, but in so doing, cut his hand on the window, and bled a rather obvious trail of blood spots in the snow all the way home, a distance of over two miles. The local constables were able to follow the spots and associated footprints. He was transported to Van Diemen's Land (Tasmania) for 10 years.[5]

On Thursday last the quiet little village of Glemsford, (which has received the *nom de guerre* of "the land of Egypt," either from the remarkable fertility of the soil, or from pressure of local taxation) was the scene of a singular freak of the rural population. It appears that on the day before-mentioned a sale had taken place at a public-house in the parish, and amongst the multifarious articles which came under the auctioneer's hammer, were several casks of old beer, which, in direct contradiction to the usual laws delay, had to be very speedily removed from the place of sale to the residences of the respective purchasers. Glemsford—like too many other parishes—has, unfortunately, a redundant population, and the novelty of an auction at a public-house had drawn together a more than ordinary quantity of the unemployed labourers, and the usual alehouse loiterers who looked quietly on whilst the various articles changed hands under the auctioneer's ivory knocker; but when it became necessary to remove the beer, the proprietors soon found themselves encumbered with help, and as carrying weights is but dry work, sundry mouths were soon seen descending and ascending from the foaming liquor. "The pressure from without" continued to increase, and the news of this portable beer spread fast among the villages. Mugs, cans, glasses, horns, cups, saucers, basins, and bowls were put in requisition. In vain the guardians of the property remonstrated, entreated, threatened, present enjoyment laughed at future peril, and "To your good health, Sir," and "my service to you," were the only replies they could get. On went the drinking bout till the blood of John Barleycorn began to do its usual work. Sundry unsteady movements were soon manifest among the crowd; numbers found it was easier to hold by the door-posts than to walk, and though with Cassio they could name correctly their right and left hands, the words "I'm not drunk now" stuck in their throats. Not a few sought a recumbent posture, and though "The night was winter in its roughest mood," the inside lining seemed to defy the severity of the cold. Many took their stations under the hedges, and mistaking the snowy banks for their beds proceeded to untie their shoes and buskins preparatory to the night's repose: others not so far gone sung the praise of good ale in strains which had more of mirth than music in them, but still merriment and good temper prevailed throughout, and though there was a sad breach of the laws of sobriety there was no breach of the peace; but the proprietors who imagined they had bought the beer a bargain, found the price of the remainder considerably increased by the free-trade system,—[*From a Correspondent.*]

Throughout the eighteenth and nineteenth centuries, **superstition** played a large part in the lives of most of the labouring classes...

At Farnham, Suffolk on Monday last a poor man suspected of being a wizard was swam (as tis called) in the river Deben in the presence of a great number of spectators who had assembled from different parts of the county of Suffolk on the occasion, he was put upon his watery trial about 7 in the evening with his feet and hands tied but to the surprise of the whole company he sunk to the bottom and had it not been for the assistance of a humane spectator the experiment would have terminated in a manner shockingly to its protectors. Mortified and disappointed the company soon dispersed, ashamed of themselves and angry at their own weakness and credulity.

Ipswich Journal: July 20th 1776

It will scarcely be believed that in this present day that there should be persons so ignorant that they believe in witchcraft, yet an instant took place in Ballingdon [near Sudbury] *this week, a labouring man named Ruggles having been afflicted since harvest and still remained so, three of his neighbours took it into their heads that he was bewitched or as they termed it 'in bad handling.' To rescue him they pared his finger and toe nails and cut off some of his hair and put the whole into a glass bottle and*

placed it on the fire using some incantations and expecting to see some evil spirit depart from the victim, the bottle burst, it so frightened these ignorant necromancers that two of them have scarce recovered. Two are tradesmen's wives; another a bricklayer's wife.

Bury Post: February 18th 1829

Inquisition at Bury on Abraham Ransom aged 2 years who was found dead in bed: it appears the child was put to bed by a little girl who at his request covered him up with bed clothes in consequence of his fear that the sweeps might get him.

Bury Post: June 14th 1837

A child of about 12-13 in Bury is afflicted with St Vitus Dance, the parents were advised the only remedy was to charm it away and accordingly on Saturday night music was provided and the child kept dancing for three hours. The charm is to be repeated until a cure is affected.

Bury Post: August 8th 1855

Give them their due, the editors of our local rags tried to educate their public or at least to let them know their opinion of some more **unlikely stories**...

In October 1874, a young woman, swimming at Croyde sands was... *driven ashore by a mermaid, who issued forth from the breakers green-haired, golden-combed and all. True, the mermaid may have been an overgrown Lundy Island seal.*

(Newmarket Monthly Illustrated Journal)

This magazine, later to become the Newmarket Journal newspaper, then described itself as a *'local magazine of useful information and instruction.'*

When Mary Toft, a woman from Godalming, claimed to have given birth to a number of rabbits, to certain people, the explanation almost seemed believable...

We have the following account well attested from Guilford in Surry, viz. That three women working in a field near that town saw a rabbit which they endeavour'd to catch. but they could not, they all being with child at that time. One of the women has since (by the help of a man midwife) been delivered at several times of a... rabbit... and is kept by the said man midwife at Guilford.

Ipswich Journal: October 15th 1726

The most unusual part of this whole story seems to have been the *'man midwife'*, Mr. John Howard, who kept the rabbits preserved in spirits. Many people came to view them and their 'mother' over the next two months, including representatives of King George I. Nathaniel St. André, the King's physician (whose appointment had less to do with his medical prowess and more to do with the fact he spoke German), published a tract on the case that sold in huge numbers. By December, in spite of having convinced a number of other leading medical figures, Mary Toft was shown to be a fraud, and imprisoned. It became the big joke of the year...

At Lincoln's Inn after the play had ended last night, there was an entertainment called Harlequin the Sorcerer, *in which the audience was unexpectedly diverted with a representation ridiculing the rabbit imposture, Harlequin assisted by a male midwife being delivered of four rabbits, which ran about the stage and raised such a laughter as perhaps has not been heard on other occasions.* Ipswich Journal: December 10th 1726

The following April, it had all been largely forgotten, and Mary Toft was allowed to return home to her family (minus rabbits), there being no further charge against her.

One of the more curious local stories involved the death of Ipswich woman, Grace Pitt, on 10th April 1744. Her remains were found by her daughter, lying in front of her empty fireplace. Her skin and bones were reduced to ashes, yet her shoes and clothes were intact and the wooden floor on which she lay wasn't even scorched. Locals put it down to witchcraft. It was less than ten years since the Witchcraft Act had (largely) been repealed. It remained a mystery.

When I started to collect old newspaper articles, I realised I had a disproportionate number of stories about **death**. I began to wonder if this said something about me. But I checked, and sure enough, there was in past centuries a definite obsession with **graveyards, coffins and funerals**. Often amusing, always entertaining, there was no doubt about it - death sold papers.

On Monday morning a fire attended with fatal results occurred at Hitcham at a place known as Box Tree farm. Part of the house is occupied by a man named Abbot, and the other half by Mr. Arthur Fayers, a retired farmer. Mr. Fayers and his daughter on Christmas Eve went away for a few days holiday so only Abbot was left on the premises. After the outbreak was discovered, Bildeston fire brigade was soon on the spot and with willing hands helping. The charred remains of the poor fellow Abbot was discovered; it could be seen that he had lain down on the bed with his clothes on and a clay pipe which indicated the cause of the fire. The property is the owned by Sir Cuthbert Quilter M P. and it is occupied by Mr Ward from Monks Eleigh. The deceased man appears to have been a remarkable character, in early life being a well known poacher and his skills were lately more lawfully exercised in the position of gamekeeper. He was a splendid shot at pigeon and sparrow matches: his first wife died, and late in life he married again but to a woman much younger than him. She ran away and left him, and after he has since led a lonely life doing for himself. Bury Free Press: Jan 1st 1898

There was nothing like a good blood-thirsty story to sell papers. So, when one turned up, you had to make the most of it. When the gun-cotton factory at Stowmarket exploded and 24 people were killed, the Illustrated Police News demonstrated why they had gained a reputation for graphic representation.

EXPLOSION OF GUN COTTON AT STOWMARKET

The illustrations for the following stories are also taken from the Illustrated Police News...

An awful tragedy occurred on Monday morning at the village of Sudbourne near Orford, the suicidal tendencies of a farmer named John Botwright involving not only his own death, but that of his son Raymond...

Ipswich Journal:
September 30th 1893

This, one of a number of detailed accounts explained how John Botwright had tried to put an end to himself a number of times before. Whilst a number of Suffolk papers dwelt on the tragedy of such waste of life, the more lurid national papers focused on the state of the bodies and the shock experienced by the witnesses. This was a far from rare occurrence. At an inquest less than a month later, the Bury & Norwich Post reported...

The Tragedy at Cockfield:
Mrs. Crick, who was shot a fortnight since on the allotments in the village of Cockfield by William Souter who afterwards committed suicide, succumbed to her injuries on Thursday evening. From the first, hopes of recovery were slight indeed, the injury inflicted being very severe. All that medical skill could devise was done to alleviate the severity of her suffering, but all efforts were unavailing...[6]

This story too received a lot of coverage, the fact of the matter being that Souter had received notice to quit his cottage and, believing that his neighbour Mrs Crick was responsible, had attempted to put an end to her. Then... *afterwards deliberately loaded his gun, placed it underneath his chin and with a freshly cut forked stick, with the result that the charge entered his head and he fell dead on the spot.*

Not all stories in local papers are local stories. Many colourful tales published were there for their entertainment value alone...

A consignment of 19½ tons of embalmed cats from Benni-Hassan, Central Egypt has just reached Liverpool. In the parcel there are remains of about 180,000 cats. They were discovered by an Egyptian fellah employed in husbandry, who fell into a pit, which, on further examination proved to be a large subterranean cave completely filled with cats. Specimens of these have been deposited at Liverpool Museum: the remainder are about to be employed as manure. It is estimated these are from about 2000 B.C.

South West Suffolk Echo: February 8th 1890

7 A CUNNING FOX.—Two travellers had halted in the desert, and had just killed a couple of fowls for their dinner. Before they could dress the birds, the hour of prayer arrived, and they turned, like good Moslems, to their devotions. A fox which had been skulking in the neighbourhood, seeing them thus engaged, came boldly up and carried off one of the fowls before their very eyes. Prayers over, they began lamenting over their loss, when, to their amazement, they beheld the thief at a little distance dragging his tail submissively behind him, and holding the fowl in his mouth ; he then deposited it on the ground, and slunk away with every sign of repentance and contrition. They at once hailed the occurrence as a miraculous testimony to their own piety, and ran to pick up the fowl which had been thus strangely restored to them ; on reaching the spot, however, they found that Reynard had only restored the skin, and in the meantime had slyly stolen round to their camp-fire and made off with the remaining moiety of their dinner.

And then there were **jokes.** Yes, our forebears had a sense of humour and to prove it, a number of our local papers carried a **'wit and humour'** column. These two items are both from 1874 and 1875 issues of the Newmarket Monthly Illustrated Journal...

The early nineteenth century was known for its encouragement of enterprise and creativity.   Apparently, it was not uncommon for the Duke of Wellington to be pestered by inventors wishing to make money from their ideas. On one occasion, we are told he asked one such man, *'What have you to offer?'*

'A bullet-proof jacket, your Honour.'
'Put it on.'

The Duke rang a bell and sent for the Captain of the Guard to order one of his men to load with ball-cartridge.
[At which] *The inventor disappeared.*

A paper speaks of a man who 'died without the aid of a physician.' Such instances of death are rare.

Occasionally, we are given a view of how Suffolk might have been very different had other circumstances prevailed. An account in the 1814 magazine *'The East Anglian'* gives detailed plans regarding the proposal to build naval dockyards at Havergate near Orford, sounding entirely enthusiastic about the scheme. Other articles suggest developing Shotley. I can't say I'm sorry that they decided otherwise.

Shotley

Halesworth

One of the most endearing characteristics of old newspapers is the way they became more and more parochial. Up until the 1950s, some of our local rags reported every tiny insignificant event in the most amazing detail. A typical wartime story from 1943 involved Sonny H. Wright of Halesworth who was fined £5 for 'wasting petrol'. He had driven from his home in Halesworth to Maldon to pick up some furniture.

These three extracts are from the Stowmarket Recorder for 1936 and demonstrate perfectly what local papers were all about. (Report from 'The Stowmarket Parliament') *Appointment of new attendant at the ladies lavatory came next for recommendation. The present attendant had given notice of leaving and as a result of applications having been invited for the vacant post, that of Miss D. M. Andrews of 35 Regent Street be accepted. If services are satisfactory, Miss Andrews is to be provided with a mackintosh.*

JOCK OF STOWMARKET

Old age and summer heat has taken toll of poor Jock whose kennel home was at 14 Tavern Street. He was a faithful canine friend and possessed remarkable sagacity as can be vouched for by his owner. Regularly and unbidden would he trot along each morning over the Market Place and along into Ipswich Street, fetch his master's morning paper and deliver it to the breakfast table. He had no occasion to fear the Police Station; neither had the kindly officers there to fear him. Kindness begat affection but a loving kindness (and there's a difference between the two) will get gentle devotion. Jock liked little snips from the larder next door and he got them, but he could not accept them unless they were wrapped up, then he would take them home and enjoy them with the pleasure and delight of a child. He would take his walk and come home respectable. Obedient and docile to the last. His end came quietly at home a few days ago after eight years sojourn.

Yes, it really was an obituary to someone's dog! In a way, you had to feel a bit sorry for the poor editor. Each week, he had to fill a newspaper with exciting reading material, even though most weeks nothing of any significance happened in Stowmarket. So, what was the eye-catching front-page leader article that week?

A Traffic Jam at Stowmarket

Ipswich Street, Stowmarket was the scene of an unusual traffic jam last Tuesday morning. at about 1:30 a.m. an Eastern Counties Omnibus was proceeding up the street and at a point approximately opposite The Palladium, a laden motor lorry belonging to Mr. J.R.G. Williams was coming down the street. Offside contact

A slightly later model
from the Ipswich
Transport Museum

was made by the vehicles in passing with the result that both came to an enforced halt. This involved the hold up of other miscellaneous vehicles, 12 in one direction and 15 in the other, which lasted several minutes.

Chapter 6
Fact or Legend?
Superstition in Suffolk

How much of what we dismiss as 'old tales' is actually part of our history? Take for example a tale that comes down to us from around AD 930 that first appears in ancient Bury Abbey documents written by Archdeacon Hermann and Abbot Sampson. On Mayday, as was the tradition, the Shire Reeve (or Sheriff), Leofstan was to hold his great assembly on the hill near Bury known as the *Thing-hoe.* Cases to be dealt with that day were few. Leofstan was in a foul mood, perhaps disappointed at the lack of fines he might impose. One woman who should have been there to answer certain charges was not. Instead, he learned, she had absconded to the Shrine of St. Edmund. Furious, the Sheriff sent his Bailiffs to apprehend her. However, though these men were afraid of their master when he was in one of these moods, they were reluctant to profane the sanctuary to which the woman had fled. Not so Leofstan himself! Having drunk copious quantities of fiery mead and oblivious to potential dangers, he shrugged off the attempts of priest and deacon to stop him. Almost immediately, we are told, the Devil gripped Leofstan, leaving him writhing on the ground, foaming at the mouth and gnashing his teeth whilst his victim escaped. There this impious man died, but his soul would know no rest. Variously described as a ghost, a ghoul, a vampire; Leofstan would haunt that area so that nobody near there could get a wink of sleep, until his corpse was dug up, sewn into a calf-skin and plunged into a stagnant pool.

Since it was first told, the story has appeared in a number of books about the area, and doubtless is still told on ghost-walks around the town. Where do these stories come from, and how

The Angel Hill, Bury
St. Edmunds c1820

much truth can we attach to them? Much of this tale is quite believable, as is the reaction of superstitious people to what might have been a fairly ordinary but, nevertheless, disturbing and ultimately fatal fit. But it was some time before anyone would write down what they had been told of this series of events.

Other less plausible legendary events have hung about, being retold through the centuries: the green children of Woolpit, the merman of Orford, the fearful Black Schuck at Bungay, the slaying of a dragon at Bures, to name but a few. Mythical creatures appear not only in folk-tale and legend. A remarkable number of Suffolk churches carry pictures and carvings that might appear a bit out out of place to our way of thinking. On the outside of Peasenhall church porch, are pictures of dragons and woodwoses (wild men of the woods).

Dragons are fairly plentiful in Suffolk churches. They appear as pew-ends in Weston, Wordwell and Withersfield, as wall paintings at Troston, Bradfield Combust and Wissington, in stained glass at Elveden and Stowlangtoft (St. George's) and on the spandrels of the roof at St. Margaret's in Ipswich. In all, I have counted at least 15. Woodwoses are just as plentiful, carved into fonts at Sibton, Orford and Bildeston, on the parish chest at Chevington and on the West door at Cratfield, to mention a few. Other mythical creatures appear alongside angels in this illustration from Erwarton Church and in pictures overleaf.

Whether dragons and woodwoses, together with other assorted mythical beasts, were a representation

Below: The font in St. Matthew's, Ipswich.
Left: The font at St. Mary's, Bentley

of evil or a recognition of the mystery that was our world is unclear, but churches in this county were for centuries picture books of the imagination of their congregation.

I love the story told of an ancient font that was removed during the Cromwellian years from St. Peter's in Sudbury by a Puritan mayor. It was altogether too ornate for the tastes of the time, but proved also too elegant for the purpose he intended. Meaning to use it as a horse trough, his horses shied away from it as if sensing it was being put to a use that was well beneath its design. As it proved useless as a horse trough, it was eventually returned to the church and mounted on a new pedestal. [1]

We've always had a respect for the mystery of nature, and so many old beliefs spring from there. The intelligence and industry of bees has long fascinated our ancestors. Whenever there is a death in the family, you are meant to tap on the hive and whisper the news, as if the bees were part of the family. For that reason, swarms of bees are never supposed to be sold for money, but given, or, at a pinch, exchanged. Ravens were reputed to visit and croak when a death was imminent. Now long gone from this county, they are recorded as having nested annually at Woolverstone in trees beside the Orwell at least until the 1840s.

Across the Orwell from Woolverstone

If your foot or that of your horse was lamed by a nail, it was said, never just treat the wound and throw away the nail. Instead, keep the nail in a safe place, well greased, and the wound will heal. What is more, if the nail is in your keeping, it isn't finding its way into someone else's foot, so a certain amount of sense prevails here.

In his book, 'The New Suffolk Garland' (pub. 1866), Ipswich historian John Glyde tells of the many villages in Suffolk that were still able to boast of a *'professor of the healing art.'* Cures such as *'placing a live flat fish'* on the chest of a child with *'hooping cough'* are described. Other remedies include eating a roasted mouse, drinking milk from which a ferret has lapped or dragging the patient underneath a gooseberry bush or bramble. A cure for the ague involved going to the four cross-ways as the clock strikes twelve and, turning about three times, driving a tenpenny nail into the ground up to the head; then walking away backwards before the chimes finished. The next unfortunate soul to pass that way would step on the nail and take the disease from you. Cures involving Biblical chants, the eating of bread baked on Holy days, the swallowing of the hair from the cross on a donkey's back and the use of jewellery made from old coffin handles to prevent cramps are all listed here.

To touch the hanged man at a public hanging was supposed to be particularly efficacious.

Long after the dissolution of the monasteries, people in Suffolk prayed to holy relics, and took the water from Holy wells as medicinal treatments. The Lady Well at Woolpit had a reputation for curing complaints of the eyes.

Superstition belonged to a time long before Christianity, and continued unabated once it had taken a foothold. The laws condemning witchcraft in England effectively only lasted from 1563 until 1736. Though most parishes had their wise woman (or wise man), before that time, they were respected and tolerated for their usefulness to their community. Laws regarding heresy might have been used against them occasionally in the fifteenth and early sixteenth centuries, but regarding them as servants of the Devil seems to have been rather an extreme response in the middle ages. Instead, these people were more commonly accepted as their community's healers, midwives, counsellors and layers-out of the dead.

But for a hundred and fifty years, a kind of paranoia would prevail, whereby an assortment of witchcraft trials would lead to the imprisonment and death of a number of unfortunate characters.[2]

Matthew Hopkins, the Withchfinder General; son of a Suffolk vicar, who brought to trial 117 'witches' (17 of whom were men) at the Suffolk Summer Assize of 1645. At least 30 of them were hanged.

It is what happened after 1736, I find most interesting. The superstitious people of Suffolk, far from abandoning their former ways, continued to fear, respect and occasionally to persecute those they believed possessed powers beyond their understanding.

Most local papers reported the swimming of Isaac Stebbings, reputedly a wizard from Wickham Skeith in 1825. The Bury & Norwich Post in 1886 told of Matilda Lee, a Stradbroke gipsy who was known widely as *'The Suffolk Witch,'* and had conned any number of people out of large sums of money through fear and ignorance. A year later, the same paper had the story of the evil Mrs D____ from a village *'not far from Ipswich'*, whose *'hell broth'* had bewitched enemies of those prepared to pay her. In Fressingfield in 1890, the death of a child in its pram (from whence smoke had billowed) had been widely reported as believed to be down to witchcraft on the part of the child's step-grand-mother.

Modern conversions of old houses have turned up all kinds of witchcraft-associated paraphernalia.

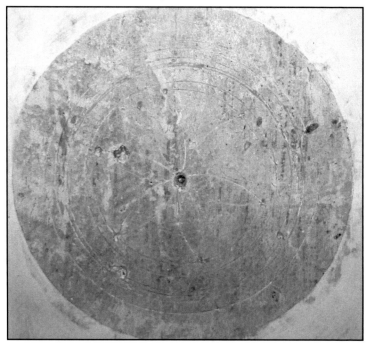

Renovation of a house in Brent Eleigh revealed this geometric design hidden beneath a coat of limewash. It was created on plasterwork that was where a window had once been. This was added protection from witches who were believed to be able to breech such barriers. The same house has revealed a number of objects placed there for protection. Mummified cats, broken broomsticks, wooden and leather objects - all have turned up in hidey-holes in old Suffolk houses. Witch bottles were frequently placed beneath floors, in cavities; even under the

entrance-way. These tended to be Bellarmine bottles, often with faces on them with magical items inserted and sealed up. These usually amounted to pins, needles, hair, nail-clippings, pierced felt hearts and small amounts of human urine.

A house in the village of Combs inexplicably revealed a quantity of Bulls' horns beneath the doorway. A large old farmhouse at Old Newton, near Stowmarket had the items pictured below in a space between the walls, apparently dropped from the attic room above, probably by servants. Having found these, the present owners have now replaced them, because ...you never know!

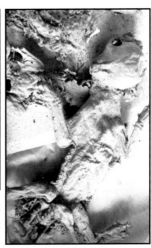

Mummified cats, leather and wooden items; even a broken broomstick

179

Even people who did not believe in witchcraft enjoyed reading about it. Newspaper items from the eighteenth and nineteenth centuries recounted the swimming of witches and wizards, the burning of effigies and other bizarre rituals. The burning of a witch or sorceress in Lisbon in November 1748 appeared in the Ipswich Journal. In 1751, the paper told of a murder at Tring, Herts whereby a man had drowned an old lady, believing her to be a witch, a crime for which he was later executed. Reports of a ceremony involving a witch-bottle filled with crooked pins and horse urine appeared in 1792. In 1849, readers were told that 10% of the population of Henton in Oxfordshire were witches, and many more were described as hag-ridden. In 1857, a brief was presented to a Norfolk magistrate requesting permission to swim the local witch.[3] A year later one of a number of stories appeared, again in the Bury Post involving the Essex wizard, Cunning Murrell. Here police protection had to be given to a young lady, Emma Brazier of East Thorpe. And so it went on. In eighteenth and nineteenth century Suffolk, 'witches and wizards' were 'swam' at Monks Eleigh, Stanningfield and Wickham Skeith.

Tom Paine

Then there was that time-honoured way of dealing with your enemies: to burn an effigy of them. Not everybody's favourite, Thomas Paine of Thetford was 'executed' at Saxmundham in January 1793... or at least, a model of him was. Several places in East Anglia burned effigies of Napoleon during the early years of the 1800s. Likewise the Emperor of Russia in 1855 (Crimean-War time).

Bonfire-night antics in Woodbridge and Orford often involved burning a 'Pope' or prominent local Catholics. But it could get a whole lot more personal...

James Claxton looked out of his window in Ixworth on Guy-Fawkes night 1862 and was shocked to see what looked like a figure of himself set alight. Earlier, a riot at Bungay in 1845 where an effigy was burned had led to the imprisonment of six of the rioters. David Garwood, the blacksmith at Brockley, following a similar demonstration, had to take out an injunction to force his neighbour John Mead to keep the peace.[4]

Edward and Frederick Kerridge found themselves up before the Beak at Ixworth in 1863. Their fire had been built in the middle of what is now the A143. Even quiet, well-behaved Bradfield St. George saw an effigy burned in December 1892 of a farmer who had cut the hourly-rates paid to his labourers. Local leading-lights were often the victims of such indignity. These included the Vicar of Needham Market and the Brandon Churchwarden, both in 1886. In an election-night fracas in Stowmarket in October 1892, the effigy of Oliver Parker was stolen before it could be burnt, so the mob made one of his wife and burnt that instead, leading to what we'd probably describe today as a right-old punch-up.

In January 1895, the effigy of an unpopular Alderman of Lowestoft, Mr. Adams, was burnt.[5] This was one of a series of similar events in Lowestoft during the late nineteenth century. Just across the Waveney in Harleston, Norfolk, a local businessman, by the name of Mr. William Bunn [the baker?], was burned in effigy instead of Guy Fawkes on November 5th 1875 (though eye-witness accounts suggested that the effigy looked nothing like him). By that time, it was over two hundred years since we'd hanged a witch in Suffolk, and a century and a half since we'd been allowed to try one in court. But as has been seen, you can change all the laws you like; however it takes an awful long time to alter the ways people think.

Just across the Waveney in Roydon near Diss in October 1893, six men were imprisoned for riotous assembly, having built and pulled apart the effigy of Mr. Todd, the agent to local Lord of the manor, Mr. Frere. The locals didn't have a lot of time either for the Freres or their representatives.

Which is all very unfortunate when you learn that Mr. Frere ought never to have been living there in the first place. Once of Finningham Hall, his great, great grandfather, Sheppard Frere, had been expected to inherit the manor of Campsea Ashe near Wickham Market, being the closest surviving member of the wealthy Sheppard family. However, on one of his visits, Sheppard Frere offended the old man by ordering drinks after his host had gone to bed, and for his cheek, was struck out of the will. An expensive mistake!

The house he should have inherited - High House, since demolished

Chapter 7
Suffolk characters

This chapter could be very long indeed, but I have attempted to tease out stories that have not become over-familiar, and may hopefully include tales long-forgotten and ripe for unearthing.

Millicent Almond was the last landlady of the Three Mariners Inn at Slaughden near Aldeburgh. Slaughden is no more, having been swallowed up by the sea and the pub with it. W.A. Dutt's book 'The Norfolk & Suffolk Coast' describes the village early in the twentieth century as *'a small sea-threatened cluster of cottages bordering a primitive quay and grouped around an ancient inn with a huge bone of a whale suspended over its front door.'* [now in Aldeburgh Moot Hall]

For years, Slaughden had been at the mercy of wave and tide. Early seventeenth century reports describe ships of over 350 tons belonging to the town being at anchor there. Today, all you will see is the beach on one side of a bank, and the river and yacht club on the other.   A hundred years ago, Milly Almond, it was said, refused to allow the encroaches of the sea to drive her out, even as the rest of the village submitted.   Newspaper accounts from February 1882 describe *'boats and punts plying along the road to and fro in readiness to remove the inhabitants.'*   On several stormy nights, Millicent would pile fish boxes in her room and sit on an armchair atop them. Local people would warn her of the danger she was in, but she sat fast, time after time until eventually, the sea won, as it was bound to.   The picture here shows the inn in its final days.

Fergus Menteith Ogilvie was born in London in 1861. He was educated at Rugby and Kings College Cambridge before specialising in ophthalmology at St. George's Hospital in London. His passion was British Birds and he was to become one of the foremost 'sportsman-naturalists' of his day. At his death in 1918, his collection of stuffed birds (197 different species) was donated by his mother to Ipswich Museum. Many of these cases, preserved by T.E. Gunn of Norwich are still on show today. Most were shot around Ogilvie's home at Sizewell House.

If a letter sent to Mr. Packard in 1900 is anything to go by, improvements had been needed in the museum's collection. Writing from the British Museum, E. Ray Lankester wrote, *'Go round and destroy by burning more than half of your stuffed bird and animal skins - they are hopeless caricatures and only disgrace what would be a very fine and creditable town museum. You need to require to trust someone to do this and to give him dictatorial power. I would come and do it for you some day if you would give me unquestioned authority.'*

The downside of the activities of sportman-naturalists like Ogilvie was that rare birds became rarer, something that was not confined to Victorian times. As long ago as 1618, Robert Reyce in his *'Breviary of Suffolk'* was writing of a decline in certain species, especially the *'Sparhauke and Gosse Hauke'*.

Stuffed Bitterns shot by F.M. Ogilvie, exhibited in Ipswich Museum

However, it is in later years, the problem has become more acute.   W.H. Hudson's notes on 'Lost British Birds' (pub.1894 updated 1923) is particularly pessimistic on this matter. He names a number of birds that had once bred in this country, yet by the beginning of the nineteenth century could only be regarded as rare visitors. It is interesting to look at his list and see how some have made comebacks - others may yet do so.

Snipe Shooting in Suffolk[1]

Spoonbills were recorded as breeding at Trimley until the late seventeenth century. They have tended to appear regularly in recent times, but are a long way from being regarded as a breeding species again. The avocet, Hudson lists as being extinct as a breeding bird. Fortunately, Suffolk coastal visitors know it to be widespread again. Several birds of prey come to his attention, including the goshawk, kite and the marsh-harrier. Whilst the goshawk once bred here (says Robert Reyce in1618) it had ceased to do so by the nineteenth century, but along with the kite has begun to reappear as a breeding species. Marsh-harriers, whilst not common, are well established in the marshy areas of the county. Bitterns, hunted to extinction for their feathers will probably always be 'red-list' birds, but at least for now are back as regular breeders in Suffolk.

Not so the Great Bustard.   This unfortunate item appeared in The Graphic in 1891...[2]

THE RURAL CALENDAR years hence will bear against February, 1891, the entry, " A great bustard killed in Mildenhall Fen." This splendid bird was said in 1878 to be extinct in England, a remark which we always welcome, as it is almost invariably followed by a reappearance of whatever creature has been thus hastily denounced as "obsolete." So it certainly was with respect to the great bustard, three specimens of which were shot in 1879, and two in 1880. Since the last year, however, a whole decade elapsed without a capture, and fears began to be felt that the bustard had really gone the way of the large copper butterfly, of the beaver, and of the crane. It is, of course, a thousand pities that this particular bird was shot, but the slayer did not recognise his prey until it fell.

The egg-collectors and sportsmen-naturalists have a lot to answer for, but at least we can still see, over a century later, the fruits of Fergus Ogilvie's obsession.

There are many tales told of the **Maharajah Dhuleep Singh**, another great shot of his day. He purchased the Elveden estate near Thetford in 1863 and was renowned for bagging hundreds of game in a day, rarely missing. Even on his journeys away from his estate, he would travel well prepared for hunting, taking 'hooded falcons and muzzled hounds'[3] wherever he went, even as far as India. It is his death and funeral however that leave us with a tale that is both wonderful

187

and quite horrific. There was supposed to have been a lady in Elveden who, having 'died' was buried in the churchyard there.

Body-snatchers coming to her tomb that night were horrified to discover that she had actually been buried alive and had torn her shrouds to pieces.

The body-thieves ran for it, screaming, whilst the woman came to her senses, climbed out and went home to frighten the living daylights out of the husband who believed he had been widowed. She lived, we are told, a number of years after that. The Maharajah was so troubled by this story, he left instructions that on his death, after the body had laid out a while, his throat should be cut before the coffin lid was screwed down. He had no intention of waking up below ground. Though I'd like to be able to say otherwise, I must confess, I have unfortunately been unable to find a single piece of evidence to corroborate this remarkable story.

Not a million miles from Elveden is the tiny village of Eriswell. In Eriswell church is a weatherbeaten stone once erected to one **James Paul**, a North American Indian who died in 1820 at the age of just sixteen. The church believed in 'converting the heathen of the world,' and the New England Company saw fit to apprentice some Indian boys to tradesmen in England. James Paul found life as a carpenter in the damp and the cold of Suffolk too much. American servicemen, keen to see him remembered have, in recent years, erected a new memorial to James Paul.

Also buried at Eriswell, in a tomb far exceeding her station is a servant by the name of **Patty Turk**. She seems to have caught the eye of the eccentric third Earl of Orford, **George Walpole**, whilst he was still a young man at the family estate of Houghton Hall, near Fakenham in Norfolk. George was attracted to Martha (Patty) Turk and left home to live with her in a run-down parsonage at Eriswell. Though the family arranged assorted political posts for him, he showed himself to be neither interested nor particularly able as a member of Parliament. He was prone to bouts of insanity but enjoyed his sport, and probably chose

Eriswell because it lay close to the Newmarket racecourse and the Fenland marshes where he liked to hunt and shoot. The rector of the parish at the time, Thomas Ball was himself referred to as a 'jockey parson', meaning he spent more time racing than preaching. In the summer of 1774, George Walpole and his mistress spent three weeks exploring by boat the creeks and marshes between Eriswell and Peterborough. They were together a number of years and it was widely believed that her death in November 1791 hastened his. He lived only another three weeks.

When Suffolk lawyer **Joshua Grigsby IV** of Drinkstone Park died in March 1829, he was known to be a strong non-conformist in more ways than one. He left instructions that he was to be buried in a tomb in the garden. Though his house has now gone and been replaced by another, the tomb and its monuments remain. Local legend has it that he was buried standing.

Though there is no evidence to support such an idea, two reasons are given for this. Some will tell you he loved his garden (he was known as keen botanist) and wanted to be able to view it in death as in life. The suggestion was that he was keeping an eye on his gardeners, to check they weren't slacking. Superstitious garden workers felt uncomfortable about being overlooked when working near the tomb, and a low wall was built around it to conceal it. The other reason given for his unusual interment is given by others less charitable, who have been heard to say that his widow had him placed like that as he had spent too much of his life horizontal, so to speak.

THIS SPOT IS HALLOWED
FOR
HERE REST THE REMAINS
OF
A TRULY GOOD MAN

His life was in conformity with all the precepts of the
He bore the trials allotted to him with unshaken const
Leaving us a bright example of *Christian Resignati*

A DEVOTED ATTACHMENT
TO THE SURROUNDING SCENES
INDUCED A STRICT INJUNCTION
TO BE HERE INTERRED

It was a fondly cherished wish consistent with
His own peculiar but *firmly religious* principles.

Home burials, though far from common occurred on a number of occasions across the county. **Absalom Feaveryear** of Wingfield, having fallen out with the church over the matter of tithes, set about building his own mausoleum in the garden of his house, even carving his own gravestones, though of course he never carved the date of his death. For much the same reason, John Reynolds of Felsham was interred in the grounds of what is know known as Mausoleum House. In 1863, John Moseley of

Glemham House put in an application to build a burial vault at his house.[4]

Some of Suffolk's grandest tombs are to be found at Framlingham, where several Dukes of Norfolk were buried along-side their wives, though not always together. The fourth Duke, **Thomas Howard** was married and widowed three times, not always happily. His third marriage to Elizabeth Dacre came as part of a remarkable family deal, whereby three of her daughters would marry three of his sons. Two of Thomas Howard's wives were supposed to share a tomb at Framlingham, though when the vault was opened in 1842, little more than a single skull was found.

Tradition says that the townsfolk of Framlingham emptied it in 1745 to make room to hide their valuables, being afraid the Young Pretender, Bonny Prince Charlie would, if victorious, ransack the town. I have two problems with this story. The Dukes of Norfolk had espoused the Catholic cause longer than most and if any town in East Anglia was to be spared, it would be Framlingham. Also, although the Pretender and his troop reached as far south as Derbyshire, accounts in the Ipswich Journal of the time seem remarkably unconcerned, the story being given less importance than you might expect. The rebels, as they were described, were seen as more of a rabble than a serious threat...

'They seem'd to be extremely out of humour and stripp'd some persons of their cloaths, &c. ... His Royal Highness put himself at the head of the Horse and Dragoons and a thousand volunteers... we hear the rebels are retiring Northward with great precipita-tion.'[5]

Having money meant you could make extravagant gestures. **John FitzGerald** of Boulge (brother to Edward) would always, whatever the weather, protect himself from sun or rain alike with a large gingham umbrella. On one occasion, having gone to London and forgotten it, he sent a servant back to Woodbridge to fetch it, costing him far more than the price of a new one.

Some Suffolk men rose to great heights in spite of what those around them believed regarding their potential. John Glyde tells a tale of **Sir George Biddell** of Playford, who became Astronomer Royal. According to other family members, he had to become a scientist as *'he was found not to have sufficient brains for farming.'*

Tudor times enabled intelligent men of modest means to rise to positions of great power and authority. **Nicholas Bacon,** son to Robert Bacon of Drinkstone in Suffolk, though far from a pauper, made a spectacular rise in fortune. His father was a yeoman farmer who had himself risen to the position of sheep reeve with the Abbey of St. Edmundsbury. This gave him the financial clout to seek a good education for his second, highly intelligent son, Nicholas. By the age of just seventeen, Nicholas Bacon had graduated from Corpus Christi College, Cambridge. He then followed the path of other great men of his time. By the middle of Henry VIII's reign, the power once exerted by church-men like Cardinal Wolsey and Sir Thomas More had passed to lawyers, and it was here Nicholas would make his mark.

Acquiring wealth had not always made it easy to move into the realm of the landed gentry. But Nicholas did particularly well out of the dissolution of the monasteries, snapping up the manors of Redgrave, Botesdale and surrounding parishes as well as lands further afield. Surviving the ups and downs of changes of monarch, he rose to the position of Keeper of the Great Seal to Elizabeth I. Robert Reyce wrote of him... *a man of such deep witt and experience of all matters of state and policye, that in forreyne countries hee was reputed of great fame and admiration, and at his death was accounted one of the greatest statesmen for wise counsell and deep policye that these parts of Christendom afforded in those dayes.*

When he died in 1579, he was buried in St. Paul's Cathedral and among his six children, we particularly remember his youngest son Francis, philosopher, scientist and Lord Chancellor to James I. Not bad for a shepherd's son!

Unfortunately, there were others born to wealth who failed to make any great mark on the world at all. **John Elwes**, who inherited the manor of Stoke by Clare, was born John Meggott in 1714. According to the writer Ada Whitlock, he was educated at Westminster but *showed himself so indifferent to books that after*

he left school he never again opened one. All in all, he appears to have been pretty ignorant and was soon parted from much of his inheritance by promises of a high rate of interest which lured him into investing in wild-cat schemes run by an assortment of plausible rogues. Having lost £24,000 in an iron-works in America that never materialised, he became a bit more wary. A wealthy uncle came to his rescue. Harvey Elwes had no children of his own and was taken with his unfortunate nephew. By now, Meggott had a bit of guile, and when visiting his uncle would change at a nearby inn into tattered and much-darned clothes so as to appear needy. At the age of 49, he got what he wanted. Uncle died and Meggott changed his name to **John Elwes** in memory of the man who had ensured his future.

John Elwes would become renowned for two things: he would be an inveterate gambler, often losing thousands: but at the same time he would be the most pitiful miser. He would never dine at an inn. He would travel taking crusts of bread and hard-boiled eggs for the journey. He chose routes with the fewest turnpikes and would escape paying tolls by making detours across fields. When he inherited what is now Stoke College, he could never bring himself to keep the place repaired. It was said he move his bed around the room as leaks appeared in the roof. When he was 60, he consented to stand as M.P. for Berkshire, as long as no outlay was required. He was elected, but he rarely attended the House. The only time he was really frightened was when Lord North proposed he be offered a peerage. Terrified that he might have to keep a carriage and a house full of servants (all perhaps better dressed than him), he declined. Though he amassed a fortune of £800,000, his mansion went to rack and ruin and was known locally as 'the poor-house.' *"When he died in squalor and haunted by fears of poverty,"* Ada Whitlock tells us, *"he had not a friend in the world and his death was regretted by no-one."*

But before we are too condemning... A poem entitled, *'Epitaph on John Elwes Esq.,'* appears in John Glyde's *'New*

Suffolk Garland' (1866). It adopts a kind of, *'there but for the grace of God go you or I'* attitude, seeking to present Elwes as much like all of us - a mixture of good and bad, no better or worse than most. This is a short extract from the beginning and end of the rhyme.

Here to man's honour, or to man's disgrace,
Like a strong picture of the human race,
In ELWES form - whose spirit, heart and mind,
Virtue and vice in firmest tints combined...
    Learn from this proof, that in life's tempting scene,
    Man is a compound of the great and the mean;
    Discordant qualities together tied,
    Virtue in him and vices are allied:
    The sport of follies, or of crime the heir,
    We all the mixtures of an ELWES share.
    Pondering his faults - then ne'er his worth disown,
    But in his nature recollect thine own;
    And think - for life and pardon where to trust,
    Was God not MERCY, when his creatures dust?

Many of the best Suffolk stories concern the sea, and it is one of these I turn to next. It was commonplace for ships leaving large harbours along the east coast to call at Suffolk ports to pick up crew. So, ships sailing south from Hull and Newcastle or north from the Thames would often begin journeys quite light on crew, hoping to make up their company at Lowestoft, Harwich, Aldeburgh or along the Orwell.

In early May 1553, three ships set out from the Thames, commanded by **Sir Hugh Willoughby**. The largest was one hundred and sixty tons burden. Progress up the East Anglian coast was slow, as winds became changeable and the ships moved to Yarmouth, then south again to Aldborough (Aldeburgh) and the Orwell. This at least enabled them to stock up with supplies and to set sail with a full contingent. Having passed Orfordness on June 23rd that year, they made their way north in search of a north-east passage above Russia to China. Though still only August, Willoughby's ship met a great deal of ice and, becoming separated from the other two ships, was forced to remain the winter aground on the Arctic island, Novaya Zemblya.

A year later, the bodies of all of them would be found, apparently frozen to death. Poets romanticized about their deaths, describing their having been found frozen to their stations, dutiful to the last. A more likely account came from the Russian fishermen that found them. They had shut themselves in a cabin, sealing up all draughts and lit sea-coal to warm themselves. It seems probable that with no ventilation, they died of carbon-monoxide poisoning. Ironically, Willoughby's family had made much of their wealth from trading in sea-coal.

Meanwhile, the other two ships, the largest being the *Edward Bonaventure* commanded by **Richard Chancellor**, were more successful, making progress as far as the White Sea and the port of Archangel. Chancellor was transported by sledge from there to Moscow for an audience with the Czar, Ivan the Terrible.

He would return home in triumph, only to drown returning from a similar mission in 1556. Though these are the names that survive to this day, it is fair to assume that as crew were gathered from Aldeburgh and Ipswich, Suffolk seamen were in no small way responsible for this great exploration.

Philip Staffe of Ipswich, ship's carpenter with the great explorer Henry Hudson, spent the early years of the seventeenth century sailing those same northern waters seeking a north-east passage to China as well as heading west to navigate Canada's northern waters beyond what is now known as Hudson Bay. It is remarkable to consider just how small the ships used on these voyages were. The *Hopewell* was eighty tons; the ship used on their final voyage, the *Discoverie* was only fifty-five tons. This last ill-fated journey in 1610 led them by way of Iceland and Greenland to the Hudson Bay, where food ran low and morale among the crew ebbed away. Led by one of the crew, Henry Green, the men mutinied and were in the process of capturing Hudson and his Boatswain, when the carpenter tried to reason with them. He was offered a chance to join the mutineers but chose instead to be cast adrift with his captain. Philip Staff, Henry Hudson and King the boatswain were never seen again. The mutineers did not fare much better. Green and three others were killed by *'esquimaux.'* The survivors, on returning to England were tried for murder.

John Collier's painting of Hudson, Staffe and others cast adrift

The sea and what lay beyond it once proved a haven from religious intolerance, and a number of Suffolk people were early founders of colonies in places that today still bear the names of Suffolk towns and villages. My collection is far from complete. Someone might like to research this more fully. Sothold in the county of Suffolk on Long Island owes its name to **John Yonges** and his wife from Southelmham St. Margarets who sailed to the new world from Southwold in 1637 by way of Holland (They were not permitted by the authorities in Yarmouth to sail directly from there). Many Suffolk place-names appear in Massachusetts - Ipswich, Framlingham, Wrentham, Sudbury and Haverhill (there are at least 5 Haverhills in the USA). Melford appears both in

Maryland and Nova Scotia. There are at least three Woodbridges and four Grotons in America today.

Much of this is down to those who sailed in the wake of the Pilgrim Fathers; who left the place of their birth to begin a new life where they could worship as they wanted without interference... Thomas & Nicholas Danforth and Thomas Warner of Framlingham, Thomas & Elizabeth Paine and John & Margaret Thurston of Wrentham; and John Winthrop of Groton, who rose to be Governor of Massachusetts.

John Winthrop was born in Edwardstone in Suffolk. His family came from Lavenham.

A maritime story I'd love to believe crops up in the family papers of the Newson family, lodged at Lowestoft Record Office. This is the tale of **Mary Ann Bulley**, daughter of a Yarmouth sea Captain. No date is given. It appears, she was taken by her father on a journey to Gibraltar, but what started as a treat turned into a nightmare. Returning laden with goods, they were attacked by pirates, and their ship the *Amelia* was carried across the Atlantic to the West Indian port of Laguira [possibly La Guiara on the northern coast of Venezuela, which in the eighteenth century was a haunt of buccaneers]. The cargo being unloaded, the crew were freed but succumbed to an epidemic, which wiped out all but Mary Ann and the cabin boy, John Wilson. Exchanging her female attire for jacket and trousers, Mary Ann Bulley is supposed to have hired two black sailors and successfully navigated the ship back to Liverpool.

Though it seems an unlikely tale, Lloyds register for 1824 names a Brig '*Amelia*', from the port of Gt. Yarmouth captained by a J. Bulley.

Added to that, the Norfolk Chronicle for November 3rd 1827 states...

The Amelia of this port, John Bulley master, from Seville to London, has been taken by a Colombian brig of war, under suspicion of the cargo being Spanish property, and was carried into Puerto Cabello about the 16th August - Letters have been received by the owners of the Amelia mentioning the death of the master at Puerto Cabello.

The Liverpool Mercury in February the following year in its Naval Intelligence listed a ship the *Amelia* (no Captain named) as having reached Kinsale in County Cork, bound for Liverpool from Laguayra [suspiciously like La Guira] and St. Domingo.

With so many miles of coastline, Suffolk was bound to produce its fair share of sailors and aquatic adventures. These included **Henry Seckford**. Whilst his brother Thomas was making a name for himself in and around Woodbridge as a lawyer and businesman, but particularly for his charitable works, Henry was making his money in an altogether different way. Henry Seckford was a pirate and, living at a time when dealings with the Spanish were often conducted at the point of a cannon, he sucessfully plied his dubious trade, not always being fussy whose ships he attacked. In 1580, complaints came that he had seized the cargo of a Hamburg vessel. There was no doubt as to who had been responsible. His name, alongside that of his ship, was painted in the brightest of colours on the ship's bow.

The rescue of the Sarah & Caroline

Over the centuries, many lives have been lost to the sea. In 1801, in an attempt to do something about it, **Robert Sparrow** of Worlingham Hall near Beccles founded the Lowestoft Lifeboat Society, soon to become known as the Suffolk Humane Society. With the help and sponsorship of **John Rous, 1st Earl of Stradbroke**, the first British sailing lifeboat the *Francis Ann* (named after one of the Rous daughters) was built and launched in 1808 . It sailed under the command of **Lt. Samuel Carter** and in its 42 working years, saved about 150 lives. Lowestoft people affectionately named the boat *'Old Mawther'* In October 1820, just before the founding of the R.N.L.I., Carter and his crew made a particularly daring and successful rescue of twelve sailors from the Woodbridge sloop, the *Sarah & Caroline*. This dramatic picture of the event was a lithographic print from a painting by Yarmouth painter, William Joy.

Suffolk's connection with the sea has often had a lot to do with smuggling. Famous sites along the coast and up the estuaries found their way into the newspapers of the eighteenth century on a regular basis - Benacre, Minsmere (or Misner) Haven, Sizewell Gap, Pin-Mill, Ramsholt and so on. But it was not the sailors themselves who were the great smugglers of their day. No, that was much more down to the criminal master-minds who organised the storage, distribution and sale of the goods.   **George Cullum** of Brandeston, **John Harvey** of Pond Hall, Hadleigh and even the **Reverend Ready** of Wadham in Norfolk, who did rather more than just fail to notice the activity that was going on in his parish (and his outbuildings).

Church property has long been associated with smuggling - Theberton near Sizewell, and the two-aisled church of Westhall where the valley roof was reputed to store many a cache of contraband.   Philip Meadows, rector of Great Bealings during the early nineteenth century was known to turn a blind eye when his carriage and horses briefly disappeared from their stable, enabling local smugglers to move goods around freely. No-one was going to search the parson's chaise. According to a letter from Edward FitzGerald to his friend, Charles Keene (artist for Punch), in Theberton Church contraband was hidden beneath the altar, in the full knowledge of the rector, Benjamin Taylor.

My favourite tale of this kind involved an Aldeburgh captain called **H.P. Clodd** who used a similar trick to the one described on page 319 (the old fake burial routine) to run contraband almost under the eyes of the preventative officer, through to Blyford Church for safe keeping.   B. Granville Baker describes in his book about the Waveney (pub. 1924), how around Beccles and Worlingham, *'the ghosts of furtive figures of long ago revisit old haunts, deep cellars where all manner of illicit goods were hidden from the excise men, to be carried away across the marshes by tracks known only to the initiated.'*   The marshland beside the Waveney was a formidable place, best avoided by anyone not familiar with the area.

One more smuggling tale with less of a happy ending is in the *'Recollections of a Smuggler'* which according to the Leiston Observer is to be found in the British Museum.   It was also reported in the Ipswich Journal of 27th June 1778.   Six cartloads of spirits had been brought ashore at Sizewell and were being held at a farm on Leiston Common. This apparent activity attracted the attention of the revenue men, but the smugglers were too quick for them, moving it all to a vault in Coldfair Green. This was particularly well-disguised, being under a stinking manure heap. Some time later when it became necessary to move the tea and spirits under there, Robert Debney and William Cooper were the first to clear a way to the trap-door and enter. But the build-up of noxious fumes overcame them and they died down there. Though the other smugglers were later able to move the contraband again to the Parrot & Punchbowl at Aldringham, this was too well-known a haunt and they and their stash were taken.

All that remains today to remind us of this is a heavily weathered stone to the two who died there.

Robert Debney & William Cooper   Died 22 June 1778
R.D. aged 28 & W.C. aged 18
All you dear friends that look upon this stone
Oh! think how quickly both their lives were gone;
Neither age nor sickness brought them to decay
Death quickly took their strength and sense away
Both in the prime of life they lost their breath,
And on a sudden were cast down by death,
A cruel death that could no longer spare
A loving husband, nor a child most dear,
The loss is great to those they leave behind,
But thro' Christ 'tis hoped true joy will find.

One character I remember reading about, and disregarding as highly improbable is the **Reverend William Cratfield**. Just about the only book I know telling of the 'highwayman parson' is *'Colourful Characters from East Anglia'* by H. Mills West. My first thought was to question whether this unlikely and undated account had any truth to it whatsoever. However, this turns out to be a much older story than I had first assumed.

William Baret de Cratfield was introduced to the parish of St. Mary's Wortham near Diss in 1401. Yes, there is a list of past rectors in Wortham Church and, sure enough, his name is there (much earlier than some web-sites suggest). According to tradition, he showed himself to be an unpopular and slovenly parson whose parishioners canvassed for his removal. His tenure only lasted until 1408, when he was defrocked, and he left Wortham to begin his second career. On his departure the people of Wortham had a great celebration, burning an effigy of him.

Wortham Church

William Cratfield met up with a criminal named Thomas Tapyrestone (or Tepyrton), and the pair of them for a while followed the lucrative trade of robbing folks on the highway around Newmarket.

We tend to think of highway robbery as an 18th century crime, but it was going on a long time before that!

Some accounts suggest they managed the criminal business of the area, extorting money from lesser criminals for the privilege of working on 'their patch.'

London trial records survive for 1416 (Calendar of Letter Books of the City of London) naming the two men as having been found guilty of robbing William Boton(er), 'goldsmyth of London' of a sum of money. The Inquisition report describes them as *'notorious highway robbers and murderers.'* It is unclear whether Cratfield was hanged this time. The name reappears and it seems likely that following a trial in 1432 for *'divers felonies'* he finally met his predictable end.

William Cratfield was far from the only Suffolk parish priest to demean his cloth. **George Wilfred Ellis**, rector of Wetheringsett turned out not to be the real thing at all. This story was carried far and wide and to prove it, this account is from the Hawke's Bay Herald, published in New Zealand (six months after The Times had reported the trial) in late September 1888...

The career of imposture laid bare in the case of Rev. George Ellis, late rector of Wetheringsett, Sussex [by which they mean Suffolk] is as extraordinary as any of its kind. Mr. Ellis seems to have been the illegitimate son of a woman who married a rabbit-skin seller in Lincolnshire and first worked as an ordinary labourer. But he had wits and somehow got employment in a Roman Catholic School at Salford. Finding out that the Church of England admits converted priests from the Roman Communion without re-ordination, he forged papers of ordination in Latin with the signatures of the Roman Catholic bishop and canon of Salford. On the strength of these he was admitted to the Church by the Bishop of Truro, now the Primate and passed into the Diocese of Norwich. Here he married and was presented to a living worth £800 a year by his father-in-law. Unfortunately prosperity appears to have at length turned his head. He quarrelled and behaved in an unaccountable way towards the village till suspicion was aroused and reference made... brought the truth to light.

The not-reverend-enough George Wilfred Ellis received a sentence of seven years penal servitude and, to appease all those horrified to discover their marriages were false and their children technically bastards, special legislation was passed to make those marriages retrospectively valid.

With the passage of time, what was once a scandal seems to be viewed locally with more than a touch of humour. Even the Wetheringsett village sign displays two past rectors - one (Richard Hakluyt), remembered for writing a significant sixteenth century book - *'The Principal Navigations, voyages and discoveries of the English nation'* - the other (shown here on the right), George W. Ellis, the unordained rector.

I am sure most parish priests took their calling seriously. And even when their moral standing was drawn into question, it wasn't always their own fault. During the Cromwellian years following the English Civil War, parsons who were seen by their Puritan masters to be too high-church were eased out. The Committee for Scandalous Ministers was set up to examine any rector, vicar or curate who had given them cause for concern. Evidence and general tittle-tattle was gathered and used as evidence against anyone who might be viewed as a Royalist or was too attached to a non-PC form of worship. Now there may have been a few who gambled, drank and resorted to ladies of questionable morals, but it is fairly remarkable the extent to which men they wanted to get rid of were found wanting.

At Finningham, **Edmond Major** found himself up before the Committee accused of saying prayers in support of the King, refusing even to read the orders sent out by Parliament and being *'a common haunter or frequenter of innes, alehouse and tippling-houses.'* Major was ejected from his living, but he was later allowed to return. Many other Suffolk ministers were less fortunate.

Thomas Newman of Little Cornard faced a host of accusations including bowing at the name 'Jesus', celebrating Christmas, and giving sermons that were *'full of bawdry not fitt to be repeated by modest and sober men.'* **Nicholas Stoneham** at Eyke even attended a game of Camp-ball on a Sunday (see page 251). In the case of **John Ferrour**, rector of Trimley St. Mary, it was sufficient to say he hadn't done enough to discourage his household servants from playing games on the Sabbath. **William Walker** of Winston was supposed to be *a common gam*[e]*ster at tables and hath wonne and lost much money.* Whereas **William Gibbons**, rector of Great and Little Bealings... *in a suspitious and lustfull manner putt his hands under the clothes of Susan Scott, a noted harlott.* But most of the accusations were of a political nature. The other stuff was just the icing on the cake, and was especially useful should priests come on all high and mighty.

Between 1644 and 1646, over forty *'scandalalous ministers'* were examined by the two Suffolk committees. Most were found wanting and ejected.

At Mellis, they clearly toed the line. A document[6] describes... *a solemn league covenant for reformation and defence of religion and the happiness of the people and King and the peace and safety of the three kingdoms of England, Scotland and Ireland according to the ordinance of the Parliament on 10th March 1643.*

Not only parsons found themselves out of favour during the Commonwealth period. A great chef and writer of cookery books at that time was **John Murrel** of Oakley. In the words of the time, *he improved his knowledge of the continent* during the Cromwell years, returning only at the restoration of Charles II.

For some Suffolk men and women, their fifteen minutes of fame was little more than that. This county may not have sired James Watt or Isambaard Kingdom Brunel, but we do have **Mr. Snell**, landlord of the Star Hotel, Newmarket, inventor of *'Vestipluvia'*, a waterproof fabric that in 1875 was sold to the London manufacturer, Luck & Sons, so producing the first leisure clothing for *yachting, riding, driving and walking.*[7]

Suffolk has had more than its share of eccentrics. **Orlando Whistlecraft** of Thwaite was no exception. He was, in his time schoolmaster, shopkeeper and farmer in the village of Thwaite. Whistlecraft died in 1893 at the age of 82, leaving a remarkable legacy. As well as leaving paintings and poetry, he was an avid recorder of the weather. His *'Rural Gleanings'* of 1851, published at his own expense, are so detailed they are regularly referred to by writers examining changes in our weather patterns today.
A typical entry is this...

1832 March 7th; a tree at Boxford riven to atoms in a sharp storm of thunder at noon. June 9th: Exceedingly heavy rain, thunder and lightning, over all Suffolk; especially Ipswich and Woodbridge. The thunder continued near or distant, all the day.

July 12th; in the evening, and till near midnight, a most terrific whirlwind, with vivid lightning and thunder, throughout Suffolk. It came on S.W., and whirled up the dust, and twisted trees to pieces in every place in its course. A mill at Sudbury lost its sails; a stall of rich earthenware was upset at Stowmarket; very many trees disarmed and torn up; a barn at Stoke Ash, and another at Eye, thrown down. Many mills dismantled; two at Bury, one at Ixworth, and one at Stonham, lost sails; another damaged at Beccles; one at Loddon, Norfolk, uncapped, and two men killed by its fall. Great Thornham mill lost a sail, and was otherwise injured; and Mr. Rose's barn and other buildings and stacks, were burnt by lightning, at Palgrave. To the East of Norwich, the corn was destroyed by hail.

Orlando Whistlecraft's books offer advice on prediction of the weather. *'When the wind settles between S.S.E. and S.W. on or near March 21st, the following Summer is almost generally showery. But if the wind sets in at north-east or from north to east near this time, we shall have generally a fine summer in that year.'* He was a countryman through and through, and well understood the seasons. Writing about the frosty winter of 1841, he wrote...

No stately swan or ostrich can supply
So fair a vest as here attracts our eye;
'Tis beauty perfect all! our theme must soar,
Amid the grandeur spread without our door -
O'er woodland, glade and vale, or rustic farm;
Each amply proves each season has a charm.

Another great eccentric of his time was **Jemmy Chambers**, the Wandering Poet. Born in Soham in Cambs. in 1748, he became a pedlar. Though he could read a little, it was only in later life he learned to write and began selling his poems at a few pence a time. As his fame grew, so did his commissions and his poems commanded a higher price.
On the death of Nelson, he wrote...

Mourning dress succeeds to fashion,
Sadness reigns from shore to shore;
Sorrow glooms the illumin'd nation:
Brave Lord Nelson is no more.
...Many victories fame'd in story, Gallant Nelson did acquire;
But the last with zeal for glory Did each loyal mind inspire.

Jemmy Chambers,
the wandering poet

More often, his poems came from the harsh wandering life he led. *Morning Winter* was written after he had woken up in a cart shed to find his limbs covered in snow blown through the crevices. At one time he resided in a shed at the back of Framlingham Castle. Mr. Cordy of Thorndon and Lord Henniker of Thornham among others tried to ease his latter years with sponsorship and providing a cottage so he had no more need to roam. But he was rarely able to stay more than a month at a time, preferring a bundle of straw to a couch or a bed.

I think a fairer judgement of the quality of his work can be made from this rather special poem. *'The wounded soldier's return'* seems years ahead of its time, recounting of the failure of this country to care for its troops and to supply a land fit for heroes to return to...

The rattling drums beat loud, the fifes began
My King and Country seem to ask my aid,
Through every vein, the thrilling ardour ran
I left my homely cot, my village maid.

In loathsome vessels now like slaves confin'd,
Now called to slaughter in the open field,
Now backward driven like chaff before the wind
Too weak to stand, and yet asham'd to yield.

Through burning deserts now compelled to fly
Our bravest legions moulder fast away,
Thousands of wounds and sickness left to die
While hovering ravens mark'd them for their prey.

Now may this tale which agony must close,
Give deep contrition to the self-called great,
And teach the poor how hard the lot of those
Who shed their blood for Minister of State.

John Glyde, who researched Chambers' life, describes his face as having been furrowed by time and surrounded by long matted grey hair to which both comb and brush had evidently been great strangers. His hands and face showed his antipathy to soap and water. *"His whole aspect was of an unusually repulsive kind and his rude covering scarcely protected him from the blasts and frigid visits of the wintry storms."* Yet he continued to shun the efforts of others, and died at Stradbroke in 1827. Today, he is a largely forgotten figure.

When writing of Suffolk poets, you can't really ignore **George Crabbe** (1754 - 1832), whose long narrative poen *'The Borough'* would eventually give rise to the Benjamin Britten opera

'Peter Grimes' (libretto by Montagu Slater). Crabbe, at the centre of five generations of George Crabbes, grew up in Aldeburgh but does not seem to have had a high opinion of the place and its people. Aldeburgh from the sixteenth century was in Crabbe's day still a Chartered Borough, run by a collection of Bailiffs & Burgesses, its tiny electorate returning two Members of Parliament until 1832. Though centuries of attrition from the waves of what was known as the German Ocean had driven the town inland, there was still a good bit more to Aldeburgh and neighbouring Slaughden than there is today. By the time of Crabbe's death, over 200 fishing boats still worked from its shores.

'The Borough' doesn't really show anyone in a good light. The fishermen and working people of the town are a shifty, drunken contemptible lot. Officials like the parish clerk and the vicar don't fare a lot better. The system allows workhouse boys to be 'apprenticed' to the likes of fishermen like Peter Grimes, and whilst the town may deplore what Grimes may have done to bring about his apprentice's death, there is little desire to change things.

The Cottage where George Crabbe grew up in Aldeburgh

212

Crabbe would be fortunate enough to receive a good education and would leave Aldeburgh just as fast as his legs could take him, but he would still be drawn at times in his life, back to the area which would be such a source of inspiration for his verses.   George Crabbe had little time for the lower classes of Aldeburgh from which he had come: and even less respect for the clergy, even though he would end up as a west-country parson.   It is probably for his lines about the Suffolk coast: its wildness and its wild-life that we remember him best...

Here, dull and hopeless, he'd lie down and trace
How sidelong crabs had scrawled their crooked race,
Or sadly listen to the tuneless cry
Of fishing gull or clanging golden-eye;
What time the sea-birds to the marsh would come,
And the loud bittern from the bullrush home,
Gave from the salt ditch side the bellowing boom:
And nursed the feelings these dull scenes produce,
And loved to stop beside the opening sluice.

Provided you could find a sponsor, the Church was a good way of finding a respectable (and often well-remunerated) position. Paying a curate a pittance to do the boring stuff, left you time to indulge in the things you most enjoyed. Suffolk parsons have been notable writers, historians, scientists and archaeologists.

William Bulleyn became rector of Blaxhall in 1550. He was already a renowned writer on medical matters, and saw no reason why a change of profession should inhibit him from continuing to research and publish what he was actually quite good at. Unfortunately, his medical musings involved a certain amount of pro-protestant rhetoric and on the crowning of Catholic Queen Mary I in 1553, took himself off to Durham, where understandably, at a distance from London, he felt a little safer.

Professor John Stevens Henslow was one of the leading scientific figures of his day and teacher to none other than Charles Darwin. Yet at the height of his academic sucess, he took Holy Orders and settled in Hitcham to be their rector for the rest of his life.

Ever a champion of help for the poor, he established a decent school to replace *'that of a wretched dame,'* ensuring

those who could afford it paid regular subscriptions; himself included. He, along with **Sir Charles Bunbury** of Great Barton, pioneered the Allotments scheme, persuading reluctant farmers to part with small parcels of land so that the *'deserving poor'* could spend their few hours away from their labouring duties producing food for their suffering families. Actually, the scheme was hardly a new idea. Between 1589 and 1775, by Act of Parliament it had been determined that no new cottage should be built unless four acres of ground were attached to it.

John Henslow's subject was Botany and he inspired a passion for it by way of the lessons he gave himself at the village school. He was a founder of Ipswich Museum and continued to work with Cambridge University on a number of projects. In later years, he led archaeological digs, such as one at Eastlow Hill, Rougham in 1844. At his Henslow's death in 1861, his son-in-law, himself an eminent botanist, wrote to a friend, *'Henslow has left a blank in my existence never to be replaced.'* The same might have been said by the poor of Hitcham, to whom he had dedicated much of his life.

Through the years, Ipswich played host to a number of great performers of their day. A decade before his death in 1870, **Charles Dickens** gave readings of a number of his most popular works. [8]

Mr. CHARLES DICKENS
WILL READ AT THE
CORN EXCHANGE, IPSWICH,
On Monday Evening, Oct. 10, 1859,
At EIGHT o'clock, his
CHRISTMAS CAROL,
AND
TRIAL FROM PICKWICK.
(5802
PLACES for the Reading (numbered and reserved) 4s.; Second Seats, 2s.; Back Seats, 1s. Tickets to be obtained at Haddock's Library, where the PLAN OF RESERVED SEATS IS NOW READY.

In 1873, **Charles Blondin**, the man who had tightrope walked across Niagara Falls came to the Royal William, Ipswich and performed in a fireproof suit, walking a rope, pushing a wheelbarrow from which fireworks exploded. **Wombwell's Menagerie** came to Suffolk many times. Bramford Road in September 1898 was the scene of a visit from the great **Barnum & Bailey** Circus.

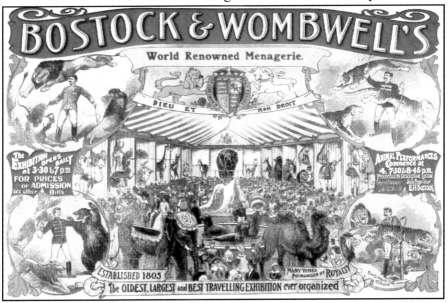

Not every celebrity who came to the town is remembered so well today. In January 1879, the American pedestrian **Edward Payson Weston** set out to walk 2000 miles in 1000 hours of consecutive walking (Sundays excepted). This task, taken on as a bet caught the public's imagination and thousands turned out across Suffolk to  cheer the man as, that February, he walked into the county from the North, from Beccles to Ipswich, then on to Bury, before making for London. Unfortunately, he fell behind in his schedule and failed to complete the distance in the agreed time by just 22 miles.

General Booth, founder of the Salvation Army visited Suffolk a number of times, his later visits being marked by a cavalcade of motor-cars, generating a great deal of excitement. Early twentieth century visitors to Ipswich included suffragette leaders **Sylvia** and **Christabel Pankhurst**, **Lloyd George**, **Sir Ernest Shackleton** and even **King George V**.

Back in the reign of Edward IV, the court-jester or fool was a Bury man called **Scogan**. It is written that he was an educated man from a good family but had a passion for practical jokes and trickery that sometimes went too far. In raising money for the building of a church in Normandy, he used a bit of psychology. He claimed to the congregation he was addressing that he had in his possession a skull which was endowed with the power of speech. He said that this relic had spoken to him, requesting that a church be built above where it was to be buried. But, the skull added, no money should be accepted from faithless wives, as their sin would corrupt such a venture. As a result, all the women of the town flocked to make their donations.

On another occasion, when Scogan had borrowed money from the king that he was unable or unwilling to repay, he feigned his own death and arranged for his 'funeral procession' to pass close by His Majesty. On the king expressing his sorrow at the death of his fool and announcing his wish that he could absolve Scogan of the debt, the jester sprang out of the coffin and blessed the king for restoring him to life. When he returned from Normandy, some time after one of a number of his expulsions from England, he landed in England with his boots filled with Normandy earth, claiming immunity from prosecution as he was not standing on English soil.

His last request was to be buried under one of the water-spouts on Westminster Abbey as he said, *"I have ever loved good drink all the days of my life."*

But I like to think the real Suffolk heroes are those forgotten and unsung heroes of yesteryear. In his book, 'Blithe Waters,' B. Granville Baker tells of the remarkable **John Jennings** who died in the early 1800s at the age of 95. He had followed his father and his great uncle into becoming postman over a wide area between Ipswich, Needham Market and Stowmarket, travelling over thirty miles a day until he was 71. After that, he cut his workload to enable him to serve just the villages of Coddenham and Barham, his home parish, for a further fifteen years.

The Gentleman's Magazine for November 1826 describes the death of **'Blind Tom' Batley** of Gazeley at the age of 75 who had been blind since his youth, yet had been a conveyor of parcels and letters from Gazeley to Higham *without the guidance of a fellow creature or dog.* Possibly even more remarkable was **George Rope** of Blaxhall who, in 1908, was still acting as church-warden in that parish at the age of 94. He was father to George Thomas Rope, the renowned artist, and sculptor, Ellen Mary Rope.

One of the most productive lives explored in this chapter concerns the printer, **John Daye** (1522 - 1584). There has been an assumption made that the printer of such works as Fox's Book of Martyrs was born at Dunwich in the parish of St. Peter's, now long since disappeared into the sea. However, as parish registers began some years after Daye's birth, we have no real proof of this.

The John Daye memorial at Lt. Bradley in Suffolk

Local writer and historian Allan Jobson is one of a number of Suffolk historians to make this claim, based largely on the fact Daye owned a house there. I sometimes wonder where these stories come from. And are we supposed to view them with suspicion, or respect that what is passed down is likely to have at least an element of truth about it? What is certain is that, after a life dedicated to printing and publishing a host of beautifully illustrated books at a time when the Renaissance had just reached Britain, John Daye died at Saffron Walden in Essex, but was buried at Little Bradley in Suffolk. His memorial in the church reads... *"Heere lies the Daye that darkness could not blynd... Tow Wyves he had... Each wyfe twelve babes and each of them one more."* Yes, a productive life in every sense!

Less dramatic, but equally meritorious, in 1873, the town of Beccles was lit by 136 lights, all of which were lit nightly by a **Mr. Brown**. According to the Suffolk Chronicle,[9] Mr. Brown could trim 60 wicks in an hour and regularly covered the four-mile route, lighting all the lamps in an hour and a quarter. He was known as *'The Nimble Lamplighter.'*

East Bergholt appointed **William Clarke** as their village schoolmaster in 1797. His salary was to be just forty pounds a year, not a great deal for an educated man. This was something below what many curates might expect to earn and about a third of what was paid to the governor of a small workhouse. Nevertheless, when he lost his sight in 1809, you might expect him to have been thrown out on the street. Give the village their due, he continued to be employed until his death some twenty years later with the help of one or more assistant teachers. Heartwarming stories like this from the past are less uncommon than you might suppose.

Black sheep in the family are part of the deal that comes with wealth and power. Suffolk families, from the Herveys at Ickworth (Earls & Marquesses of Bristol) to the Jermyns & Davers of Rushbrooke Hall, have tended to find that sooner or later the intermingling of noble genes will produce one of the family line whose extravagance and irresponsibility goes beyond even their extensive resources. Correspondence between George Henry

Fitzroy, VIth Duke of Grafton and his son, **Lord Charles Fitzroy**[10] is particularly revealing. To begin with, we read of a father in 1818 warning his son of the evils of gambling, but agreeing to pay his debts at Drummonds. It didn't work. By 1822, Charles was writing to his father about certain *'financial difficulties'* he was experiencing in Florence. A year later, his problems were clearly nearer home, as he was being advised to remain abroad to avoid his creditors. Four years after that, he informed his father[11] that he was ashamed to admit he had *'led his family to the brink of ruin'*, incurring debts amounting to £38,000. Some people never learn.

Euston Hall, family seat of the Dukes of Grafton.

The seventh (and last) baronet in the Barker family (of Ipswich) would be one **John Fytch Barker**. He only lived to the age of 24, but made the most of his few years in the world. Inheriting Sproughton Chantry along with other lands at just 16, he fell for a pretty teenager, Lucy Ward of Hintlesham Hall.

The elegance of Hintlesham Hall

They eloped and subsequently went on the mother of all spending sprees. Though he died young in 1769, the Ipswich Journal published long lists of creditors seeking payment for his debts. It would be over five years before the dust would settle and what remained of his inheritance would be sold to pay his bills.

After John Fytch Barker's death, others, notably the Collinson family would enlarge and renovate Sproughton Chantry[7]

As we move towards the chapter devoted to Suffolk criminals, the final name in this chapter might well belong there. **William Stevenson Fitch** was an avid collector of pictures and documents of the county. He was an Ipswich pharmacist, postmaster; but also a trader in valuable manuscripts. But it is the means by which he acquired both his own collection and items sold to others that is rather more debatable.

When W.S. Fitch married Rachel Alexander, she was acting as house-keeper at Ham House in Surrey. That and Helmingham Hall in Suffolk were the homes of the elderly seventh Countess of Dysart. It is rumoured[13] that Fitch's wife had been the illegitimate daughter of the sixth Earl. This would have placed her in a position of trust, whilst as a mere servant may have given her cause to feel hard done-by. Whatever the actual truth, Fitch was able, unsupervised, to plough through the archives at both Ham House and Helmingham Hall.

Helmingham Hall

Sytematically over a few decades, W.S. Fitch helped himself to a treasure-trove of documents, keeping what interested him, but selling huge volumes of rare and valuable material. These included some of the earliest printed books in the country from the presses of Willam Caxton, letters and state papers dating back to the times of Elizabeth I; also unique publications that he knew collectors would give their eye-teeth for. Certainly a number of people must have known what he was up to, but had plenty of good reason not to disclose his secret. They were the ones who benefited from filling their collections with his stolen material. He even plundered the Ipswich Corporation Chest when nobody was looking for the treasures contained therein.

In his defence, some of what he discovered and 'liberated', especially among the Helmingham papers, was already suffering from being kept in damp mildewed corners, and might well not have survived. But whilst Fitch may have been able to raid the shelves of a blind octogenarian, he was very carefully watched should he ever turn up at the British Library or any other place where his reputation had gone before him. On his death in 1855, much of what he had collected and held onto was sold at auction. Now, his collection of illustrations of Suffolk, arranged in 30 volumes resides at the Suffolk Record Office.[14] Some were torn from books, some raided from collections: others I am sure were acquired quite legally. They include sketches by George Frost and water-colours attributed to Thomas Churchyard. The lovely watercolour painting of an approach to Eye on the following page is reproduced from that collection.

Several other pictures from the same source have been used in this book, so I guess even I have reason to be grateful to William Stevenson Fitch, chemist, postmaster, antiquarian and thief.

Eye, attributed to
Thomas Churchyard

Chapter 7
Documents about Crime & Punishment

Newspapers are a great source of information about our ancestors' behaviour, good and bad, as can be shown in parts of chapter 5. When George Nunn murdered Eliza Dixon at Wortham in July 1899, it wasn't only the local papers that went to town on the story. The Illustrated Police News filled two pages with it.[1]

Mrs. Dixon had rejected his advances and he had cut her throat, leaving her body on the village green whilst he went home to change his clothes and clean up. Though he was only eighteen, appeals for mercy fell on deaf ears and he would be hanged in Ipswich Gaol in November that year.

But where anti-social activities are concerned, there are plenty of other places to look for information. And they go back a very long way. The most local of courts were those governing the manor in which you lived and reports were kept in the Manor Rolls. Many of these survive and may be of some antiquity (hence, they can take a bit of unravelling).

At Buxhall the former village green, known as the Tye was part of the Lord's domain and therefore not common land as such. In 1553, John Richar, we are told *made trespass upon the separate soil of the Lord called 'Le Tye' in Buxhall with a horse depastured there.*[2] It could have been an expensive mistake. He was fined 3d but warned if he did it again it would cost him 20d.

Fasbourn Hall, Buxhall, built around a medieval Hall, once the seat of the Copingers, the major family in the parish since the fifteenth century.

Even the parish priest was not immune from prosecution. In 1603, Rev. George Dickenson was summoned for playing bowls on the same green and warned that *noe manner of parson shall at any tyme playe at any bowle or bowles in open places out of his garden or orchard vnder the payne to forfeit for every tyme soe offendinge 6s 8d.* Dickenson was minister at Buxhall for nigh-on fifty years (died 1619), but as far as I can see wasn't a popular preacher. At an examination of the parish in 1603, he had just three regular communicants. Perhaps he was better at bowls than preaching.

The misdemeanours of a past age make fascinating reading. William Pretyman translated and transcribed the Cotton Manor Rolls in the early 1900s. An early entry reads... *"and that Margaret Cook has not repaired the tenement called Pepres: for default in repairing the woodwork and plaster: through much default, the aforesaid tenement is in great dilapidation."* Similar comments appear throughout such Manor Rolls.[3]

A Cotton judgement of 1566 warns that tenants guilty of opening up gaps in hedges to facilitate easier movement of animals are risking forfeit of their land. In 1564, the court issues a warning against idlers, gamblers, and generally against immorality. And then there is violence - At the Leet Court held in 1583, *Thomas Sanders alias Hugh* (a 'Hugh' was a servant in Middle-English) *insulted and affrayed upon William Sanders alias Hugh, howling oathes at him and did tippe up his heles with great strength and threw the said William upon the ground, striking his head against a stone, fracturing his skull against it. He is amerced 22d.*

That, though violent, was clearly a family matter. Far worse in a way was to attack your betters. In 1569... *"That Alice Halke, wife of Thomas Halke made affray and insult on George Tyrell, gent., the present Bailiff of this manor, over the rights and liberties of this manor and at the same time struck George, which is against the peace of the Lady Queen. Thus at the same time is brought to pass a calamity to be subject to, and a pernicious example is given to others - amerced 7s 8d."*

The Manor Court did not like people taking the law into their own hands. In 1581, when Richard Dade believed his neighbour, Giles Walton, owed him money, he *'entered by means of a hole in the hedge'* and helped himself to *'three pigs and 3 little pigs called sholtes.'* For this he was fined and *'ordered to close the same field before the Feast of the Assumption.'* In the meantime, the court ordered that no-one was to seize animals *'by reason of defective enclosure.'*

Sometimes justice could seem harsh. In 1569, when William Berte cut down a big ash *'called a fellynge ashe, growing on the copyhold of this manor without license but belonging to him and for necessary repairs to his plough,'* he had his land seized by the Bailiff. The land might have been his, but timber-cutting in the Lord's demesne was a different matter.

Even the administration of simple punishments might run up costs that had to be met by the parish. This is quite convenient to historians, as where money was involved it tended to be written down Aldeburgh Corporation accounts include...

1579   8d paid to Kedall for his cart when vagabonds were whipped. [They were tied to a cart's tail and whipped out of town.]
1583   Robert 4d for whipping of a maid [a man's labour was cheaper than the hire of a cart]
1584   a payment to widow Cooper for beer when Brymble's wife was ducked.

As mentioned on page 125, most Suffolk towns and villages had a serious fire at one time or another. One village even remembers it in its name - Bradfield Combust, though the story behind the name is long forgotten. Most of these fires were probably dreadful accidents. When Walberswick saw a quarter of its population displaced by fire in 1633, they were quick to point the finger of blame - and to ensure those responsible got what was coming to them. The Churchwarden's accounts for Walberswick include these three entries...

Pay'd for keeping the Prisoners that Burnt the town   5 - 0
Pay'd to two men and two horses that went with the
          said Prisoners to Ipswich   12 - 0
Pay'd more to sending Vatryne Toby and Richard
          Sommers by the Appointment of the justices
                    to bury Prisoners   10 - 0

Walberswick Church c. 1800

As late as 1824, being widowed could present a woman with all kinds of problems. When Harper John Gibson died at Laxfield, he left plenty of lands, messuages, tenements and premises (and a windmill), but his wife could not inherit them. Instead, she had to go to the Manor Court and claim the right to live in and administer the family property and to be guardian to her own children (Barnabus aged 11, Penelope aged 9), on the under-standing that she render accounts until they became of age: at which point, they had the right to put her out of her home. [So for the next ten years, mum had better be nice to them!]

A lot of what were strictly local matters were the responsi-bility of the district magistrate. At Ipswich Record Office there is a revealing little book[4] that appears to be the notebook of a local magistrate during the Cromwell years around 1652. It contains first-drafts of what would be written up as warrants and other legal documents. This was a grim and a dour time. Along with warrants against certain undisclosed misdemeanours and empowering constables to search 'suspicious places', there is a recognisance against 'games prohibited,' levies and distraints against all manner of 'tipplinge' (especially on fast days) and instructions to overseers and churchwardens to deal with problems in their parishes. Contracts between masters and servants feature - both to search for a fugitive servant and to prosecute the master who has turned out a servant, in breach of their contract.

Long after those times, local justice was often swift and harsh. In 1794, boys were warned by the Clerk at Metfield that should they be caught at any illegal play on a Sunday they would be put in the stocks.

Devereux Edgar was a Justice of the Peace in East Suffolk during the reign of Queen Anne. His notebooks, transcribed by S.R. Schofield, can be seen at Ipswich Record Office. Almost on every page (and there are many) is a story to be told. In 1701, *Elizabeth, wife of Edward Bond of Somersham*, we are told, was *a lewd and disorderly person; a common mover of discord in the neighbourhood.* Some like her would be handed back to the Churchwardens and Overseers of the parish to sort out in what -ever way they saw fit. Others, like *Sarah Bird (an idle person)* who had *deserted her service with Mr. John Dines of Nettlestead* was to be *carried to the house of correction at Needham Market and set to labour till the next Ipswich Quarter Session.*

William Cobbald of Willisham was brought before the magistrate on complaint that he had cut and carried away *wood and divers bundles of thatching stuff* belonging to James Harlwyn of Needham Market. Robert Kerridge of Coddenham complained that Daniel Horsom *did in a violent manner assault, beat and bruise the complainant in his head and body and then did further threaten bodily harme and then did beat him within an inch of his life and all without any just provocation.* My favourite has to be James Berry who not only deserted from Major General Churchill's regiment, but pawned his army coat to give him a bit of ready cash with which to make his escape.

Other entries during the early years of the eighteenth century include the duty payable by Thomas Seabourn of Stutton New Mill for refining 150 bushels of salt. It's sometimes forgotten the importance to the Suffolk economy of salt refining, especially along the coast and tidal rivers. Wherstead Church has a gravestone dated August 27th 1618 dedicated to Robert Gooding, 'salt-finer'.

Wherstead Church

Devereux Edgar's notebooks contain a complaint made upon Susan Cabourn of Washbrook for *profane swearing oathes*

231

contrary to the late statute and distress to the poor. John Blackham of Culpho, *a very idle ladd* was giving cause for concern as he was (aged 12) *becoming very dangerous and incorrigible* having attempted to fire a house.

It is interesting to note that it was not always the employer who won in disputes between workers and their bosses. *John Lylly of Ffoxhall* in 1702 complained that *Thomas Rolling, his husbandman hired for one yere had absented himself from complainant's habitation.* It turned out that the master was *a Dissenter of the Independent Congregation* and demanded that his workers either go with him or be sent *hedging & ditching or picking turnips.* Thomas Rolling objected, as he was not a dissenter and wished instead to attend the parish church. Magistrate Devereux Edgar was clearly most sympathetic and must have made his position perfectly clear, as the final sentence reads... *Had he not humbled himself and desired to discharge his servant and promise reformation, I would have bound him to appear or committed him to Goal.*[gaol]

All of this often began with an *'official complaint.'* A number of these are kept at Ipswich Record Office.[5] Such as the nosey neighbour who reported farmer John Cottingham of Laxfield in 1792 for having wagon wheels less than 9 inches breadth on the turnpike [the A12] at Melton. Narrow wheels on heavy vehicles had a tendency to dig deep ruts in the road. One of my favourites of these complaints has to be one from 1796 where George Clublee said that George Cullum of Orford ...*did keep and use a certain dog called a greyhound, being not qualified to do so.* 'Long-dogs' were trained as poachers' dogs and local laws were passed to make sure they didn't get into the wrong hands.

These complaints include a lot of suggested abuses of apprentices by their masters. Blacksmiths in particular seem to have been a rough lot. Thomas Woolnough of Wickham Market and John Pannfer of Hollesley come in for particular mention, accused of violence, beating, assault and denial of food and clothes, in spite of having signed indentures making it clear this was unacceptable. In the Woodbridge/Wickham Market area of Suffolk, in the 1790s, the slightly better-off trades people were legally bound to accept a certain number of servants and apprentices from poor local families. There are plenty of cases, especially of farmers, refusing to take on poor children in Campsey Ash, Ufford, Sutton and Bredfield.

An awful lot of stories regarding servants have unhappy endings. They had so little security. The sketch on the left is one I discovered[6] with a story attached. The picture is of Timothy Hammond of Clare, and was drawn in 1842.

Apparently, he was taken on by a Mrs. Spalding as a child. He worked for and resided with her for many years, expecting on her death to be provided for. But this wasn't to be, and for the rest of his life he had to scrape a living by selling fruit and vegetables about town. He was known locally as 'Old Tim.'

Suffolk's prison records are far from complete, but where they survive, they give us a fascinating insight into the criminal world of the nineteenth century.

The earliest Gaol books from Beccles[7] date from the very beginning of the nineteenth century. They are beautifully presented, though they give less detail than later registers. They were filled in weekly. Amongst other things, the books list the work that prisoners were put to.

Richard Nicholls' six months hard labour for larceny was apparently spent *'at his trade'*, which was making shoes. Robert Tilney (33) was convicted of being a rogue and a vagabond. Against his employment is offered the word 'blind.' Others are described as 'not well' or 'lame'. Those who could work were generally set spinning wool or tow [flax], mending clothes or knitting mittens. And I thought hard labour meant stone-breaking!

Age, crime and even the prisoners' behaviour was listed. Most were described as 'orderly.' George Marshall, aged 10 was described as *disorderly*. No employment was entered up against his name.

The early books of the Woodbridge House of Correction[8] describe the behaviour of nearly all as 'decent'. One exception is John Pizzey who was on remand to answer a charge of stealing silverware from Hannah Hubbard. He escaped from prison on July 8th 1823, six weeks after his arrest.

In the Woodbridge books, quite detailed descriptions appear regarding the crime which led to the person's incarceration. Instead of merely 'chicken stealing', Roger Revett in 1823 was *'charged upon the oath of William Harper of Stratton Hall in this county, Gen[t.] on suspicion of*

having in the night of the Twenty sixth day of Feby. last or on the morning of the twenty seventh day of the same month feloniously stolen, taken & carried away Two Hen Fowls from the premises of the s^{d.} William Harper, his property.'

Another case lists William Prentice, who in 1824 was arrested for *'Poaching and useing a certain Engine called a Snare to kill game and destroy Game in the parish of Nacton in this county.'*

'Hard Labour' in Woodbridge gaol at that time meant pumping water, cleaning the yards, limewashing the prison and making straw hats.

The Ipswich Gaol books date from 1840, a time when a lot of people were leaving the land and drifting towards the towns. Also, with the coming of the railways, there were large numbers of itinerant workers who could not always find employment. It is common to find outsiders arrested and given a month for vagrancy. Most were illiterate or could only read imperfectly. All this is clear from the records. There were, of course, no pictures of those imprisoned, but detailed descriptions allow you to get an idea of what they looked like.

A large number were imprisoned for trivial offences such as petty thefts, drunken assaults or what are merely described as midemeanours. This frequently meant such as breaking windows in the workhouse. By repute, the prison food was better, and some regularly used this means to improve their diet. However, it could work against you if later caught for a small theft. Regular offenders could end up being transported to Australia.

Earlier records are particularly entertaining. Presentments at Bury Quarter Sessions in the seventeenth century included Will Bridgeman for *'suffering his hoggs to goe without a keeper,' 'Widow Gren at ye Horse Shoe for keeping a disorderly hous,'* several cases of people who had failed to attend their parish church three Sundays running and all manner of tradesmen conducting business without having served their seven years apprenticeship. These included an ironmonger, fishmonger, grocer, linen draper,

RECEIVING BOOK.

Prisoner's name. *William Goshawk*

Last Residence. *Helsell*

Trade or Occupation, and where learned. *Labourer*

Age.	Height.	Complexion.	Colour of Hair.	Colour of Eyes.	Visage.	Marks, &c.
		Fair	*Light*	*Grey*	*round*	

Apparent state of Health. *Good*

Is he Lame or Ruptured? *Neither*

Has he any infectious Disease? *none*

Hats.	Smock frocks.	Coats.	Guernsey Frocks.	Jackets.	Waistcoats.	Flannel Waistcoats.	Breeches.	Trowsers.	Pantaloons.	Drawers.	Gaiters.	Stockings.	Shirts.	Handkerchiefs.	Caps.	Boots.	Shoes.	Knives.	Purses.	Watches	Pocket Books.	Tobacco Box.
/				/			/			/	/	/		/								

	DATE.	MONEY.				
Observations on the state of Prisoner's Apparel as to Cleanliness and Decency. *Clean*		Received.			Paid.	
		£	s.	d.	£	s.
				/		

Place of Nativity. *Helsell*

Father's { Name *Joseph Goshawk* { Trade *Labourer* { Residence *Helsell*

Is Prisoner single, married, or a widower? If married, Wife's residence, and means of subsistence. *Married*

Number of Children. Age of { Eldest { Youngest

Hard Lab.

Convicted of an offence aga...

One of thousands of entries from Bury gaol books. It seemed appropriate that someone called Goshawk should have been caught hunting game. His sentence was 6 weeks. It was his 7th offence.

bricklayer and confectioner. Mark Wilkinson and William Brydon were indicted for simply *'walking about on a Sunday in time of divine service.'* You've got to ask yourself, who was around to notice?

And then there was the problem of filth - In 1674, John Pond was accused of *'not amending his Gutter annoyed by a frequent Dungell which he layes in the Kinges Highway.'* Likewise, in 1686, John Curtis was brought to court for *'Annoyeinge the street with his house of Office muck.'*

Amongst the more intriguing cases is that of Joseph Fordham of Rickinghall, found guilty of *'disturbing the congregation during divine service'* at Diss and given 21 days to consider his ways. According to the register, he had seen the inside of Ipswich gaol 23 times before.

William Moyes of Needham Market was given the remarkably merciful sentence of 3 months for feloniously killing and slaying his wife Sarah. At a time when murder almost always led to a public hanging, the same Assize court sentenced William Andrews to just one year in prison for *'feloniously killing and slaying Thomas Wilkinson.'* Just what was going on here?

In the case of William Moyes, at 79 he was struggling to cope with a wife suffering from dementia. It seems he just snapped and hit her harder than he intended. The court saw fit to be merciful. In the other case of unlawful killing, Thomas Wilkinson had turned on a boy who had been bullying his son and struck him. The boy died a day or two later. Again there seemed no point in exercising the full power of the law.

The surviving Bury Gaol Receiving books[9] date from the 1840s, but are numbered and indicate there were once many more. Book 20 covers 1847 - 1848. It describes the visual appearance, state of health and apparent cleanliness and decency of prisoners. It was unusual to find anyone not described as *'clean'* and in a good state of health. Many cases involve men who were refusing to support their families and therefore leaving them chargeable to the parish. There was much *'misbehaviour in the workhouse.'* There was even Thomas Wales (17), convicted of *'having lewdly exposed his person on the streets at Ixworth to insult certain females.'* For this, he was to serve two calendar months in Bury Gaol.

But one crime in the Bury area far outweighed all others. In just the first half of December 1847, Robert Grimwood, Richard Rowe & George Gladding of Rattlesden, James & Duncan Dyson of Dalham, William Radley of Wissington, William Sale of Barrow, Robert Humphrys, Henry Smith & John Barrell of Hartest, Thomas Willingham of Bures, Abraham Saggs of Lt. Cornard, Robert Kemp of Troston, Samuel Brewster of Boxford, James Booty & John Warren of Walsham-le-Willows and George Ralph & John Balls were all gaoled for 1-3 months for *'an offence against the game laws.'* Yes, West Suffolk thrived on poaching!

'Catching a poacher' [10]

Prosecutions were not always straightforward. Poachers at Cowlinge often got away with 'night adventuring' as the local authorities could not determine whether their crime had been conducted in Suffolk or Cambridgeshire. This was the basis for an unsuccessful plea in January 1887, when Walter Pledger,Thomas Wollard, George Ginn, James Wright and Joseph Isaacson were proved to have bagged game on the Suffolk side of the border and each spent two months with hard labour bemoaning the fact.

In 1844, the crime of the moment was arson. Lucifer matches were a fairly new invention and had taken their time to make their way to Suffolk. Once they were for sale in every village shop, they made it a whole lot easier to set light to something. Even small children could light fires when all they had to do was strike a match. Skimming the pages of the Suffolk Herald for the first half of 1844, I found nearly fifty Suffolk villages hit by cases of 'incendiarism.' It was a copy-cat crime that often involved the young. The victims tended to be farmers, seeing their fields, haystacks and houses go up in flames. There had always been fires, but these were usually accidental. In 1844, it was the topic of the moment. Questions were asked in the House of Commons. There were attacks in Essex, Cambridgeshire and Norfolk, but Suffolk suffered far more. Around the country, there was a certain amount of public sympathy for the incendiarists as this Punch cartoon *'The Home of a Rick-Burner'* shows. But in Suffolk opinion was very much more divided between the haves and the have-nots. The Rector of Woolpit, Rev. L. Page, published four sermons on the subject of incendiarism.

Culprits were not often caught; even then, it could be hard to prove guilt. So, those who were found guilty tended to discover the book being thrown at them.

At the Suffolk Spring Assize that year, seven would be tried for arson. Four were found guilty and transported to Australia for life. The Summer Assize that year, ever-after referred to as the *'Fiery Assize'* saw at least fifteen cases of arson leading to a dozen convictions. Some were as young as 11 years of age. Sentences of transportation were given to nearly all.

After that it all calmed down a bit. There were still a few cases of suspicious fires that autumn, but far fewer than before, though the Suffolk Herald did report a couple of cases of fields set on fire by passing steam engines. At least 22 Suffolk men (and boys) would find themselves banished to Australia in the late 1840s for setting light to things.

For a few, merely threatening to fire a farmer's property would be enough to bring down the wrath of the law upon them. James Friend of Tunstall ended up in Van Diemen's Land (Tasmania) for just that.

The Earl of Ashburnham owned a good bit of land in mid-Suffolk at the time of the Fiery Assize, though he lived in Sussex and rarely visited Suffolk. His stewards wrote copious letters to him, keeping him informed of how his estates were performing and matters concerning them. Many of John Kirby Moore's letters, written from Badley Hall near Stowmarket, survive. In 1844, he wrote of two attacks on Columbyne Hall at Stowupland, which would untimately result in the conviction and transportation for life of Samuel Jacob. Columbyne Hall, though owned by Lord Ashburnham, was let to an unpopular local tenant farmer, Mr. Boby. It seems likely that this fire-raising was not the work of just one man. Most of Boby's labourers had axes to grind. A keen issue at the time was (see page 214) allotments. Farmers were being persuaded to make available small parcels of land at peppercorn rents to help the *'deserving poor'* to help themselves. Not all farmers were that keen, and demand for allotments far outstripped their supply. Especially, it seems, in Stowupland. In Newmarket, workers were more suspicious of the scheme, which seemed to many to increase the workload of the working man. Their allotments, located in the shadow of the workhouse were known locally as 'Van Dieman's Land.' But allotment land was at a premium in Stowupland and most of the local people put the blame squarely on Mr. Boby.

One aspect of the Columbyne Hall case above that makes itself clear is just how much it cost to bring felons to trial. In 1844, criminals were prosecuted not by the crown, but by private citizens. Though they could claim back some of the expenses incurred - swearing of warrants, witnesses expenses etc. - they could still be seiously out of pocket once the dust settled, even if they obtained a conviction. John Kirby Moore explains in one letter how the whole process would amount to well in advance of £80, only £50 of which could be claimed back from the County.

Columbyne (more recently, Columbine) Hall

One letter among the Ashburnham papers at Ipswich Record Office[11] is unsigned. It begins *'It is with extreme regret that I write to inform your Lordship that another wilful fire has taken place on your estate at Columbyne Hall.'*
What begins informatively slowly becomes a little darker, not exactly threatening, but making the reader aware that should change be further delayed, more fires are only to be expected. Though the letter is imperfectly drafted, it is cleverly enough worded to avoid the charge of it actually being threatening...
'To prevent more fires, then let more small parcels of land to the poor.' The last comment being, *'Boby has a bad name.'*

People in positions of wealth and power were vulnerable to all manner of threats. Among the Churchman family papers[12] is a thoroughly chilling letter. Unsigned, but dated February 1st 1898, once again it begins reasonably, addressing the two brothers William and Arthur, who at that time managed the tobacco company founded a century earlier by their great grandfather...

Gentlemen

I must begin with an explanation. I am a Private Detective, investigating a case at Ipswich and when watching in some evergreens, behind some palasading [sic] *I overheard a conversation which places you both in great danger   two men met   after looking round, they placed there* [sic] *backs against the irons* [iron railings?]   *one said he had orders from Old Sol to see the boys they were to meet at the old place and take orders about kidnapping one of your children and they would have a thousand pounds down in gold for its reliece* [release] *and five hundred a year as long as you live. It will be sent to an old hag who will soon brake* [sic] *it in starvation... Old Sol have a grudge against you and he mean to ruin you, there is a paid spy in your works helping them who will put a poisonous powder into all the goods you manufacture which will make people ill who smoke your goods and they will news it fast and hear* [spread the news so everyone hears] *about it and it will be your ruin.*

After they were quite [quiet?] *I thought I should save you both your little children and business and the dread that must hang over you which is worse than all. The reward I ask (I shall not do it without) is you must help a widow with a family who once helped me and saved me going to the bad you must agree to give her two hundred pounds down and two hundred pounds a year as long as either you live that is all I ask for what I do for you the other way I am on my oath you loose* [sic] *all. Now if you agree to my terms Advertise in East Anglian Times Personal 'H. I agree to your terms, signed C' on Thursday, Friday and Saturday of this week... and I will write and tell the widow to meet you on Ipswich platform on Monday next (as soon as the noon train is gone which I believe is about half past one and* [she will] *bring letter I write to her you are not safe after Saturday night and it will be better for you not to go out alone after dark and to keep your children close and be as secret as the grave about it all for your own sake I persuade you not to think lightly of this letter... I am on my oath it is genuine and you are in great danger. I shall let Old Sol know his plot is found out on Monday if you meet the widow and agree to the terms.*

By all accounts, William Churchman was not a man to be easily frightened, but on Saturday February 5th 1898, this advert appeared in the personal column of the East Anglian.

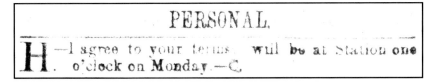

And like so many historical tales, that is as much as we know. Did the Churchman brothers pay protection money, or did they have their own special way of dealing with charcters like this. As the letter was still in the family's possession and not with Police records, we have to assume they did *'keep as secret as the grave'* about it all.

Records of some Suffolk Assize Courts can be seen at the Public Record Office at Kew, but these are far from complete. The local papers are a far more reliable reference. However, the Quarter Sessions, held four times a year in four different parts of the county are easier to unearth in Suffolk Record Offices.

Around the county, most minor crime was dealt with by Petty Sessions courts, the fore-runners of modern Magistrate's Courts. Most of these leave little surviving paperwork from much before 1900. However, those that are available make fascinating reading.

The 1893 Lowestoft Petty Sessions[13] include countless drink-related charges. Children aged from 11 upwards appeared for such offences as *'stealing pencils'* for which they were to spend *'one day in pit'* and *'receive around 6 strokes of the birch rod.'* More serious juvenile offenders were moved to a place of correction for long periods. Bertie Lee (13) and Ernest Allen (14) were sent to the Kerrison Reformatory (Thorndon) for 5 years for theft. Beatrice Mary Painter, for stealing two coats, was ordered to be detained in Ipswich Girls' Reformatory for four years.

Where the Magistrates' Court was unable to handle the gravity of a particular crime, those accused would be sent to the Quarter Sessions or, in the most serious cases, to the Assizes. William Nobbs was twice charged with stealing nets in 1893. Almost all local theft was handled by this court, but in Lowestoft, this kind of theft was deemed more serious and he was sent to the Sessions for trial. H.G. Frosdick was remanded to Norwich Gaol for *'attempting to shoot'* and committed to the Assizes, as was Laura Wilby in 1894 for the concealment of her baby. This was one of the more difficult crimes met by judges. Bastard children often died soon after birth. It was not unknown for mothers to be charged and found guilty of their murder. It was often easier for the mother to bury the infant rather than report its birth and death. This meant that should the authorities later discover such a case, it might mean more than just concealment - it might mean the child was murdered.

Among the more intriguing cases cropping up in the Lowestoft Sessions in the 1790s are G. Heard, charged with selling adulterated butter, Thomas Leggett for polluting a well, James and Hannah Worlledge for keeping a brothel and John Lay who was fined 1/6d + costs for *'furious riding of a bicycle.'*

The records of Mutford and Lothingland Petty Sessions,[14] also held at Lowestoft, date back to 1880. Drink again had a lot to answer for, as cases commonly included *'drunk & disorderly,'* *'drunk & riotous,'* *'refusing to leave licensed premises when asked,'* *'opening licensed premises during prohibited hours'* and one John Grimmer *'drunk in charge of a horse and cart'* (for which he was fined 2/6d + costs, or prison for 7 days).

Common crimes coming to trial were *'failing to support one's family,'* *'neglecting to send children to school'* (compulsory education had been introduced ten years previously), cruelty to one's horse and an assortment of petty thefts. Also there were cases of *'Lying to a pawnbroker'* (whether about where an item came from or what it was made of, I don't know), apprentices jumping ship and James White, who in 1882 was found to have *'an unjust weight in his shop.'*

The Thingoe and Thedwastre Petty Sessions Books,[15] amongst the minor thefts and assaults include the cases of Robert Cuthbert of Wickhambrook (1876) *'having a bad privy,'* John Otley of Bradfield St. George (821) *'exercising his calling on the Lord's Day'* and four boys found guilty of stealing a duck at Rougham. In this last case, they were ordered to be whipped, but only with their parents' consent. I was unable to discover whether or not that consent was given.

Surviving Ixworth (Blackbourne) charge books[16] go back to 1869. I probably shouldn't be surprised, but the same names do crop up an awful lot of times, and for a variety of offences.

Over a three year period, Fred Plummer of Ixworth (aged 22-25) found himself accused of malicious damage to a door, being drunk and incapable, conducting himself in a disorderly manner by refusing to leave the Greyhound Inn, committing a breach of the peace by fighting in the street and taking game at Stowlangtoft. Similarly, William Clarke of Hopton (aged 38) used a gin trap to kill game, for which he was fined £5 (or two months in gaol). This was a stiff fine for those times. He was probably already a regular in the magistrates' court. After that he escaped conviction for highway robbery at Wattisfield but was fined or imprisoned for trespass in search of game at Tostock, fighting, assault and using *language leading to a breach of the peace at Walsham.'* And I am sure if I had looked in later registers, he'd have been there too. Even worse was William Baker of Hepworth whose crimes included stealing wood, using threatening language, failing to support his family, poaching game at Market Weston, being drunk and riotous on two separate occasions and conducting himself in an indecent manner at Pakenham Parish Church (whatever that meant).

Pakenham Church c1820

You never know what you are going to find when you wade through the catalogues at the Record Office. At Bury, they have a register of wanted criminals from the first decade of the twentieth century.[17] These include a number of Suffolk criminals at large, as well as an assortment from around the country and in most cases include photographs. Their descriptions are quite detailed, with identifying features of all kinds. I like the one pictured overleaf from 1901: John George Carlton who was considered most likely to give himself away by singing in pubs. It seems he always sang the same song, which is probably the popular music-hall song of the time, *'After the Curtain Falls'*.

How oft we watch the players and they seem so light and gay,
We wonder if they really feel the happy parts they play;
The dancer, as she lightly trips in the footlight's glare,
She is to us the brightest one of all assembled there.

Refrain: *But could we only linger, could we only see,*
The actor and the dancer, how different they would be;

Chorus: *After the curtain falls, when the lights are low.*
After the play Is over and merrily home we go-
Many a cry of sadness is heard within those walls,
The scene is shifted, the veil is lifted, after the curtain falls.

Of the names and faces in the Wanted Register, a number were ex-soldiers; several were deserters. Many had aliases; some any number of them. Others just had names bracketed with the word 'false'. Alice Brockland, wanted for fraud was also known under the surnames Clarke, Marlow, Geary, Austin, Long etc. Of all the crimes listed to these once-wanted felons, I felt rather sorry for William Hewitson who'd had a leg amputated and was accused of obtaining money by false pretences, claiming he was collecting for the purpose of buying an artificial limb.

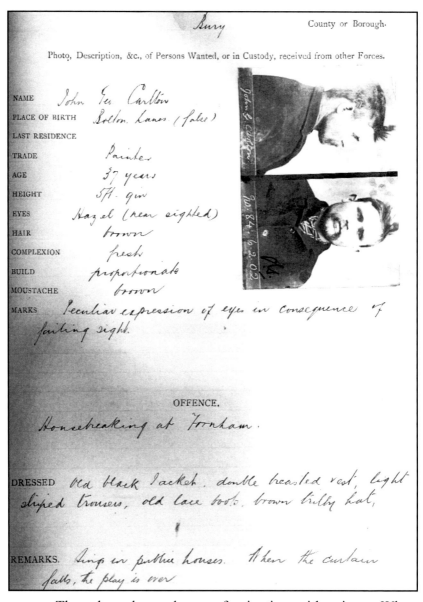

Bury   County or Borough.

Photo, Description, &c., of Persons Wanted, or in Custody, received from other Forces.

NAME   John Geo Carlton

PLACE OF BIRTH Bolton. Lancs (false)

LAST RESIDENCE

TRADE   Painter

AGE   37 years

HEIGHT   5ft. 9in

EYES   Hazel (near sighted)

HAIR   brown

COMPLEXION   fresh

BUILD   proportionate

MOUSTACHE   brown

MARKS   Peculiar expression of eyes in consequence of failing sight.

OFFENCE.

Housebreaking at Fornham.

DRESSED Old black Jacket. double breasted vest, light striped trousers, old lace boots. brown trilby hat,

REMARKS. Sings in public houses. When the curtain falls, the play is over

There has always been a fascination with crime. When particularly high profile crimes came to court, there was naturally a great deal of public interest. Nowadays, newspapers seek to outdo one another in order to sell copies and to a certain extent that

248

was true in the past. But, go back a couple of centuries and you'll find separate pamphlets and broadsheets were sold giving a kind of detail that four-page weekly newspapers couldn't match. These tended to report the trial and execution of the accused, sometimes including their life-story and untimate confession. These were sold in large numbers and sometimes survive in county and national archives.

'The Authentick Account of the Life of Mr. Charles Drew', (priced 6d) who murdered his father in 1740 can be found at Bury Record Office.[18] This was a remarkable case involving a wealthy and respected family in Long Melford. Almost certainly Charles Drew and his accomplice Edward Humphries shot and killed Charles John Drew, an obnoxious and cantankerous old attorney.

Early on, Humphries was arrested and evidence was collected against him. Meanwhile, Charles Drew, showing little sorrow for his father's death, set about trying to persuade witnesses to swear Humphries had been with them at the time of the murder. His eagerness to see Humphries freed led

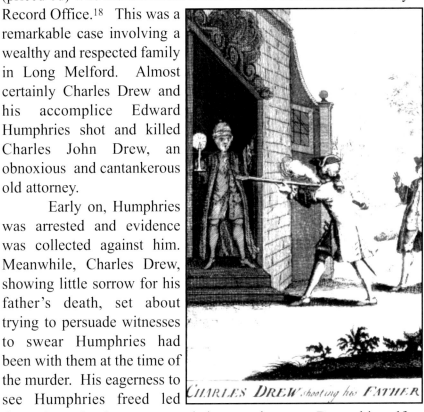

CHARLES DREW shooting his FATHER

those investigating to turn their attentions to Drew himself. Eventually, having fled to London posing under the assumed name of 'Roberts,' he was arrested. He was to bring more suspicion on himself by attempting to bribe his gaoler to help him to escape. Eventually, Drew was brought for trial at Bury Assizes. Those prosecuting realised there was not enough firm evidence to secure the conviction of either man. They then agreed to free Humphries on the understanding that he serve as a witness for the prosecution. What had been merely circumstantial evidence became an open-and-shut case and Charles Drew was found guilty. He was hanged on April 9th but spared the ignomony of being gibetted. Humphries walked free.

Before the days of local newspapers, we have to rely on those who conveniently left titbits of information; some being kind enough to complete the story for us. In the Freckenham parish register, appears this entry for 1614...

Geoffrey Hopkinson, a Miller (who had but one eye) & hillerie Aymore, a lad his servant were found slained in Chippenham field near Freckenham y[e] 18 day of May in y[e] morning & were buried at Chippenham next day.

Shortly after appears... *Richard Button was executed for y[e] said murther nere the place where it was comited y[e] fourth day of August 1614.*

In Suffolk Record Offices, a number of reports survive detailing Coroner's Inquests (or 'inquisitions' as they were often called). Many appeared briefly in local papers. Though the majority of 'sudden deaths' were not the result of criminal activity, they usually involved a court with a jury; hence I have included them in this chapter. It never ceases to amaze me the remarkable ways in which people have been known to leave this world. They include James Reeve of Bromeswell who died in 1826, smothered under a load of rabbits and Amy Leach of Otley who drowned in 1894 in the baptismal pool of her Baptist Chapel. Mind you, I have a certain respect for William Smith of Walton who, in 1892 at the age of 78, managed to climb high enough to die falling from a cherry tree. So many verdicts are quaint to say the least - William Bann, miller of Wickham Market who died in church in 1827 was recorded as having had *'a visitation from God.'* Mary

Ann Craske of Hollesley in 1892 was apparently *in failing health* and Charlotte Choset of Burgh in 1891 died from *shortness of breath*. I think there is a case for saying everyone does. But my favourite inquest involves John Clowe of Nacton whose verdict reads *'exhaustion train journey.'* I think we've all had journeys like that at one time or another.

Sport, in its earliest forms, could offer a way of indulging in what would otherwise be seen as criminal behaviour, without too much fear of retribution. Camping or Camp Ball was violent and primitive form of 'no-holds-barred' football (The word *Camp* seems to derive from the same source as the name *Kemp,* meaning *'warrior'*). Camping was popular across East Anglia until modern-day softies cleaned it up. Mind you, if some reports are to be believed, it could get a bit rough.

From Harpers Weekly in 1865, this is a picture of a game of football at a miltary camp. So that is why it was called 'Camp-Ball!'

The diary of Adam Winthrop of Groton recounts how in February 1604, *'one Sewell was bruysd through a fall w'ch he had in Camping that he died thereof.'* Even a volume as prestigious as the Victoria County History for Suffolk (Vol. II) couldn't resist including an account of a game of Camp Ball played between teams from Norfolk and Suffolk on Diss Common in the mid-eighteenth century. Apparently each team numbered three hundred and, after 14 hours, the ground had been turned into a battlefield. Nine deaths are reputed to have ensued within a fortnight of the contest, though whether they died from the wounds they received that day or from a bit of 'afters' is not made clear.

The families from hell

Of these, there were many. When Samuel Bush of Stradbroke was transported for 14 years to Van Diemen's Land in 1844 for the pathetic crime of stealing one oak plank, one might have felt a twinge of sympathy. However, Samuel and his family were no strangers to Suffolk courts. In 1838 both he and his brother Christopher had received a sentence of transportation for larceny. This time their sentence was commuted. The family continued to make court appearances. Their six sons all faced hard labour at least once. I guess in 1844 the judge finally lost his patience with the the lot of them and Samuel was away on the punishment ship to Australia.

A lot of prison hulks never sailed anywhere but merely served as prison accommodation

John Cage of Stonham Aspal was just 18 when he was sent to Western Australia in 1854. His younger brother was already serving time in gaol. Though found guilty of a violent sexual assault, you might have felt John Cage should be given the benefit of mercy, as he had been an orphan since the deaths of both of his parents three years before. But that turned out to have been because his mother Mary Emily Cage had been hanged for poisoning her violent husband with arsenic.

The Aylward family of the Kersey area were remarkably criminally prolific. Maltsters at Kersey, they seem to have been prone to helping themselves to malt, corn, seed and even the occasional animal from nearby farms. Eight of them would face transportation to various parts of Australia between 1820 and 1848. Some people never learn!

Kersey by A.R. Quinton

Between the ends of the eighteenth and nineteenth centuries, punishments diminished. Take for example William Last, alias Denny, of Walton near Felixstowe. In 1786, he was found guilty of sheep-stealing, for which he was carted up to Rushmere Heath and hanged in front of a crowd of thousands.

Almost exactly fifty years later, Thomas Pawsey would face banishment to New South Wales for the same offence.

In 1870, just after the end of transportation, William Grimwood of East Bergholt, aged 19, would serve just two years hard labour for that same crime. However, possibly it was more about whom you stole from than just the crime itself. Drover Thomas Algar had the cheek to steal a total of 71 sheep from the Maharajah Dhuleep Singh at Elveden in January 1875, for which he found himself 'banged up' for ten years.

Which brings me to the family I'd least have liked living next door. It is still widely believed that in 1929, George 'Joe' Whistlecraft of Rickinghall Inferior got away with murder. He and Ernest Whistlecraft were poaching in Stubbly Wood near Botesdale when they encountered the keeper, Charles Cornwell. As a result, Cornwell was shot and died soon after of his wounds. Though there seemed to be a good case against these two well-known petty criminals, the case collapsed on two counts. Firstly, the dying victim's words of identification were not admissable as evidence. Secondly, the only gun found at the Whistlecrafts' house was not the one that had been used that night (Though there are those who will still tell you Joe Whistlecraft had hidden the other gun down the well).

All this appears to have been a culmination of that family's continuous criminal behaviour around the area, over a period of at least sixty years. Way back in 1862, George Whistlecraft of Rickinghall would be given six months hard labour for stealing a quantity of wheat from a barn in Gislingham. When he was tried in 1895 for being violently drunk and extremely disorderly, it was described as his sixteenth conviction. The magistrate wanted to know why the case had taken three months to be brought before him, and was told George had been in gaol for most of that time for a previous offence. William Whistlecraft, when fined for assault in 1883, already had 8 previous convictions. These were not the only family members to make regular appearances in Suffolk courts for assault, using obscene language, poaching and petty theft. They seem to have been careful to avoid (until 1929) anything that might be a bit more serious. However, I did uncover a couple of offences that were never proceeded with as certain key witnesses *'decided at the last moment not to testify'*.

It is interesting to note that in 1887 at the Rickinghall & Botesdale celebrations for Queen Victoria's Golden Jubilee, William Whistlecraft won a fork and a spade worth 6 shillings in the village sports. He was the fastest runner in the race for over 40s. A useful attribute for a habitual thief!

"A fine and healthy place to live"
'Beside the Stour near Sudbury' (possibly Wissington)

Chapter 8
Diaries, Journals and other scribblings

Suffolk is a fine and healthy place to live. This was recognised by a number of writers about the county. Robert Reyce in his Breviary of Suffolk wrote in 1618, *it is commonly esteemed that the aire is as sweet and healthfull generally as in any other country whatsoever... as well purged and refined with the northerne blasts where the aire being somewhat peircing is deemed very apt and fitt for recovery of health in decayed bodies.* Though he does warn of living too near the coast with its *marshes and fenns.. [that] doe vent in summer poysened aire, vapours and in winter cold exhalations and mists.*

Reyce also pointed out another problem caused by the *discommodities of the site of Suffolk, the nearnesse of this countrye for near and ready carriage, the fitnesse of our havens for quick conveyance of the same which hath emboldened such officers to exceed their commission.* In other words, we were a bit too close to the seat of power, and kings through the ages looking to provision their armies and navies had tended to bleed the county dry. Stowmarket between 1570 and 1590 had supplied the Royal purveyors with *ducks, wax, hens capons, cocks, pullets, chickens, sweet otes, rye, wheate, straw, butter, cheese* and *live calves.* It is unlikely they received much by way of payment. Later it became easier to demand money. The Hessett accounts include money paid to George Scott (constable & overseer) for supplying butter and cheese for the navy. When supplies of Nitre [Salt-petre] became necessary for the manufacture of gunpowder, the Suffolk clays were processed. It is not by chance that Stowmarket became in the nineteenth and early twentieth century an important centre for the manufacture of explosives. The potential had been spotted long before.

The ways in which our world has changed through the centuries cannot be over-emphasized. Early on in this book, I wrote about Dame Alice de Bryene of Acton, a lady who in all probability was married at the age of just fifteen to a much older man. It is unlikely she had a lot of choice in the matter, and once widowed she opted to remain that way. Perhaps marriage wasn't something she wanted to repeat. What is clear is that this was the status quo for ladies of her class. A number of late medieval queens and wives of nobility faced arranged marriages in early teenage. This went on for some time. The diarist, John Evelyn knew the Graftons at Euston and on August 1st 1672, wrote... *I was at the marriage of Lord Arlington's only daughter* [Isabella] *(a sweet child if ever there was any) to the Duke of Grafton.* She was

Henry Fitzroy, 1st Duke of Grafton

at that point barely five years old, and clearly the wedding ceremony was as far as it went... for the time being! John Evelyn, seven years later... *was at the remarriage of the Duchess of Grafton to the Duke, she being now twelve years old. I pray God*, Evelyn wrote, *...the sweet child find it to her advantage... to make the wife of the greatest prince in Europe.* Presumably at the age of twelve, she was now considered old enough to fulfil all the requirements of a gentleman's wife. But there is still more to this story than meets the eye. What we are not being told is that the Duke, one Henry Fitzroy, was at the time of the first marriage, just nine years old himself; and only sixteen at the remarriage. He was quite a catch, as the name 'Fitzroy' suggests. As the illegitimate son of Charles II and the Duchess of Cleveland, Henry Fitzroy had been given a collection of hereditary titles that would survive to the present day. Isabella, a bride at 12 years of age, would outlive her husband and, unlike Dame Alice of Acton, would remarry.

William Cobbett, in his Rural Rides, written in the 1820s also had much that was good to say about the county... *Coming from Ipswich to Bury St. Edmunds* [before the days of the A14] *you pass through Needham Market and Stowmarket, two very pretty market towns and, like all the other towns in Suffolk, free from the*

drawback of shabby and beggarly houses on the outskirts. I remarked that I did not see in the whole county one single instance of paper or rags supplying the place of glass in any window and did not see one miserable hovel in which a labourer resided. Cobbett claimed the place looked well-kept and prosperous and that at one point when he stopped, he counted 17 windmills within his view.

Cobbett's main complaint was what we had been doing to our trees. Pollarding was the typical Suffolk way of harvesting wood. As Cobbett describes... *trees that have ben beheaded at from six to twelve feet from the ground... nothing in nature can be more ugly.* As with coppicing, most deciduous trees survive a ten year cycle of lopping in this way, so supplying a regular harvest of firewood.

On page 126 I mentioned the seventeenth century document (or collection of documents) known as *'A Chorography of Suffolk.'* This includes some fascinating insights into the world of past centuries. Peyton Hall, at Ramsholt, we are told was an ancient seat of the Ufford family, *but as it lyes neer the Channell off the hooking grounds for whitings... and being of late account-ed no good air... it has usuall been tenanted so the house looks not great now whatever it has been.* In other words, they were saying, "It stinks so let some other poor blighter live there."

Until well into the twentieth century, landowners, tenant-farmers, tradesmen & fishermen, and a number of others paid tithes to their parish priest. Tithes, a tax paid to the church, or perhaps to the rector himself, were the cause of endless disputes. The Quakers refused to pay them at all and often had goods and property confiscated in lieu of payment. Other non-conformists raised strong objections. Until the nineteenth century, payment of tithes would usually be in kind. But different parishes operated the system in different ways. For example, a dairy farmer could not expect to pay his tithe in milk, and only so much fish at a time might be acceptable from a fisherman. According to the Chorography, Dallinghoo tithes could not be paid in cheese, but this was most acceptable in nearby Debach. Ilketshall St. Andrew had extensive orchards and hemplands. Their tithe was payable at the rate of 2d for an orchard; 4d for a hempland. This sounds a little vague, as we have no idea of the sizes set down to fruit or hemp. At Cookley, it was clearer. Hemp was tithed at 4d per peck sown. Tithe is by definition a tenth, so the arrangement at

Henstead whereby each seventh pig, calf or goose was taken seems particularly harsh.

It is all made abundantly clear in a terrier from Wortham, quoted at length in materials gathered for a 'History of Suffolk' by William Stevenson Fitch.[1] *'According to the ancient customs there time out of memory of man...'* every tenth cock of hay, every tenth sheaf of corn is detailed, along with payments in lieu of milch cows, pollarded trees and sheep's fleece (tythed by weight).

The Freckenham parish papers include some seventeenth century records of tithes paid[2] at a time when these were normally paid in kind. They include Simon Bishop, whose tithe of 1s 3½d was paid in hens, offal, calves & walnuts. Others paid in pecks of apples, lambs, wool, game hens, pigs and even a dovecote (presumably occupied).

You might think that parsons would be honest, decent and law-abiding, even where money (or its equivalent) was concerned, but in 1619, there was a fair old kerfuffle took place at Kentford. Sir Robert Vernon, Lay Rector of Gazeley had sent his servants with sticks and swords to take possession of over £5 worth of tithe corn that should have been the property of the Rector of Kentford, Mr. Thomas Barcocke. The courts were not impressed and after an unseemly exchange of views Sir Robert had to pay back what he owed.

Other snippets of historical information creep into the Chorography: items that, it seems, just had to be mentioned... Most Suffolk towns experienced a major fire at some time or other:

Sowoulde [Southwold]*was pitifully defaced by fire in 1596, upon a Fridaye. Beckles* [Beccles] *was pitifully defaced by fire... but it hath almost recovered hir former beautye agayne.*

Metfield: in this towne is that famous lane so much spoken of for myre & dirt it is in the common rode called Christmas Lane from Harleston market in Norff. to Halesworth Market in Suff.

One of the more ancient Suffolk stories that gets a mention here is the burial of the Danish King Guthrum at *Hadley* in Suffolk. It is hard to confirm this, but suffice it to say, it has been one of the more widely-accepted traditional tales. Guthrum had invaded and ruled over much of the land, but was finally defeated by Alfred the Great emerging from hiding to snatch victory from defeat. After this, Guthrum and Alfred seem to have got on quite well: the formerly pagan Dane becoming a born-again Christian, and the two leaders going on a joint tour of the realm. After that, with Alfred in Wessex, Guthrum ruled over the counties of the East Angles until his death in 890 A.D.

There has been a counter claim from Hadleigh in Essex that Guthrum's bones lie under their churchyard (but we don't believe that do we folks?)

An account in the book that seems to have a good reliable pedigree is that concerning *Mr. Cuddington* at *Ikesworth*.

The memorial to Richard Coddington at Ixworth Church

262

In the 1530s, Richard Coddington had resided at Ewell in Surrey right next to where Henry VIII intended to build his new Nonesuch Palace. Now, it might seem a little frivolous to suggest that Henry wanted a larger bowls green, but he certainly coveted the land next door. In 1536, under his instructions, the smaller monasteries began to be dissolved. Ixworth Priory was almost certainly too large to be included in these, but when the inspectors had come calling, anticipating a taxation demand, the Prior had undervalued their assets, only to discover too late that this had been a bad idea.

So, Ixworth Priory was up for sale. It was suggested that the Coddingtons might like to do a swap; to up-sticks and move to Suffolk, leaving their Surrey home to the King. You didn't tend to disagree with Henry VIII, so Ixworth became the Coddington family home and Henry got his palace, and his bowls green (there I go again). Ixworth Church still contains memorials and brasses to members of the Coddington family. Virtually nothing remains of Nonesuch Palace.

The crypt at Ixworth Priory - one of the finest surviving pieces of monastic architecture in Suffolk

One real old Suffolk character, Firman Alexander, died in 1972, aged 89. For those who have read my biographical novel, 'Lydia', Firman was one of a number of her great-grandchildren. He left, amongst his few possessions, a short handwritten account of his childhood in the village of Cotton around the end of the nineteenth century. The whole piece appears in my book, *'A Short History of the Village of Cotton'* This is part of it. Apart from a little tidying-up of spelling and punctuation, this is exactly as he wrote it.

The Story of an old Perisher

About 75 years ago when I went to school I had to walk about a mile and a half twice a day, night or morning, wet or fine and on bad roads as well. The people had to pay for their children to go to school them days, 2d or 3d a week according to age. But of course there was no buses about then, or a motor car, only a penny-farthing bike, and you may be sure that I had to get one as well as other lads. But then, low bikes come out so I had to change mine, as dad didn't like me to ride far on my penny-farthing, as of course the big wheel was about a foot taller than what I was, so when I got on I had to catch hold of something or fall off.

Well, when I started to go to school there was an old lady lived on the road the way we went to school; so three mornings a week, I used to go and get her a farthing worth of snuff and she would give me a penny each morning I went. One morning she wanted a pennyworth of tobacco so she could have a nice smoke as well as her snuff, for she had got a little short pipe about an inch long - it was her nose-warmer she used to say. And one day she wanted a pint of vinegar as well so off I went to the shop and the shop man told me all his vinegar was gone sour so I never got any for the old lady, but she told me, "All vinegar is sour boy!"

Well, on a very hot day when I was at school (of course, we had to carry our dinner as it was too far to go home) the biggest of the boys and girls said they should like to go and have a wade somewhere, so we went down to the river where a man used to get his drinking water from, and he come down there when we was all in the water splashing about and he picked up all our clothes and carried them all to school, so we all had to go naked and stand round a stove in the school room and the old teacher made us all stop in that afternoon, but still we didn't care. We all had the stick and promised not to do it again.

When I was eleven, I left school and had to start doing a few little jobs. And the first job I had was to go and keep some sows and pigs on the pea-stubble. Well of course they were all right for a little while, time they could find some peas, but when they could not find any they was all over everywhere. I would go one way and others were sure to go the opposite way because they knew where acorn trees grew round the field, and up at the top of the field there was a crab apple tree and as soon as they found that, I soon lost my sows and pigs.

So, the next morning the master come again and he said he would send another boy to help me, so perhaps we could take some turkeys as well, as they would pick some peas up for a time if they were hungry. Well, I expect I had left one or two at home and them few what we had got heard them other ones calling out at home, so we soon lost everything - sows, pigs as well. The next morning the master come again and we were gone as well for... we was afraid to see him in them days.

Well, of course, I got a little better man and had more jobs to do, for I was Jack-of-all-jobs and master of none. I had to keep sheep so long each day, although I used to be afraid, for there was one or two would knock me down. Well, of course I kept getting bigger so I had to go into the yards then. Well, I never minded that, for I got so much for killing rats - 2d each,

265

and moles - 3d each, and sparrows - 4d a dozen; and I must have catched thousands for we used to go round the hay and straw three nights a week with a big sieve and go into an old thatched shed with a lantern. They would fly round the lantern, so some nights we caught twenty or thirty. Then we would walk round the meadow and if lucky we would get a blackbird or a water-hen [moorhen]. Then mother would flour them all for Sunday dinner and although the birds was small, the gravy was all right.

Well, years ago when herrings was a bit cheaper, father used to buy them. He would buy a hamperful at a time and string them up by the heads so we could pick them when we liked. But I can tell you that when the thrashing machine come, the herrings soon went, for they used to have herrings and swede for dinner every day, for we used to steam them in the machine nearly all day and the longer they cooked, the better they was, after they was covered with soot.

Harvesters at nearby Gislingham

Well, one day, I and my old partner went to Ipswich for the day and we had a nice spree for he went into a shoe shop and asked the manager if he could set him up with two old shoes, and the man said, "Certainly, yes, for there is a large heap there, but I can't promise you there *is many your size. But what size do you require?" And my partner said, "Anything from 7 to 11, black or brown, as I am not fussy." So of course, after he got what he wanted, I had to have a go, and the first thing I asked for was an old wellington or two, so the man said, "Help yourself, as there are all sizes, black and brown."*

Well, the man in the shop where we were lucky enough to get what we asked for told us that very often a man could come and buy a pair of boots or wellingtons and only take one, as perhaps he would not have only one foot and a wooden leg. And still for all that, this is how they come to get odd boots and shoes. I don't know what ever made we do a thing like that but I expect that we had got one pint over the mark. I have not seen that man since, and I don't think I shall now, for it is over fifty years ago.

I went to the church one day with one Sunday boot and a welling-ton on the other foot. I didn't know about it till someone told me about it. Of course, I had to spit on the wellington and try to make it look like a Sunday boot.

Bessie Cooke later to become Bessie Bloomfield lived a long and interesting life. In later years, she wrote about her time in service at Coney Weston Hall and Thelnetham Rectory. Her handwritten account can be found in Bury Record Office.[3] Bessie was born at the Mill Inn, Market Weston in June 1874 and died in 1972. This has been very slightly edited.

[I] *went to Coney Weston Hall in 1890 as between-maid where there was 9 children in* [the] *family and six maids and a governess. Rev. J.S.S.* [John Sikes Sawbridge M.A.] *used to give a lot of parties, when they used to have Mr. Hogg's band. First of all, he would invite all the High-class from the villages when he had ices and cakes from Norwich. Also* [he] *always had home-made syllabub which he generally helped to make himself. Then J.S.S. would invite middle-class of farmers' wives etc, then another party would be when all the village from Barningham* [came and it] *carried on to the evening when a cask of beer was in the kitchen for anyone to have a drink. After keeping so much company,* [they] *had to get another maid. Instead of my helping in the house till*

11 a.m., I was made kitchen-maid. When the Hall was under alterations, the family all went to Lowestoft except Harriet and me and the Hall boy. Mr. Martin, who was Butler to Miss Bridgeman used to come and sleep there. I used to go and help at Thelnetham Rectory... When the flu was bad in Coney Weston, J.S.S. sent bottles of wine and dinners... Every Saturday afternoon the whole family rode out on horseback, some of the younger children on Shetland ponies and some in the wagonette. Miss Birdie would never allow her horse to be exercised before she rode it, but Miss May's horse was always exercised by the groom. Miss Birdie loved all animals and had a pet goat which she always looked after. Also she had a pet lamb she brought up till it butted her.

Thelnetham Rectory

When J.S.S. returned to Thelnetham Rectory, I went as Cook. We was 19 with company. Miss Birdie used to like to get in the kitchen. Well she says one day, "If you marry and have 19 children, you will know how to cook for them."
I said, "I am afraid I should not be able to provide for them."

...My sister who was parlour-maid got up ready a bottle of Apollinaris [sparkling mineral water] *in the ordinary way - it was kept in the cellar till wanted. When my sister opened the bottle, it poured out over J.S.S.'s face and made his collar wet. He said, "Selina, what are you doing?" She could hardly get upstairs for a towel* [fast enough]. *When she came* [back] *into the kitchen, she could not go in and finish lunch. Kitty had to go in. Another day, the maids had turned all his books out of the room for Spring cleaning. J.S.S. asked what they* [were] *doing as everywhere was in a muddle. Poor man, he said, "[I] shan't be able to put my foot down anywhere."*

He was very good for the village. Winter time, we had to make a big [vat?] *of soup for the village... When the family came home from Lowestoft, J.S.S. had brought tubs of fish to send to the villagers of Thelnetham & Coney Weston. With all our luggage and the family's and tubs of fish, it made the train 20 minutes late. Anyhow, we all arrived safe from Harling Station.*

...J.S.S. always gave the staff a bottle of wine and a bottle of cider to celebrate the birthdays of each member of the family. He gave parties at haymaking time. There was a large swinging boat in the grounds of Thelnetham Rectory. Swings, games, races were very popular... schoolchildren rode in wagons to the summer parties at Thelnetham. J.S.S. gave a threepenny piece to any boy who opened gates for him when he was riding round the Coney Weston farm. At that time, one penny was the gratuity for walking to the doctor's at Hopton - 6 miles there and back, so 3d pieces were eagerly sought.

'The Diary of a Poor Suffolk Woodman'[4] transcribes the writings of William Scarfe of Thorpe Morieux that were written in a prayer book between 1827 and 1842. They give something of an insight into the dialect of the time in that part of Suffolk. William Scarfe spelt exactly as he spoke...

1827 April 19th *young Norman fell of Cockfield Stepel*
he Died from the fall he was stopping of holes in the Stepel
the Rope Brock The Fournoon he cut his Name and age in the
stepel the afternoon fell Down and Died

1831 Sept 11th *Isaac Scarfe was Desey by Running Rond*
Sceared is Mother she Thought he had ben an died
we was All Scared to se Him

1832 June 10th *It Thunard on Wisensunday June 10*
It Rained a good Deal It was a Durty Day for to go A Horledy
Making being horledy time

He also had a way of telling you more about his neighbours than
they might have liked...

1831 October *John Bird at the Folley Farm Thorpe Mary*
North Liddy Wittel theay borth ware Hose Keepers for him
are Boath in the familey way by ther Master John Bird

1831 January *old Mr Raynes and Mrs Melton fell out*
concerning the House Keeper lie with her master
thay whent to Law Mr Raynes Left House Keeper Charlotte
Kebbell 2 hundard Pound

Other journals are more discreet, but nevertheless help us
understand the lives of those written about. Combs Tannery
ceased trading in September 1988 after at least 200 years of
business.

Lankester Webb was the man responsible for the nineteenth century expansion of the business, so that by his death in 1887 they employed around 150 people. A brief (anonymous) journal covering the years 1834 - 1838 describes the activities of 'LW', and demonstrates just how hard a young and enthusiastic manager expected to work.

July 14th   *L.W. went a round of 63 miles started at 3 o clock*
1834   *got to Thetford About 6 from thence to Kenninghall*
              and there to Diss got home about 6 o clock fine day
              did not do much business
              horse performed the journey very well.

This was not unusual. A typical week is outlined here...

Jan 29th Mr. L.W. goes a journey to Botesdale
1836

Jan 30th Mr. L.W. attends Ipswich market Horn of Kenninghall
              comes in his absence pays cash on a/c purchases leather.

Feb 1st Mr. L.W. goes a two day journey to many parts of Suffolk
              and Norfolk Lucas comes in his absence buys a small
              parcel of leather.
Feb 3rd. Mr. L. Webb attends Bury market

Feb 4th Mr. L. Webb attends Stowmarket returns 5 o'clock starts
              for Woodbridge at half past six o'clock arrives at 9 o'clock

Feb 6th Attends Ipswich market on his way from Woodbridge
              arrives at Combs half past 5 in the evening

...Remember, he was riding all these miles in the middle of one of the worst winters on record. And he still found time to attend prayer meetings and get involved in charity work. Perhaps it is not surprising to read...

March 12th   *Mr. L. W. returns from Norwich about 7 o'clock this*
              morning and starts to Ipswich directly

*transacts the usual business amongst the Butchers
and returns about 8 o'clock in the evening .*
*Is taken very ill in the night occasioned by
excessive fatigue*

At Bury Record Office can be found a transcript of the Diary of Thomas King of Thelnetham[5] covering the years 1804 - 1837. King appears to have been involved in the building trade, possibly as an estate carpenter and later as a mill engineer. As with any diarist, his entries refer to the things of interest to him...

The Weather
1816: Deep water in October the 8th, 9th and 10th ever remembered. The poor were gleaning wheat at last of the month and harvest was not done at Gunpowder Plot 1816.

1818: This summer was very dry and hot but the best wheat ever remembered, after harvest plenty of rain so that after Michaelmas the flowers of the field was plentiful.

The sharpest thunderstorm that I ever heard or see was at Kenninghall on 28th August 1830.

Local construction & demolition
Hollands Mill at Thetford removed whole it should a been only it fell down and smashed to pieces April 1818

I and Geo. Bloomfield put the irons on to Thelnetham Steeple June 12 1820.

2 Spring sails put on Mr Brooks Mill at Hopton in May 1828.

...and significant local news items
Old Playford the sweep found dead in the snow Mar 21 1817.

6 prisoners got out of Norwich gaol in April 1818.

True as you are alive Oct 23 Balloon went up at Bury 1835.

About 20 from Market Weston went to America May 9th 1838

The handwritten accounts of travels by Lady Pleasance Smith[6] may be found at Lowestoft Record Office. In her account of her European tour with Lady Lacon, she ends with several pages listing her dislike of most of the places visited, especially France, *'with its dirty narrow streets peopled by beggars and idlers.'* She has less regard for many of the hotels in which she has stayed. Added to this, she writes about *'the annoyance of Custom House searches,' 'the trouble of passports'* and *'difficulties arising from the French and German languages.'* She complains at length about waiters' familiarity and servants' rudeness; about the *'mal du pays from undercooked foreign food'* and even the weight of the money... *'To carry £20 in foreign currency requires a strong arm.'* Even *'the doleful sound of the Catholic Bells'* gets a disparaging mention. I don't think she enjoyed her holiday much!

The Fitzroy family papers include a diary kept by Lady Mary Fitzroy,[7] the wife of Lord Frederick, who travelled with her husband to the Crimea in 1855. As Colonel in the Grenadier Guards, Lord Frederick was allowed to take his wife with him. He may have wished he hadn't.

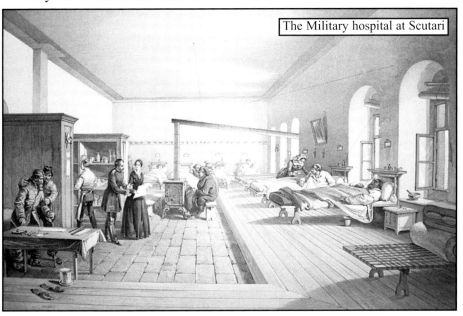

The Military hospital at Scutari

The journey across the Channel and through France was bad enough, but the boat trip across the Mediterranean was blighted by Cholera. On arriving at Athens, they were refused permission to land. A number had already been buried at sea. Finally arriving at Scutari, Lady Mary writes... *'Miss [Florence] Nightingale allowed me to have Miss Newton from the Scutari Hospital.'* - apparently as a companion, rather than for any medical skills she may have possessed. Lady Fitzroy comes across as a much more feisty lady than her timid companion. She comments regularly about Miss Newton's discomfort regarding the cold, the local butchers' shops, the unwelcome attentions received from *'the Greek gardeners at the Embassy'*, the *'dirty Jewish women with their diamonds and jewels'*; indeed anything unusual and unfamiliar seems to have disconcerted poor Miss Newton. And when they were caught out in a boat in choppy seas and *'the men put down their oars and intimated they might be swamped'*, it was Lady Fitzroy who *'entreated them to persist'*, so ensuring they survived. Before returning home in early 1856, we are told they shopped at the bazaar for amber bracelets and pieces of mosaic.

John Barber Scott was another traveller who recorded his journeys in a number of diaries also to be found at Lowestoft Record Office. Perhaps most significant was an account describing how he and a group of friends in 1814 were able to visit Napoleon in exile on the isle of Elba.[8]

First impressions were not great... *'Can this be the great Napoleon? Is that graceless figure, so clumsy and awkward the figure that has awed emperors and kings?'* At first Napoleon was reluctant to meet them, believing them to be Americans, but appears to have been won round. By all account he professed a great respect for the English and for Wellington, whom he claimed was *'the first General.'*

Of course, a year later, he would have escaped from Elba and would find himself again facing Wellington's army at Waterloo.

Napoleon coming ashore on Elba

I was rather amused by a letter that is kept at Bury St. Edmunds Record Office and appears among the Oakes family papers. Some of this material has been edited and published. This one letter however is from J.H. Porteus Oakes to his father.[9] At the time of writing, J.H.P. was taking the waters at Buxton and must have been aware of his father's problems with gout. In the letter he suggests a cure involving half an ounce of bicarbonate of potash and the same of carbonate light magnesia. These are mixed with 3 drachms of Turkish rhubarb and 1 drachm of powdered ginger. Take half to a whole teaspoon stirred into half a tumbler of water we are told, and it will effect a cure. However as this recipe had been the prescription used by the Archbishop of York who'd continued to suffer with gout for 40 years, it can't have been awfully effective.

'Lucky is the Name' is the title of a substantial book compiled from the writings of Alf Burrows (1904 - 1969). This tells the life of a farming family in mid-Suffolk. The title derives from Alf's grandfather having been bet 2/6d that he wouldn't christen his son 'Lucky'. Well, half-a-crown bought a good deal of beer in the Cretingham Bell in 1858, so Alf's father became the first of half a dozen in the family to be given the name Lucky.[10]

275

Lucky is
the Name

The true story of a Suffolk
farming family 1858 - 1969
Compiled and edited by
Pip Wright and Michael Anderton
from a manuscript written by
Alf Burrows

All manner of tales are recounted in this book, but the parts I enjoyed most involved moving farm. At the very end of the nineteenth century, Lucky Burrows and his family moved from Town Farm Stowupland to Oak Farm Wickham Skeith - a distance of over seven miles...

Lucky [Jnr.] and John were to drive the sows, an unenviable job you can imagine. These rather awkward creatures would want to turn into everybody's garden gate. They would have to be guided past the farms en-route. So off went these two boys aged thirteen and eleven, in charge of a herd of sows and responsible for getting them all the way to the new farm.

In my opinion, the other three boys had a very much worse task. They were detailed to drive the turkeys. Can anyone think of a more ridiculous problem than a flock of these birds being driven seven and a half miles on public roads by three small boys: Samuel aged ten, William eight and James only six. The story of this journey has been related to me several times in later years by Jim, as we now call him. One comfort at least was that there would be no possibility of encountering any self-propelled vehicles: it would have been rather unusual to see a bicycle, so it was just pedestrians or farm carts.

These boys had such difficulty in keeping the turkeys from flying over the field gates. When they saw a farm cart approaching, they had to manoeuvre the birds into a close pack near the hedge until the road was clear again. The last mile or so was the most difficult; the boys were tired, twilight was falling and the turkeys were instinctively flying onto gates, hoping to roost for the night.

Later in the book, we read of Alf's role in helping them move farm to Harleston near Stowmarket...

One of the most uncomfortable trips was when I moved eight iron hurdles. Iron hurdles could be described as gates on wheels, and they were supported by their four wheels. They could be dragged around to make sheep folds in a very few minutes and some of these hurdles were between twelve and fifteen feet in length. To move the hurdles to Harleston from Wickham Skeith I had a horse and tumbril. Attached to the rear of the tumbril on the left hand side, was a train of four hurdles, and on the right were the other four making two trains side by side.

I was a worried sixteen year old in charge of a mobile contraption of about seventy five feet in length and running on thirty four wheels. These wheels had not tasted a drop of lubricant since they were made, and for the first half mile they were running on rust and fairly quiet. By turning at the rate of about two thousand times to the mile, the axles dried and brightened, and began squeaking louder and louder until they sounded like a litter of fifty hungry pigs fighting for one teat. No two squeaks were on the same note. Nearly all the wheels were at an angle of forty-five degrees from upright on their worn axles. The loose chains on the hurdles were jingling and rattling like forty little devils.

The wheels were held onto the axles by a nail in a slot, and as the nails wore through, so the wheels dropped off. I had to continually watch out for fallen wheels and put them back on again. When they were completely lost, the front of the hurdle had to be chained high on to the one in front so it just ran on its back wheels.

This is a book that takes you back a hundred years and places you right there, seeing the world of yesterday through the eyes of a young child who saw little outside the farm and the family (and the chapel on a Sunday)...

Mother did insist however, that I should learn to play the violin; she thought there should be something in life besides just normal work. I had lessons for three years beginning when I was twelve. For these lessons I had to cycle three miles to the next village. Mrs. Last would let me leave school half an hour early for this purpose, as it was part of my education. By doing this, I missed the poetry lesson. I couldn't have both and finished with neither.

I sensed Father did not approve of this sissy fiddling, so I am afraid I did not put much heart into it. Periodically, Mother would say, "Just let yer father hear you play so he knows you are progressing."

With much persuasion, I falteringly played my latest pieces. After I had finished and feeling very red, I dared not look up at him and waited for a bit of encouragement. Following an uncomfortable pause he would usually say, "Cor, you should hear old Jack Tarrent play (I am not sure if this was the man's name). He could regular make his old fiddle speak." I used to feel like smashing the darned thing into a hundred pieces and chucking it onto the fire.

To reach our Chapel, the last hundred yards or so was a straight, narrow path about five feet wide. When the preachers spoke of keeping on the straight and narrow path that leads to heaven, I honestly felt that my destination was assured.

Then again, another speaker would tell us that the way is winding and difficult, with obstructions that must be encountered before reaching Paradise. My mind would instantly follow the route to the village church, a twisting uphill lane just wide enough for a hearse or wedding cabs, by brushing past the boughs. At the end of the lane, a gate had to be opened and closed, as a meadow had to be passed through where a pony and donkey often grazed. Then a second gate was opened before reaching the churchyard, which made me think that no doubt church people also went to heaven.

In my early years I could not quite fathom things out. I looked upon members of the Church of England as wealthy people, including the farmers who kept maids, the shopkeeper, girls who had left the village a few years and risen to be cooks, house-keepers and even the gardener at the Hall. I thought of them as rich as they all went to church and had a certain bearing. They walked with confidence. The chapel people seemed to think they must act with humility and appeared as if they were constantly apologising for being born.

Our preachers would read from the Bible about it being easier for a camel to go through the eye of a needle than a rich man to enter heaven...

Having got it rooted firmly in my mind that as my father took me to chapel by the straight and narrow path, it must be the best way to get to heaven. As second best, we could get there through the church if we were not rich. These problems being solved to my satisfaction, the material part of life had to be faced. This was well cared for in our village, as just beyond the chapel was the village green. Here stood the day school and the general stores. Around the green there were three farms, two pork-butchers, the windmill and several cottages, so this part of the village supplied the needs of the body.

Beyond the green, the road continued, being the widest piece of roadway we had: it went downhill and we called it the 'Broadway.' But our preachers told us not to go the way of the un-Godly. It was easy, they said, to yield to temptation, and they warned us most emphatically not to take the broad way that led to destruction. At the age of seven or eight, I thought they meant our road 'The Broadway,' which by a strange coincidence led to 'The Swan.' This was the village pub which I thought was an evil place and had to be avoided. To my tender mind, the layout of the village plainly illustrated, 'the way of the sinners,' 'the way of life,' and finally, 'the way of the saints.'[10]

To finish this chapter, I have turned to an extract from an unpublished account of his childhood by Tom Alexander of Cotton. Tom was born in 1920 and has spent nearly the whole of his life in the village of his birth. Writing in the third person, he tells of his childhood in the twenties and thirties.

The employees of J. Williams in 1934. Tom Alexander is one from the right in the front row.

It was playtime at the village school; the children were enjoying the break from class while Tom stood in the garden beside the playground watching the happy faces and feeling so sad at being the one left out. How he wished he could join the other children at school.

Although Tom was only three and a half years old, he felt he was not as good as the other children, until one day, his mother said, "I've been talking to Miss Cousins the Head-Teacher and she says you can go to school." He could not wait to go and he loved every minute he was there, but as he got older, Tom realised school was not all play. Some lessons were hard work and spelling lessons on Tuesday afternoons became his pet hate as he knew he would be kept in after hours to rewrite his mistakes.

It was no joke to Tom to be late home from school. He had his chores to do before his father got home from work: pails of drinking water to be carried home from the village pump; coal, wood and sticks to be got in, and any other tasks father had given him. Often he had to go out in the fields and gather two sacks of hogweed for his rabbits.

It was about this time that he began to take notice of nature. All rabbits looked alike to him, but his curiosity made him ask his father what he was doing when he picked the half-grown young rabbits up one by one, turned them up and examined their backside area, putting some in one locker, some in the other. Father said, "It's girls and boys: they don't have girls and boys sleep together." Then, a few days later, father told Tom to take the old doe rabbit to Mr. Rice up Cotton Lane. "Give him the sack with the rabbit in, then wait until he brings it back to you. He will tell you if it is alright or no good." It did not take many visits to Mr. Rice for Tom to figure out the purpose was for mating and the production of young rabbits.

When the young rabbits were fully grown, it was his job to take them to Tom Barker's. Tom Barker was the local coalman and carrier of anything people wished to put on the market at Stowmarket. One Thursday morning, he took a number of rabbits to Stowmarket. Old Tom Barker was already loading his four-wheeled cart. He started putting the boy's rabbits in a wooden crate, when just beside him a cockerel in another crate called out a very loud 'cock-a-doodle-doo!' Old Tom said, "You can stop that or I will rub your arse with a brick!" Tom saw the funny side of that remark and never forgot it.

As the years went by at school, Tom still had that left-out feeling. Why was it that all the boys in the upper school classes were able to go to the Bacton school one day each week to wood-work classes, except him? - He was the only boy left with the girls. He even tried his hand at needlework with the girls. He was left out because Bacton had not room for one more, and he, being the youngest, had to stay. As he often wondered, was it because he was from a larger family, so had no cycle to go on? All the other boys at school seemed to have bikes, except for one family that lived farthest away from the school at the Wimble. They all walked to school in all weathers, were always present and were usually first at school.

Tom's regular playmate was Noel who lived next door, but he was often out with other lads on his bike when Tom had free time to play. But on Winter evenings, the two of them spent hours in a back room in Noel's house. Noel knew how to play lots of card games and taught Tom to play. Hours were spent playing with Noel's real steam engine and Meccano sets. They would get up steam with Methylated spirits and make the engine drive the machinery made with the Meccano. But Tom always felt he had no real right to play with other people's toys. Why did he not have his own?

Not every Winter's night was spent in the warmth of Noel's back room. There were nights when father would say, "You are coming with me tonight," and after having had their teatime meal, Tom would be off across the meadows with Father and Uncle. On reaching a fallen tree, Father would light an old bicycle gas lamp and he had to stand, shaking with cold, holding the light for Father and Uncle to see where the cross-cut saw was cutting. Sometimes the gas-lamp leaked and flew on fire. He would throw it on the ground. Then Father would start to swear, blow the lamp out and start all over again. Tom longed to hear Father say, "Alright, that's enough for tonight." He couldn't bear the thought of another freezing evening of it tomorrow.

The boy had another job to do each year that he simply hated doing. Soon after harvest, Father would say, "Bring the cart to the allotment; no need to hurry, I have to dig the 'taters up first. So come in time to help pick them up, and you can bring them home." This went on each night until they were all home if the weather was fine. Tom hoped the crop would be poor. The cart was a big wooden box mounted on old iron hurdle wheels and it was hard enough to push when it was empty, but with three or four sacks of potatoes, it as much as he coul do to move it. Father would help him as far as the Cock Public House. Tom had it alone from there. It was not too bad down the Cock Road - a slight downhill - but the hill from the school, round the church corner nearly always proved impossible, and Mother would always have to help him up the path at home.

One evening when Tom went round with the cart, several boys were on what they called 'the Kippo' meadow playing football. He knew it would be some time before he needed to arrive at the allotment, so decided to join in the football game. "Mustn't stay more than twenty minutes," he thought. But twenty minutes isn't long when you are really enjoying a game, and he had no idea how long he had been there when he heard a shout. Father had left off and was on the road, red-faced, and looking somewhat upset. Tom ran to his cart which he had left beside the road. Father was swearing and when Tom reached the cart, he received a back-hander around the head. "I'll learn you to play football!" said Father. Again the boy was aware of the others having a laugh at his expense, and thinking "Why me? Why do I have to do this work while no other boys seem to be made to work. They can all play football. In fact, they all have football boots; not me, I only have my hobnails."

'Harvesting' by
W. G. Easton

Each Spring, Tom's father made Tom accompany him in the sugar-beet fields. Father chopped the beet out with his hoe; Tom had to follow him along the row pulling every cluster of beet plants apart and leaving just one plant at each position. Also hoeing in the field one spring was a man his father called Harry, and during the conversation, Harry told Tom's father how lucky he was to have a good boy singler. Father said, "He can single for you tomorrow evening." So, next evening, father made Tom's older sister go singling for him whilst the boy had to go with Harry. Tom thought Harry paid his father, but he was never sure. The boy certainly didn't get anything himself, but Harry was pleasant to work for. He never found fault. Tom could even crawl along the rows on his hands and knees - a thing his father would never allow. Father would say, "Stand on your feet or you will pull all the beet up with your toes as well as wear the toes out of your boots."

Towards the end of the beeting season, Tom had large blisters form on the palm of his hand. His mother walked with him to the doctor's surgery. Dr. Aveling had a room as a surgery at the Mill House. On seeing the boy's hand, the doctor said, "You have been in the beet fields, singling beet, and have poisoned your hand with a poison weed. Thereupon, he got a small pair of scissors and broke the blisters, cutting all the skin away. Tom couldn't bear to watch, but when it was over and some soothing ointment applied, and the hand bandage, he sighed with relief. He smiled to think, this had stopped him singling beet for the rest of the season.

During Harvest, he had to take Father's dinner to the harvest field. Mother had cooked the usual big meal; perhaps a beef pudding in a basin, with the potatoes, runner beans etc., all neatly wrapped and put into a large wicker basket. Tom often tried to run all the way, especially if the fields were the farthest away from the farm. He knew that if he was late there would be a box around the ears and a good telling-off.

In the autumn, Tom often went with his grandfather

gathering sloes. Grandfather seemed to know where all the blackthorn bushes grew. He also knew that his grandson liked a sweet from the village shop so before setting out, Grandfather would tell the lad to go for a pennyworth of bulls-eyes. When Tom brought them back, he would ask him if he had taken one, and then would say, "Garp for one then." Tom would open his mouth and Grandfather would pop one in.

One afternoon, whe Tom was about twelve years old, he got home from school to be told by his mother that she had found a Saturday job for him. It was to work for the District Nurse who lived in the next village about a mile away. So, he left home each Saturday about 12:30 to be there by one o'clock.

The old housemaid who worked for the nurse would let him in, whereupon Tom had to hand pump water into a tank in the bungalow's roof. It was a slow process and usually the nurse was home before he had the tank full, but if she was late it was his job to sweep out the garage and clean out her chicken hut. When she arrived home he often had to get the car washed and polished. Then during the spring and summer, he had to help with the gardening, some of which he liked doing. But the job he really detested was the grass cutting.

The lawn mower was a big heavy Ransomes cylinder mower. It was about as much as Tom could manage to move it on the concrete garage floor, so to use it on the lawns and paths, the nurse had secured a long length of rope to the front of the mower, which he had to put round the back of his neck and under his armpits, and then pull the mower while the nurse helped to push. There were the odd Saturdays when the nurse would be extra late in getting home and if Tom had finished his usual routine, with no sign of her coming, he would take to his heels and try to reach the Chapel Fields without meeting her. If he did meet her, it meant a ride back in her car and a very severe talking to. She would often tell him he must be there to help her with her gardening one or two evenings during the week. Tom didn't think she was very fair, and certainly not too generous. His pay was one shilling each week.

The number of hours or the number of times he went made no difference - it was always one shilling.

Walking to the next village every Saturday and sometimes in the evenings began to get a bit much for him, but he dared not refuse to go. He knew his father would be very annoyed and he realised the shilling he took home to his mother was a little help towards his clothes. So, he was really elated when one evening, the local big farmer asked him if he would like to be the 'farmer's backhouse-door boy'. "Yes, please," he replied "Alright," said Farmer Williams, "be here at nine o'clock on Saturday morning. Clean the back scullery up, get my wood and coal in, keep the dairy shed and the back-yard clean and you will get half a crown a week." This was just the offer Tom wanted - a job near to home, two and a half times the money and no fear of having more to do with the old nurse that he had grown to dislike.

'Feeding the chickens' by William E. Millner

Mr. Williams, the farmer, had a daughter who lived with him. Although she was very crippled, she liked to be a bit bossy and made sure Tom looked after her chickens that were on the orchard.

The chickens were leghorns and as wild as hawks. As soon as anyone went into the orchard, they flew around the wire netting run, but Tom spent as much time as he could

286

with them. He talked to them and the chickens soon got used to him and began to get very tame. Eventually, the hens went off the lay. Edna, the daughter, decided to get rid of them, and the very first Saturday that the chicken hut was empty, she ordered him to lime-wash the hut.

Tom armed himself with bucket and stirrup pump, mixed a bucket full of lime-wash, and from inside the hut started spraying all round the walls. He left the door open to help keep the fumes to a minimum; this left about an inch opening between the door and door post, which happened to be just the place he was spraying when Edna came on the scene to see how he was doing the job. She got the full force of the lime-wash all down the front of her, from face to feet and for a few minutes she was angry to say the least. The language turned blue as she let rip at him. Two minutes later, she began to see the funny side of it, told Tom he had done a good job and blamed herself for approaching the hut the way she had. All this time he had wanted to laugh, but he knew it would have been the instant sack if he had not kept a very straight face.

The month of July had arrived. The corn seemed to be ripening early, and although Tom would not be fourteen till the end of August, he was looking forward to the school harvest holidays when he could start work proper. So, he was delighted when Mr. Wiliams said, "Will you work for me when you break up from school?"

Most of the boys that went to work for Mr. Williams were bribed into learning to milk the cows by hand by being promised they would be taught to drive a tractor. But Tom was not all that interested in driving a tractor and didn't at all like cows, and somehow he kept away from both.

A lot of the time, he had to work on the Lodge Farm, which meant he had to start away from home soon enough to walk by the fields to get there on time, but he eventually talked his mother into letting him have her old bike, which had been hanging in the shed for years.

One of the first jobs he had was to go picking beans. The beans had grown so short that the binder had failed to tie a lot of them in the sheaves. It was on this job that Tom began to realise that some of Mr. Williams' sayings were true. One of his sayings was 'One boy is a good boy; two boys is half a boy and three boys is a bloody nuisance.' There were four of them picking beans. He knew that he would have picked more beans had he been alone than the four of them did together.

The corn was all cut and the fields all stood full of shooks and Tom once again found himself with Noel and old man Charlie and Bill. The four were to be the field gang to get the harvest

'Scythers' by Daniel Wright

carted in. Charlie knew what boys could be like, so on the very first day, he said to the pair of them, "I want you both to be good boys and if you are, I will give you both a shilling to go to the fair with when it comes in September."

Tom hated loading the wagons. He was always afraid he would fall off the back of the load, and each evening when he got home, he could have cried when having a wash was so painful. His face and arms were scratched so much from the corn sheaves jabbing one after another all day long, and washing made all the scratches sting. Then he would go to bed and as soon as he dozed off, he would dream he was loading again. He kept waking up and telling himself not to be so silly, then fall asleep and start loading once more.

Sundays had always been special days for him. He had always attended Sunday School in the afternoons and had been in the church choir every Sunday morning and evening. He was proud to have a Sunday suit to wear, and of course the Sunday School and Choir outings to Yarmouth were a big incentive.

Tom's wages of nine shillings and eightpence a week didn't seem to go very far. His mother gave him four pence on Saturday morning, then he went with all the other men to the Church Farm at twelve o'clock where Mr. Williams would be sitting in the carpenter's shed paying the wages. Tom would hand over his four pence and take a ten shilling note, which he took home to his mother who then gave him two shillings to spend on himself.

One Saturday when he was receiving his pay, Mr. Williams told him he wanted him to go to help the shepherd on Sunday mornings. This was a new experience to him, but he soon got the art of using a fold drift to make holes for the sheep netting stakes, and he acquired the knack of carrying twenty to thirty netting stakes on his shoulder at a time. Now going to work on Sunday meant that Tom missed his attendance at choir and when he went into the church vestry for choir that evening, Johnny Cowell the parson told him that if he didn't come in the morning he was not wanted in the evening. Tom did not stay to explain that he had to work. He just walked out and went straight home and told his mother what had been said. Now, when he got home from work on Monday, his mother said, "The parson has been to see me and wants you in the choir on Sunday evenings." A few evenings later, he met the parson, who tried to talk him into going to church again, but Tom said in no uncertain manner, "You turned me out once; you don't get the chance to turn me out again!"

It was around about this time that he spent most of his

leisure time with Biddy and Bailey. Biddy was later to become Tom's workmate, but when he first got to know him, Biddy was helping deliver milk as his main job. Bailey was helping a builder. One Saturday afternoon, Biddy asked Tom about going to the pictures at Stowmarket. Tom still had no bike except Mother's old crock. Biddy says to him, "Jump on my crossbar; we'll soon get you a bike. You only need a couple of bob." So away sped Biddy with Tom on the crossbar, straight through Finningham and on to Walsham-le-Willows. They arrived at Mr. Vincent's Bicycle Workshop. Tom got his eye fixed on a shining blue bike. Biddy did the bargaining and he got his blue bike for three shillings and sixpence. It was an old bike that had had a good service and repaint and to Tom it was beautiful. From then on, he would regard Biddy as his very best friend.

This was a very happy time for Tom - his own bike to go for rides with the other lads on Sunday afternoons; the Pictures quite often on Saturday evenings. And he enjoyed most of the work on the farm, especially leading the horse on the horse hoes, job that was continuous from early spring right through until harvest. They would hoe the fields of beans, sometimes a field or two of wheat, and most of all the sugar-beet. The first hoeing of the beet was with the disc hoes and the horsemen behind the hoes made the boy leading the horse take great care in making the horse walk in exactly the right place. The boy also had to keep both wheels moving along as he turned at the ends, or the inside turning wheel would bore a bowl shape in the ground and thus disturb the beet plants.

Years pass by, and as younger boys come on to the farm, the older boys lose the job of leading on the horse hoes and Tom finds he has to buy himself a hoe for hand-hoeing.

Before he went chopping out, Mr. Williams asked the four that were going on piece-work to meet at his house. Tom along with Biddy, who had just started on the farm, and Frank and Pokey all arrived at the back door of the farm, bikes propped up alongside the garden hedge. The four went into the kitchen. "Find a seat," said Mr. Williams. "Have half a pint of cider each." He must have known the cider was strong. Tom did not know, nor did he think anyone else knew what the price of chopping out beet per hundred yards or per acre should be. Poor Pokey did not know how to ride his bike: he mounted it, rode straight into the cow yard, where he landed. Tom thought, 'So much for price negotiations. All we shall get now is the rate set for the farmers by the Union.'

At pay-out one Saturday, Mr. Williams asked him if he could look after sheep as well as the shepherd. When he said, 'No,' Mr. Williams said, "You have got to, as I have bought a hundred and fifty young ewes to breed - It's your job to look after them." So, once again, Tom became a shepherd. He soon had the task of driving his flock to a farm at Walsham, which Mr. Williams had apparently bought off a Mr. Sykes.

When Tom first met Mr. Sykes, who still lived on the farm, he thought he was a brash, foul-mouthed bully who did his utmost to make Tom take Brownie, his collie dog to work the sheep. Even after Mr, Sykes had given him a demonstration as to how good Brownie was, Tom still refused the use of the dog. However, in time he became more than pleased to have Brownie with him.

Some time much later, Tom had his flock at Wickham; Mr Williams was making him feed the sheep lots of corn. Now, he knew the sheep were very thirsty, what with a diet of corn and very dried up sugar beet tops, so on Saturday when he took his wages, he told Mr. Williams he wanted to get his sheep some water to drink, but Mr. Williams, who always knew better than his men, said, "In no way can they be thirsty - they'll be alright."

The following Tuesday afternoon, Tom had put the corn in the troughs on the meadow. The sheep had had most of the day eating the beet tops. He opened the meadow gate and gave his usual call to the sheep, and straightaway as they always did, the sheep came running to the troughs, but today turned out to be different - not one sheep stopped at the troughs, but ran to the far end of the meadow and disappeared through the hedge. Tom ran to get them back, only to find the whole flock in a pond that he didn't know was there. There was no water in the pond as such, but there was plenty of depth of black mud, from which the sheep just could not get themselves out: seven or eight sheep were walking on the backs of the rest.

No one single person was going to pull even one sheep out of this mud on his own, so Tom ran to two men who were pulling beet in the next field. Then he ran to the farm and told everyone what had happened. Soon there were men arriving at the pond with horses and wagons, ropes and ladders, and after a few hours of heaving and pulling, the men had every sheep out. The biggest flock of all-black sheep one had ever seen! Just seven remained white. The men were filthy, covered in black slime from head to toe.

Mr. Williams always went to Ipswich market on Tuesdays. He soon heard what had been going on when he got home, and of course, he soon had his car heading towards Wickham; but all was well by the time he arrived. Tom had put the sheep in the fold for the night and was about to mount his bike to go home. "What the hell do you think you have been doing?" said Mr. Williams to him and he ranted and raved for several minutes. Tom kept quiet until he thought Mr. Williams had finished, then he said, "You can look after them yourself from now on. I've finished. You know it all, so when I told you the sheep needed water, you knew better... so, look after them yourself!"

Mr. Williams calmed down, then told him to bring the sheep to the horse yard at Wickham Farm at 8:30 the next morning. At first, Tom said, "No, I've finished." But Mr. Williams said, "You will see, I'm right. Bring the sheep there where men will be waiting with full water troughs, and you will see that the sheep will hardly touch the water." Tom agreed to take the sheep just to show him how wrong he was and next morning, he started with the flock towards the farm. When the sheep were about a few hundred yards from the farm, they could smell the water and made a headlong dash to the horse-yard gates, straight into the troughs in such a rush that the troughs all went flying. The men with their buckets could hardly get amongst the sheep to straighten and refill the troughs and it took a gang of men four hours to satisfy the thirst of the whole flock. Mr. Williams apologised to Tom, saying he would never have believed sheep could be so thirsty and he told him he would take more notice of him in future.

Tom lost his shepherd's job soon after war was declared. Mr. Williams did not want him to be called up and be left without a shepherd, so the following Saturday, he asked him if he should look for another shepherd or apply to have him made exempt from call-up. Tom said, "My mates are being called up, so I may as well go too." So, it was not long before Herman the new shepherd arrived.

Tom's girlfriend, Anne was not too pleased when he told her that he had refused the chance of being made exempt from call-up. She and Tom had been seeing a lot of each other for some time. Anne worked and lived at a farm, and on evenings off he was always there to accompany her home. But she passed by the wayside, the same as quite a few of his girlfriends in the next few years.

Poor Biddy and Bailey had already been called up for their medical when Tom got his orders to go to St. Matthews Street in

Ipswich. Biddy said, "I'm coming with you," and on the day, he did just that. They went for a drink before Tom went into the medical place. The men had to strip off in cubicles which were open-fronted and he couldn't help noticing that the man in the next cubicle had his toes bandaged up. The bandages were almost black as if they had been on his toes for weeks, and Tom wondered what the doctors were going to think about him. But he soon forgot the black toes when he was called to the first doctor. Then he went from one boarded-off compartment to another with nothing on until the last little room where he was given a small glass and told to go next door and produce a sample. Next door was an empty space, bare floor, but no toilet of any description as he had expected. The glass was not big enough. The drinks he'd had previously were causing him a little concern - where could he find a toilet? Once he started to fill the glass, he just could not turn the tap off, so relieved himself in the corner on the floor, and in doing so, could see he was not the first.

Now it was time to climb the stairs to see what they called the Attestation Officer. The other men were of the opinion that it was a waste of time as the officer would put you in the army anyway. He eventually faced the officer who asked his preference. Tom said, 'The R.A.F.' When asked why, the only answer he could think of was that he was more interested in aircraft than he was in tanks.

Mr. Sykes had moved into the Church Farm and taken over the role of Foreman. Tom thought it wrong for a man who could not run his own farm to have a say in running a collection of farms for someone else, but eventually became very friendly with him, and spent a lot of his spare time in the evenings with him, helping him with the incubators, collecting turkey eggs and so on. He got to know Brownie very well and when Percy (Tom now called him by his Christian name) asked him to take Brownie to work the sheep with him, Tom was only too pleased to take him.

Brownie was a real asset. Tom could never forget the first morning he went to get him. Mrs. Sykes greeted him by saying,

But as the head of Simon Theobald demonstrates, trouble is usually best avoided. As a result we're remarkably lacking in battle-sites here in Suffolk. And in times of upheaval, we prefer to sit on the fence and await the outcome before taking sides. The English Civil War was a case in question. Also, we dissolved our monasteries without needing to hang a single Abbot. Though Bonnie Prince Charlie never got as far as here in 1745, I bet if he had, we'd have had banners for both sides ready and waiting to see which army would be victorious before waving them.

Which brings us to **fornication**. There has of course been any amount of that, with the predictable collateral damage. When in 1884 the Hon. James Henry Fitzroy, Earl of Euston decided he'd rather his new love than the lady he had rashly married over a dozen years before, a remarkable divorce case began. He claimed

that his marriage to a courtesan by the name of Kate Cooke was invalid as she already had a husband alive when she had married him. Lady Euston, fearful of losing her inheritance, came up with the discovery that the man she had formerly 'married' had himself been married to someone else at the time, so she had been free to make the most of her undoubted charms. Witnesses were brought from across the world. The petition was rejected.[6] As a result, they remained married, but separated. He shacked up with his younger model whilst her Ladyship enjoyed a substantial settlement as part of the deal.

So, there you have it. History from all kinds of places. Fragments of a past that may not be a foreign country so much as a foreign **county**. Meanwhile, we can all go on looking for those precious hints of the way things used to be. Old artefacts prompt all kinds of enquiries. This picture from the early twentieth century[7] seems to sum up Suffolk and its people. A remarkably relaxed gentleman in the Stowmarket railway sidings, looks across at us as if to say, "Now what could possibly go wrong?"

"Do wait a few minutes while I pack his lunch bag." The few minutes passed, then she came to the door with a haversack which she handed to him saying, "Brownie will run alongside you on your bike, but in no way can you tie him up: he has never had a collar."

Brownie turned out to be as good as gold. He would lie down on a sack or Tom's jacket all day if need be. He would sit beside him at lunch time, and there were times when Tom ate Brownie's ham sandwiches and Brownie had Tom's bread and jam. As a sheep dog, Brownie was the best. He didn't want to be told what to do. When they moved the flock, he would walk in front and as long as he could see Brownie behind, he knew all was well because if a sheep got into a ditch Brownie would not leave it. If a car came from behind, Brownie would come right through the flock onto the right-hand side to clear a way for the car, then lie down on the side until the flock was all in front of him again. And Tom never had to speak to him; he just seemed to know exactly what to do.

Percy helped him over the lambing period; nearly every other night Percy would sit up with the sheep and let Tom go home for a night's sleep. So all went well, the lambs grew well and some were bigger than those of the old shepherd's, although they were mostly at least a month younger. The old shepherd seemed displeased with the way he was being treated and appeared to dislike him. The time for the Diss lamb sale was drawing near. With a week to go to sale day, Tom had to take his sheep and lambs out onto the same field as the shepherd, the idea being to get all the lambs used to one another so that they could be driven to the sale in one lot.

The sheep had separate folds and each fold had a lamb hurdle: this consisted of upright rollers, set wide enough apart for the lambs to get through but too narrow to let a sheep through. This meant that the lambs from both flocks were able to get together and should have made it easier to separate the lambs from the sheep on the Thursday morning in order to be on their way to Thrandeston.

Thursday morning arrived: the shepherd and Tom made sure the old sheep were alright in their fresh folds. Then the lambs were all shut away from the sheep and all was ready for the walk to Thrandeston. The shepherd used his two dogs to try to get the lambs into the lane but with such difficulty it took three quarters of an hour: Tom thought it should only have taken five minutes. The shepherd was leading the way. Tom had by now tied the two dogs to the fence where the bikes were left and all now seemed to be going well, but about half a mile on, what should come chugging towards them but an old Trojan van. Now the lambs did not like the sound of the van and they mostly turned to face the way they had just come. He did all he could to stop any lambs getting past him but they eventually got the better of him and after a score or two had passed him and were heading as fast as they could run back to the old flock, he could see it was hopeless and just stepped aside to let the lot go.

Now tempers were getting heated. The shepherd swore at Tom, of course putting all the blame on him. Tom did not please the old shepherd when he suggested jumping on his bike and fetching Brownie. Much as the old shepherd, told him not to, that is what he did.

About half an hour later he was back with Brownie at his side and Brownie's food bag on his shoulder. The shepherd was livid, but Tom stuck out and made him tie his dogs up again. Then he told him to go into the lane and start walking towards the road. He added that Brownie would have all the lambs behind him by the time he reached the road. The old shepherd started towards the lane. Tom told Brownie to round them up, and in minutes the lambs were all on their way again.

Now that Tom had Brownie behind him, there was no chance of any lambs chasing back again and all went well. They reached the Church Farm at Thrandeston and put the lambs on a meadow. There was no fear of the lambs being any trouble; like

References and thanks

These are far from exhaustive but in most cases, where references are not included, information regarding the source of the material can be found in the text.

SRO - Suffolk Record Office
(I) Ipswich
(B) Bury St. Edmunds
(L) Lowestoft
SFHS - Suffolk Family History Society

Page 4 - SRO (I) HA87/D3/1/14

Preface:

1 The Household Book of Alice de Bryene, ed. V. Redstone,
        Suffolk Institute of Archaeology & Natural History, 1991
2 Materials for the History of Wherstead, Rev. F.B. Zincke, 1887
3 The History of Stowmarket, Rev. A.G.H. Hollingsworth, 1844
4 SRO (I) HD 480
5 Census (Suffolk) 1881

Chapter 1 - Mostly about Ipswich:

1 The Illustrations collected by W.S. Fitch, SRO (I) HD 480
2 'A History & Description of the Town of Ipswich,'
        G.R. Clarke, 1830
3 The New Suffolk Garland, John Glyde Jun., 1866
4 Notes of John Glyde, SRO (I) qs9
5 SRO (I) Stowmarket vestry minutes FB221/A3/2
6 Notes of John Glyde, SRO (I) qs9
7 'One Day from the Diary of a Stag,' Mrs David Hanbury, 1846
8 Illustration from 'The Autocar,' Feb. 21st 1903

Page 34 - from the illustrations collected by W.S. Fitch,
        SRO (I) HD 480

Chapter 2 - Frolic, Fervour & Fornication

1 SRO (B) FL602/4/1
2 SRO (B) FL507/4/5
3 SRO (I) FB 62/D1/2
4 SRO (B) FL 639/4/2
5 'The History of a Parish', Rev. G.H. Butler, c1910
6 SRO (B) FL 513
7 SRO (B) FL 637/4/1
8 SRO (B) FL 580/4/4
9 SRO (I) FC 59/D1/1
10 SRO (I) FC 22/D1/2
11 SRO (B) FL 629/4/1
12 SRO (I) FB 6/D1/2
13 SRO (I) FC 94/D4/2
14 SRO (B) FL 541/4/14
15 SRO (I) FB 94/D1/1
16 SRO (I) FB 151/D1/10
17 SRO (I) FB 6/D1/2
18 SRO (I) FC 52/D1/4
19 SRO (I) FB79/D1/3
20 SRO (1) FB 51/D1/10
21 SRO (B) FL 640/4/11
22 SRO (B) FB 82/D1/1
23 SRO (I) FB 75/D1/1
24 SRO (I) FC 94/D4/2
25 SRO (I) FC 104/D1/1
26 SRO (I) FC 93/D1/1
27 SRO (B) FL 620/4/1
28 SRO (B) FL553/4/2
29 SRO (I) FB157/D1/2
30 SRO (L) 109/D2
31 SRO (L) 110/D1/1
32 SRO (I) FB125/D1/1
33 SRO (I) FB189/D1/1
34 SRO (B) FL620/4/1
35 SRO (I) FC65/D1/1
36 SRO (I) FC44/D1/1
37 SRO (I) FB75/D1/2

38 SRO (B) FL620/4/1
39 SRO (B) FL694/4/2
40 SRO (I) FB6/D1/2
41 SRO (I) FC105/D1/1
42 SRO (B) FL602/4/1
43 SRO (B) FL649/4/2
44 SRO (I) FC69/D1/1
45 SRO (B) FL 590/4
46 SRO (I) FB 125 D1/1
47 SRO (I) FB160/D2/1
48 SRO (B) FL566/4/1
49 SRO (I) FB221/D2/2

Chapter 3 - The Parish Notices

1 The title for this chapter is borrowed from the title of a CD
     by Jez Lowe & the Bad Pennies.
2 SRO (I) FB 23/I1/2
3 SRO (I) FB 19/I1/I2
4 SRO (B) FC 500/9/1
5 SRO (I) FB 159/I1/3
6 SRO (I) FB 159/K1/1
7 SRO (B) FL 601/2/1
8 SRO (B) 2368/8/2/6
9 SRO (I) FB 23/M1/1
10 SRO (B) FL 571/1/12/4
11 SRO (B) FL 506/7/44
12 SRO (I) FC 125/G5/1
13 SRO (I) FB 220/A7/1-3
14 SRO (B) FL 507/56-9
15 SRO (I) FC 121/G9/2-9
16 SRO (I) FC 89/A3/2
17 SRO (B) FL 506/1/13
18 'Pakefield - the church & village' pub. 1938.
19 SRO (L) 119/G5/1
20 SRO (I) FB 151/69/1
21 SRO (I) FB 155/G14/1
22 SRO (I) FC 116/G3/1
23 SRO (B) FL 562/7/3

24 SRO (I) FB 160/G6/2
25 SRO (I) FB 159/64/156
26 SRO (I) FB 93/G2
27 SRO (B) 2368/7/16/2
28 SRO (I) FC 105/G2/3/5
29 SRO (B) FL 536/7/44/31
30 Taken from SFHS journal May 2001
31 SRO (I) FC 121/G5/1
32 SRO (I) FC 111/G3/1
33 SRO (B) FB 78/G7/1-16
34 SRO (I) FB 151/G12/2
35 SRO (I) FB 136/G1/6
36 SRO (I) FC 117
37 SRO (B) FB 78/G8/1-14
38 SRO (B) FL 521/9/2
39 SRO (B) FL 582/7/22
40 SRO (B) FB 136/G6/1
41 SRO (I) FB 159/G6/3
42 SRO (I) FC 99/G6/57
43 SRO (I) FB 160/G9/1
44 'Wherstead - Territorial and Manorial' F.B.Zincke pub. 1893
45 SRO (B) FL 574/7/9
46 SRO (B) FL 504/7/1-3
47 SRO (I) FC 121/G1/2
48 SRO (I) FC 121/G1/1
49 SRO (I) FC61/G8
50 SRO (I) FC67/G1/2
51 SRO (B) FL 510/7/36
52 SRO (B) FL 570/1/13
53 SRO (B) FL 582/7/46
54 'East Bergholt in Suffolk' T.F. Paterson pub. 1923
55 SRO (B) FL 578/13/2
56 SRO (B) FL 508/7/8
57 SRO (B) FL 610/1/1
58 SRO (I) FB 221/G3/1
59 SRO (B) FB 79/E1/1
60 SRO (I) FC 97/D4/1
61 SRO (I) FB 134/M1/2

62 SRO (B) FL 510/12/1
63 SRO (B) ADB 559/1/3
64 SRO (B) ABD 559/1/5
65 SRO (B) FL510/12/3
66 SRO (B) ADB 569/4/2
67 SRO (B) SLV 9
68 SRO (B) ABD 546/3/1
69 SRA (B) SPV 1
70 'Hadleigh: The Town; the Church; and the great men who have been
    born in or connected with the Parish.'
    Rev.Hugh Pigot pub. 1860
71 SRO (I) FB 126/M1/1
72 SRO (B) FL 586/13/4
73 SRO (I) FB 5/D1/5
74 SRO (B) FL 522/13/20
75 SRO (I) FB 96/A7/1
76 SRO (I) FC 70/C3/1 & N2
77 SRO (I) FB 93/G5/34
78 SRO (I) FB 19 I1/I2
79 SRO (B) FL 552/8
80 SRO (B) FL 639/1/5
81 SRO (B) FL 556/4/1-13
82 SRO (I) FB 22
83 SRO (I) FC 104/A4/1
84 SRO (B) FL 522/1/21 & 29
85 SRO (B) FL 627/3/36
86 SRO (L) 116/E1/1
87 Published by Boydell Press for the Suffolk Records Society
88 Published by Boydell Press for the Suffolk Records Society
89 SRO (B) FL 621/5/1
90 SRO (B) FL 618/3/28
91 SRO (B) FL 535/13/1
92 SRO (I) FC 205/L1/1

Chapter 4 - Directories

1 Most references in this chapter relate to 'History, Gazetteer and
    Directory of Suffolk' by William White pub. 1844,
    subsequent issues being in 1855, 1874 & 1885.

2 SRO (I) FC 30/L3/1
3 'A Chorography of Suffolk' ed. Dairmaid Macculloch,
    pub. Boydell Press for Suffolk Records Society
4 Ipswich Journal: April 9th 1878
5 'Medieval Gentlewoman - Life in a widow's household in the late
    Middle Ages' by Ffiona Swabey pub. Sutton Publishing, 1999

Chapter 5 - Newspapers

1 Photo from the Finbow Collection, Cotton
2 Bury & Norwich Post: October 5th 1850
3 The Bury & Suffolk Herald: October 30th 1844
4 The Bury & Suffolk Herald: February 28th 1844
5 Bury & Norwich Post: March 22nd 1843
6 Bury & Norwich Post: October 24th 1893
7 Suffolk Chronicle: April 12th 1873

Chapter 6 - Fact or Legend: Superstition in Suffolk

1 'History of Sudbury' by C.G. Grimwood & S.A. Kay pub. 1953
2 see 'Witches in and around Suffolk'
    by Pip & Joy Wright pub. 2004
3 Bury & Norwich Post: April 21st 1857
4 Bury & Norwich Post: October 17th 1876
5 Ipswich Journal: January 19th 1895

Chapter 7 - Suffolk Characters

1 Penny Illustrated Paper: December 27th 1862
2 The Graphic: February 21st 1892
3 Norfolk Chronicle: January 30th 1864
4 SRO (I) FC 121/E5/1
5 Ipswich Journal: December 14th 1745
6 SRO (I) FB 123/A3/1
7 Newmarket Journal: August 1875
8 Ipswich Journal: September 1859
9 Suffolk Chronicle: Dec. 27th 1873
10 SRO (B) HA 513/5/154
11 SRO (B) HA 153/5/173
12 'Sproughton Chantry' by Pip Wright pub. 2014

13 see 'The Postmaster of Ipswich' by Janet Ings Freeman
14 SRO (I) HD 480

Chapter 8 - Documents about Crime & Punishment

1 Illustrated Police News: September 25th 1899
2 'History of the Parish of Buxhall' by W.A. Copinger pub. 1902
3 see 'A Short History of the Village of Cotton'
        by Pip Wright pub. 2012
4 SRO (I) HD 88/3/6
5 SRO (I) HB 10/50/20
6 SRO (I) HD 480
7 SRO (I) Beccles Gaol Books 1122/1,2 etc.
8 SRO (I) 106/3/8
9 SRO (B) Q/agr
10 The Graphic: October 1874
11 SRO (I) HA 1/HB6/61
12 SRO (I) HA 421/B1/4
13 SRO (L) 350/1/1/1
14 SRO (L) 351/1/1/1
15 SRO (B) BB 511/1/1
16 SRO (B) ED 500/D2
17 SRO (B) ED 500/D4/1
18 SRO (B) 344.205 2523

Chapter 9 - Diaries & Journals and other Scribblings

1 SRO (I) qS9 - Hartismere
2 SRO (B) FL 513/3/1
3 SRO (B) HA 542/1/12
4 'The Diary of a Poor Suffolk Woodman' by P. & J. Wright
       & Léonie Robinson pub. by Poppyland Publishing 2004
5 SRO (B) 920.KIN
6 ref.12/ 1&2
7 SRO (B) HA 513/1/93(a)
8 SRO (L) ref. 89/1/13
9 SRO (B) HA 535/2/24
10 Though 'Lucky is the Name' is now out of print, the complete
       text of the book can be read at www. pipwright.com

Chapter 10 - A Suffolk Anthology

1 SRO (I) HA 244/M/2/25
2 'History and Antiquities of Hengrave' by J. Gage pub. 1822
3 SRO (I) HA 11/8193
4 SRO (I) HA 119/6837/1

Afterthoughts

1 SRO (B) HA 513
2 SRO (I) HA 244/M36/12
3 Ipswich Journal: November 22nd 1845
4 from Suffolk Archaeological Assn. report 1846
5 Norfolk News: December 12th 1846
6 Bury & Norwich Post: April 8th 1884
7 Picture reproduced courtesy of David Kindred

Thanks are owed to a host of people without whose help this book would not have been possible.

The wonderful front cover picture comes courtesy of Alison Merry. Her work can be viewed at **www.merryilluminations.co.uk** Thanks to staff at all three Suffolk Record Offices. In addition, I am grateful to Nic Portway (Combs Tannery Archive), Pauline Scruby & the Finbow family, Hazel Richards David Kindred, Tom and Roy Alexander, Daniel Wright, The Cobbold Family History Trust and my wife Julie who says I am impossible to live with when I am giving birth to a book.

Blythburgh Church

Tom, they were tired and leg-weary and were glad just to lie down.

By now, Percy had arrived in Mr. Williams' old Morris car and after he had seen for himself that all was well and promising that he would be at Diss lamb sale early next morning to help pen the lambs, he said, "Come on Brownie." But Tom

was having none of it. "Hang on," he said, "If you take Brownie, you also take me." Percy and the shepherd argued with him, but he would not change his mind, and Percy had to leave the dog. Tom knew that next morning there would be scores of flocks of lambs all converging on the sale yard and if two flocks managed to get mixed up it would be an awful task to pick them out again.

The next morning, they set off at first light and arrived at the sale yard with no trouble. Percy kept his promise and arrived almost as soon as them. After the lambs had been put into the pens ready for the sale, Tom asked Percy where the car was and could he put Brownie in the car. Percy agreed, saying it was parked in the Cherry Tree yard. Now Tom did not have Brownie to keep an eye on, he decided he could relax and have a look around the sale ground. After about an hour strolling around, he made his way back to the car, where he had left some cakes in his haversack. The shepherd's temper having cooled down, he invited Tom to the pub for a couple of pints.

Now he had not given a thought that Brownie might not be happy left alone in the car, so he was not on his guard when he opened the car door. Brownie flew out in a flash and Tom could not see where he'd gone in a car park full of cars. He called to Brownie and hunted the near vicinity - but no Brownie! He then had to find Percy to tell him the bad news. Percy revealed that Brownie was his wife's dog and he dreaded going home without him. They spent the rest of the day hunting the sale yard and all the surrounding gardens. They even reported Brownie as lost to the Police, but there was still no sign of the collie. It was no good. They had to give it up as a bad job, go back to the car and make for home. Tom told Percy he needed to go to the 'Gents' at the bottom of the yard, only to be greeted there by Brownie who had apparently been laying just inside the toilet entrance all day. Brownie's tail was wagging with pleasure at seeing him, but it was nothing on the relief to Tom on seeing him, and it gave Percy much pleasure in going back to the Police Station to report that Brownie had been found.

A new shepherd arrived in answer to an advert that had been in the paper, which meant the old shepherd getting the sack and the new man taking over both flocks. Tom had to work with him for a couple of weeks, treating the old flock for foot-rot as the old shepherd had seen the 'red light' and rather let the state of his flock deteriorate. He did not really like the new shepherd, who had a vile temper, and had warned Tom to keep well away from him if things upset him. So he was glad to get away from the sheep and start doing a few different jobs on the farm.

Then, when he arrived home to tea one afternoon, Tom found he had an O.H.M.S. letter, which he opened right away. The letter had orders for him to report to R.A.F. Cardington; all the instructions and the rail warrant included.

Chapter 9
A Short Anthology

Mr. Swainson, enumerator for Brockford cum Wetheringsett in the 1851 census, completed his work with the following rhyme...

So here you have the people all
From Brook Lane Farm to Puddingpoke Hall.
And here in these mysterious pages
You'll find the girls mysterious ages!
The sheep, the wolves, in each vocation,
the Parson, Clerk and Congregation:
the Deaf, Dumb, Blind, the Wise, the Fools,
The Maids, Jades, Wives and Sunday Schools:
Publicans, Tailors, young Beginners,
Farmers, and different sorts of Sinners.
Carpenters, wheelwrights & some Sawyers,
But free from Surgeons and from Lawyers!
Long life to all! and may the blushing maids
Next Census swell by splicing Brockford Blades!

Record Offices collect their material from a variety of sources. Old historians sometimes leave behind their notes and collections. In Lowestoft record office are the papers left by Janet Becker of Wangford. The daughter of renowned artist Harry Becker, Janet wrote and spoke on a number of local history subjects in the early decades of the twentieth century. Amongst her papers are some fascinating items, such as words to the Suffolk folk song *'The Old Plum Pudding Song.'*

Janet tells us that this song was regularly sung at Christmas events by 'old Eastaugh', who had been the sexton at Wenhaston church from 1888 to 1924. He lived in a house, opposite the

Compasses, and had learned the song from his father who had learned it from a boy in the harvest fields.

Now it's old Dan Tucker will sing you a song,
Not very good, nor yet very long;
'Tis very funny, you all will say
To have a great plum pudding on a Christmas day

> Chorus: Out of the way said old Mother Gooding
> Stone your plums and stir your pudding,
> Lads and lasses all in a row,
> Kissing under the mistletoe

Old Dan Tucker beheld something nice:
Three thousand great shiploads of spice,
Five hundred thousand sacks of flour,
And a ton of apples, sweet and sour.

Five hundred barrels of brandy and rum,
Lumps of suet as big as a plum,
Eggs as big as an old tom-cat,
And fifty thousand barrels of fat.

Ten tons of candied lemon peel,
Each lump as big as a large cow heel,
Currants twice as big as a pig,
And fifty thousand loads of figs.

They got ten thousand cooks, 'tis true,
As big as Gog and Magog too.
They made a cloth in half a day
That reached from London to Bombay.

They went to work and so complete:
They were mixing three and
                          thirty weeks.
They bought a kettle, I do declare,
As big as Asia and Africa.

It boiled three months, a week and a day,
When a hundred thousand men did say,
With picks and shovels they went to work,
And they sweated like a lot of Turks.

Three weeks and a day, they chopped about;
At last the steam came rattling out:
When it caused such a fog all over the land,
For a month you couldn't behold your hand.

Now on Friday night at twelve o'clock,
A plum flew out with a trembling shot.
It flew from London so swift along,
That it struck St. Peter's church in Rome.

Now to cut this pudding it required strength.
They bought a knife, three miles in length.
When half the pudding it plunged on through,
Why it broke the knife right slap in two.

Now this good plum pudding, I do declare
Would serve old England fifty year;
Scotland, Wales, Ireland too,
And half of it they won't get through.

Now perhaps good folk you will think it wrong,
What I have said in my Christmas song.
But if it's not true, I wish I may die,
So help me God, it's not a lie.

…shades of the 'Derby Ram!'
Janet Becker comments, *'The
chorus was repeated twice
after each verse, once by
Eastaugh and once by the
audience, so it took a long
time.'*

Suffolk views from the past

The picture above is of All Saints Church, Dunwich, the last major building of Dunwich to topple into the sea around 1920. These two smaller photos from Pakefield in 1898 and 1903 show Dunwich was not the only Suffolk place to suffer in this way.

Opposite: Fine buildings that still exist today...
Above: Giffords Hall
Below: Butley Priory gatehouse
          West Stow Hall
Overleaf: Gedding Hall
          & Hengrave Hall

The 'cod-bangers song' from Orford and Aldeburgh was once sung
by smacksmen visiting the towns...

When we come to Harwich Pier
The folks all flock from far and near,
To see us heave our cod on deck
And smack'em on the head with a bloody great stick.

Orford by J.M.W. Turner

In a book entitled 'Chronicles of Theberton' (near Saxmundham),
the author, Henry Montague Doughty includes a rhyme pertaining
to a past village surgeon, Dr. I Lettsom...

When patients come to I,
I physicks, bleeds & sweats 'em,
Then if they choose to die,
I letts 'em.

We are told in Granny Spall's book about 'My Village,
Stonham Aspal', that they had a rector called Robert Baynes in the
mid-eighteenth century who was particularly proud of his flock of
geese. Apparently, he arrived home one day to discover the geese
gone and the gander weighed down by a heavy purse that had been
hung from its neck. The purse was full of coppers and a note,
which read...

'Dear Mr. Baynes, do not trouble your brains
Or let your thoughts to wander
We have purchased your geese at a penny a piece
And left the change with the gander.'

When the Duke of Wellington came to join a shooting party at Wherstead in January 1825, he had the misfortune to unload part of a barrellful of shot into his friend Lord Granville. Happily, his Lordship sustained no serious injury, but it prompted this poem in the Suffolk Chronicle the following week...

His Grace, in shooting enemies, for many years expert
Though now they're dead or helpless grown, is ever on the alert
Lest foes against him should arise - so sharp he looks around
And shoots his friend, whose head appeared just above the ground.

A.B.

A picture from 50 years later that seems to match the story in every way (but the costumes)

If you were loaded, like the White family of Boulge in the late nineteenth century, then the whole family would take extended holidays, travelling around Europe, using a variety of forms of transport. Young Robert Eaton White wrote an entertaining ditty entitled *'Pa's precious bag'*, now deposited with the family papers, emphasizing how just difficult such experiences could be when he was responsible for his parents' luggage.[1] They certainly weren't travelling light but clearly felt his public-school training would make him ideal for the role. He wasn't so sure.

Here are a few selected verses and chorus...

If ever you have travelled across the raging sea,

You have had a feeling that you at last were free,

But if you were a lonely boy, you must have heard this cry,

Raised every other station by your anxious family - of -

Ch: *Oh, dear, where can the luggage be,*
          Where can the rugs and the shawls and the parcels be?
          What have you done with the sticks and umbrellas
          What's a boy's use but to fag?
          You said you would put them all neatly together,
          But now I can't say very certainly whether
          You've not left them all at the previous station,
          Including your Pa's precious bag.

When first you cross the channel and near a foreign land,
You think more of your feelings than the luggage in your hand.
But as you try to cross the deck without a nasty spill,
You hear this cry of horror raised by one who isn't ill...

When travelling in the railway train, you speed upon your way,
And from the thoughts of luggage, your mind begins to stray.
You venture to suggest the fact that you enjoy the view,
When, ah that cry like thunder bursts once again on you...

When you return to Dover, and reach your native land,
A swarm of English porters takes every piece in hand;
When every bag is safety stowed, you homeward 'gin to fly,
Still from sheer force of habit, your friends renew the cry...

And now I'm back in England, you'll scarce believe my word,
I even miss the echo of the cry so oft I've heard:
If in a cab or railway train, I ever move about,
I even now expect to hear that long-remembered shout...

R. Eaton White

The poetry of George Crabbe, once of Aldeburgh has already been mentioned on page 211. Amongst the most atmospheric of voices from the area, he was at his best when writing of the coastal marshes he remembered from his childhood...

High o'er the restless deep, above the reach
Of gunner's hope, vast flights of wild ducks stretch;
Far as the eye can glance on either side,
Into a broad space and level line they glide;
All in their wedge-like figures from the North,
Day after day, flight after flight go forth.

Robert Bloomfield (1766-1823) was one of a number of Suffolk working class poets. His reputation was made on the strength of the rural poem, *'The Farmer's Boy.'* His success owed much to the sponsorship of local barrister, Capel Lofft (see page 131). Born in Honnington, he lived awhile on Austin's Farm at Sapiston in Suffolk (shown below). This is an extract from *'Richard & Kate'* one of his finest country ballads.

> Come Goody stop your humdrum wheel
> Sweep up your orts and get your hat
> Old joys revived once more I feel
> Tis Fair day, aye and more than that.
>
> Have you forgot Kate, prithy say
> How many seasons here we've tarryd
> Tis forty years this very day
> Since you and I old girl were married
>
> Look out the Sun shines warm and bright
> The stiles are low the paths all dry
> I know you cut your corns last night
> Come be as free from care as I.

Evidence survives of our fore-bears' love of the arts [those who could afford it]. The Household Books of the Kytsons of Hengrave Hall show how large sums were spent on music and musicians. The accounts for 1572-1573 include amongst many such entries...[2]

In rewarde to Johnson the musician at Hengrave   10s
To the Quene's players   6s
In reward to Maud of Norwich for mending the virgenals   3s 4d
For a treable violin   20s
In reward to the blinde harper   12d
For stringing, tuning and fretting my lute   2s 6d
To the musicians of Swanne Alley for many times
*   playing with their instruments before my M^r & M^{res} 8d*

Suffolk Scenes

Above: Downham Reach on the Orwell c. 1840
Below: Woodbridge harbour c. 1830

This inscription comes from the kitchen of the Grade II listed Gippeswyk Hall...

He that seteth down to mete and leteth grace pass seteth down leik an oxe and ryseth leik an ase. [He that sitteth down to meat and letteth grace pass, sitteth down like an ox and riseth like an ass.]

Gyppeswyk Hall, Ipswich

In 1696 a window tax was introduced in this country. It was widely unpopular, but seen at the time as preferable to an income-tax. Like income-tax, it was assumed it would take the most money from the rich who lived in bigger houses (more windows) than the poor. Many avoided this by bricking up windows, to enable them to fall into a more lowly rated tier of taxation. This inscription from the window of a farmhouse in Worlingworth appears in a commonplace book[3] at Ipswich Record Office...

To the memory of a window which, having long lived
a useful friend, giving light and understanding
to the inhabitants of this house,
Died Oct. 1784
of a political pestilence call'd a tax:
generated in the bowels, and issuing like a vapour
from the mouth of a noxious Pitt;
proved dreadfully fatal & destructive,
even in the remotest corners of this island.
'Life is a jest & all things shew it.'
Say you 'tis not? - Pray, look on me
The gift of light, exchang'd for tea.

Newly appointed Prime Minister, William Pitt the younger had been faced by the problem of a mounting national debt. Instead of raising taxes on traditionally highly taxed items like tea and coffee, he lowered these and looked elsewhere - an increased window-tax was one of his new measures. Cutting revenue on tea was an attempt to fight back against the smugglers who pretty much ruled the roost in East Anglia. Most people in Suffolk in 1784 were buying their tea from sources that paid not a penny to the Exchequer.

Suffolk man Sir George Pretyman Tomline had been Pitt's tutor at Pembroke College, Cambridge and was for many years one of his key advisors. One of the more bizarre objects at Ipswich Record office, catalogued with the Pretyman family papers is a lock of hair from William Pitt the younger.[4]

In an earlier chapter, the old practice of gleaning is discussed. A slightly longer version of this poem appeared in John Glyde's *'New Suffolk Garland'* in 1866. The writer is unnamed, and may be Glyde himself.

Why, listen yow - be quiet, bo'! - the bell is tolling eight!
Why don't yow mind what yow're about? We're allers kind o'late!
Now Mary get that mawther dress'd - oh dear! how slow yow fare -
There come a lot o' gleaners now - Maw', don't stand gawkin' there!

Come Willie - Jane, where is he gone? Goo yow and fetch that child;
If yow don't move them legs of yow'rn, yow'll maak me kind o'riled!
There, lock the door, an' lay the key behind that 'ere old plate;
An Jemmy, yow run on before and ope the whatefield gate.

Well, here we be at last - oh dear! how fast my heart do beat!
Now Jane, set yow by this 'ere coach , an' don't yow leave yowr seat
Till that 'ere precious child's asleep; then bring yow that 'ere sack,
An' see if you can't try, today, to kind o' bend yowr back.

Yow'll all wish when the winter come, and yow ha'ent got no bread,
That for all drawlin' about so, yow'd harder wrought instead;
For all yowr father 'arn mos' goo old Skin'em's rent to pay,
An' Master Last, the shoemaker; so work yow hard I pray!

Dear me, there goo the bell agin - 'tis seven, I declare;
An' we don't 'pear to have got none - the gleanin' now don't fare
To be worth nothin'; but I think - as far as I can tell -
We'll try a comb, somehow, to scratch, if we be 'live an' well.

Local papers in past times loved publishing poems from a variety of sources. This, from the Ipswich Journal in June 1721 is an inscription added to a tombstone by a boy with a piece of charcoal. The stone had been erected to a Mr. Isaac Rot, which prompted the boy to add these lines...

As Death one day was passing by
Rot's door, on Rot he cast an eye;
And cried in language somewhat boisterous
"What, Rot above ground? O Preposterous!"
With that in hand, he takes his dart
And sends it clever through Rot's heart
Whose body then (Heaven take his soul)
He threw into this dirty hole
"There lye," quoth he, "for such thy lot is.
Low in this grave, the appointed place to rot is."

Engraved into an ancient pew in Blythburgh church - DIRCK LOWERSEN VAN STOCKHOLM ANNO N 1665 AG 12. From the days when Blythburgh was an international port.

Views of Blythburgh today

Good epitaph writers are like hen's teeth, few and far between. When they finally erect a stone to me, I wish they could have the services of the fellow who penned these words. These great lines appear on a stone in the chancel of Huntingfield church, dated September 21st 1575...

This earthly coulord stone behold with weeping eyes
Under whose cold and massy weight John Paton buryed lyes.
A gentleman by birth & deeds the second sonn to one
S'r William Paston worthy knight deceased long agone
This gentill esquier in Huntingfield a widow tooke to wife
That hight Anne Arrowsmyth w'th whome he led a loving life
Eleven yeers space and somewhat more by whom he also had
One only childe a Virgine milde his aged heart to glad
In youthfull yeeres this gentillman a gallant Coutier was
With rarest vertues well adornd to Coutiers all a glasse.
A Pensioner to Princes fower Henry the eight that Roy
To Edward King to Mary Queene to Elisabeth our ioy
Which fower he served faythfullye, the Court Laments his end
His country neighbours all bewayle the losse of such a frend
To poore a present remedy, to honest men an ayde
A father to the fatherlesse, the widows plaint he wayde
Against the hungry traveller his dores were never shut
Against the seely needy soule his purse was never knit
When he had lived three score yeeres and fowre,
      death closed up his eyes
He lived well and dyed well
      and buried here he lies.

In Moulton churchyard lies Lettice Manning, who died in July 1737, aged 49. Her epitaph reads...

O cruel death, to please thy pallate,
Cut down Lettice to make a sallet.

The last resting place of Jacobus Bacon at Burgate is marked by a rhyme, part of which reads...

Such was I once Living as yea now be
Such as I am now Dead shall yea once be
They who strive to Dye as I did Living
They shall surely Live as I do Dye.

[I know, I've read it many times and I still don't quite understand it]

And finally an epitaph from Henstead churchyard in memory of blacksmith Thomas Pleasance, who died on 20th December 1795, aged 47 years...

My Sledge and Hammer lies reclin'd,
My Bellows, too, have lost their wind,
My Fire's extinct, my Forge decay'd,
And in the Dust my vice is laid,
My Coals are spent, my Iron's gone,
My Nails are drove, my work is done.

The Old Hundred Bridge, Henstead c 1850

Afterthoughts

Details from our past are to be found in all kinds of places - libraries and record-offices, museums and private archives: but also in the drawers and attics of our homes where treasures still lie undiscovered or undisclosed. People come to me with items they have hung onto, unsure of their importance; reluctant to throw them away: and so they should be! Too much of our history has been a victim of minimalist living. In other words, be cautious what you discard.

Amongst the family papers in Suffolk Record Offices are revealing documents that are very much of their time and place. The Fitzroy family archive includes items brought home from the Grand Tour:[1] pressed violets from Carracalla, consecrated wafers from Milan Cathedral and a set of beads reputed to have been blessed by Pope Gregory XIV.

Amongst another family's items, most of which are of a legal nature, there is a tracing of a design for a monogram to be painted on the perambulator of one Robin White of Boulge.*[2]
Now how special is that!

*probably Robert Charles White, born 1904. As they had been christening the first son Robert for nine generations, I guess calling him Robin helped avoid confusion.

Record Offices don't only house old documents. Amongst the items listed for Trimley St. Mary are historic artefacts - a constable's staff of office from the reign of George III and an ornately decorated hammer and trowel from the laying of the foundation stone of the parish room in 1902.

And then there are the items that don't make it that far. The font cover from Long Melford Church, was sold at auction to a Quaker from Clare who used it as a top for his summer house.[3]

History is, as I have often shown, half-story. For example, Lowestoft had a bit of a problem with some of their vicars. In 1698, they appointed the eminent William Whiston, one of the greatest scientists of his day. But he'd only been there four years when he got a better offer and left to take up the post vacated by Sir Isaac Newton of Professor of Mathematics at Cambridge University.

St. Margaret's, Lowestoft

In his short time at Lowestoft, he was asked to sign a licence to open a new ale-house in the parish, part of his duties as parson. He replied that he would sooner sign a warrant to demolish one than build another. Perhaps it was just as well for the mariners of Lowestoft that he didn't hang around!

His brief successor was one James Smith, an ardent Scot who refused to accept an English monarch as head of his church.

So then they settled for a young man with no great reputation. As a result, John Tanner remained as vicar at St. Margaret's for fifty years. Yet his epitaph meekly reads...

If I have taken any pains
And ought that's commendable remains,
Be that my monument;
If not, let me forever be forgot.
Now that would never do!

Parsons by nature are meant to be trustful of people, some overly so, it would seem. Francis Cunningham (Vicar of Lowestoft 1830-1860) was woken one night by a sailor begging him to attend a dying member of his crew. The parson did so, arriving apparently with the man at his last gasp. The following evening he was informed that the man was dead and a request was made to conduct a rapid burial before the ship sailed on the morning tide. A coffin was brought and lowered into the grave, but when the sexton arrived in the morning to finish the interment, coffin and body had vanished. At first it was feared grave-robbers had been at work, but locals knew the vicar had been hoaxed and had read a funeral service over a coffin stuffed with valuable lace. It was just another trick of the smugglers.

Mysteries crop up in the most surprising places. Out of sight and out of reach of the congregation, some remarkable examples of graffiti have been discovered during cleaning of a clerestory window in Cotton Church. This seems to be of some antiquity. The longest piece of writing is similar to the lines,

"Were kisses all the joys in bed, One woman would another wed", which comes from a Shakespearean Sonnet. 'Who did this?' 'why?' and especially 'how?' we want to ask. And another set of questions goes unanswered.

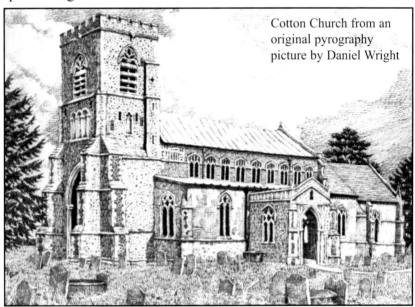

Cotton Church from an original pyrography picture by Daniel Wright

A memorial in Gazeley Church records what a jolly good person Alice Pier (died 1717, aged 39) was, but ends cryptically...

Unfortunate she was, yet here she lies,
At rest secure from all her enemies.
...Wouldn't we love to know what prompted that remark?

Which brings us to the title and, in a way, the point of this book - **Frolic, Fervour and Fornication**

Looking at life across the centuries, we've always enjoyed a good **frolic** - a celebration... a jolly... any excuse for a bit of a do! Whether it be a royal anniversary, a military victory, an annual knees-up or a once-in-a-lifetime whoopee, Suffolk people certainly know how to make the most of an event.

When Sir John Howard and Thomas Brewse appeared at Ipswich in April 1467 for their election for Knights of the Shire, they laid on quite a spread. The meat eaten included *8 oxsene, 24 calves, 24 shepe, 20 lambes, 30 pygges* as well as *fesawntes, capons, chekens, rabettes and pegenes.* Many *hoggeshedes and barrelles of wyn, bere and ale* were supplied to wash it all down. The shopping list included the most expensive spices - *peper, cloves, mases,*[mace] *safron, sawndres,* [sandalwood] *powdr of synam'o, gyngr* & that most rare commodity, *sugr.*[4]

On Monday 7th December 1846, they staged the official opening of the Ipswich-Bury Railway and what a day it was! Two engines pulled twenty carriages carrying hundreds of the 'great and the good' of Suffolk. *'They whistled the death knell of some half a dozen coaches and snorted as if in fretful impatience to display their superior prowess.'*[5]
Crowds lined Stoke hill to cheer them off. At Needham, *'ladies waved their pocket handkerchiefs on the top of sticks, poles and umbrellas.'* At Stowmarket, *'bells rang merrily and several discharges of cannon added to the universal din.'* On arrival at Bury, 400 bigwigs sat down to dinner and speeches at the Angel

Hotel whilst lesser folk entertained themselves in a manner more befitting their station in life [no, that wasn't meant to be a pun!].

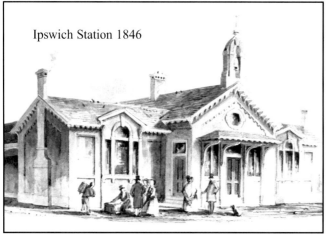

Ipswich Station 1846

The railways, probably more than any other single change during the time covered by this book, would affect the lives of all who celebrated that day and widen all their horizons.

Where **fervour** is concerned, we've tended to stay clear of as much of that as possible. Yes, there is still a church in Sudbury with a skull in a case to prove that we've shown a bit of zeal from time to time. It was hacked off during the Peasants' revolt and later returned to Sudbury, the parish of its owner's birth.

Index of places

Combs Ford, once part of Combs parish, now part of Stowmarket

The Old Cloth
Hall, Ipswich

Kentwell Hall, Long Melford

Described
by the artist
J.J. Hissey as
'A Suffolk
country
scene'

In a quiet corner of Suffolk, not a million miles from Elmswell